"Jottings from Dixie"

"Jottings from Dixie"

The Civil War Dispatches of
Sergeant Major Stephen F. Fleharty,
U.S.A.

Edited by

PHILIP J. REYBURN *and* TERRY L. WILSON

Louisiana State University Press   *Baton Rouge*

Copyright © 1999 by Louisiana State University Press
All rights reserved
Manufactured in the United States of America
First printing
08 07 06 05 04 03 02 01 00 99 5 4 3 2 1

Designer: Michele Myatt Quinn
Typeface: Caslon
Typesetter: Crane Composition, Inc.
Printer and binder: Edwards Brothers, Inc.

Library of Congress Cataloging-in-Publication Data:
Fleharty, S. F. (Stephen F.)
    Jottings from Dixie : the Civil War dispatches of Sergeant Major
Stephen F. Fleharty, U.S.A. / edited by Philip J. Reyburn and Terry
L. Wilson.
        p.   cm.
    Includes bibliographical references and index.
    ISBN 0-8071-2347-1 (cloth : alk. paper)
    1. Fleharty, S. F. (Stephen F.)—Correspondence.   2. United
States. Army. Illinois Infantry Regiment, 102nd (1862–1865)
3. Illinois—History—Civil War, 1861–1865—Regimental histories.
4. United States—History—Civil War, 1861–1865—Regimental
histories.   5. Illinois—History—Civil War, 1861–1865—Personnel
narratives.   6. United States—History—Civil War, 1861–1865—
Personnel narratives.   7. Soldiers—Illinois—Rock Island County—
Biography.   8. Rock Island County (Ill.)—Biography.   I. Reyburn,
Philip J., 1948–   . II. Wilson, Terry, 1956–   . III. Title.
E505.5 102nd   .F57   1999
973.7'473'092—dc21
[B]   98-51114
                                                                   CIP

For Pat, Matthew, and Adam;
For Charity, Abraham, and Peter

Contents

ILLUSTRATIONS

PREFACE

The genesis of this edition of Stephen F. Fleharty's published letters came about in the fall of 1995. At that time each of us was pursuing separate interests in two local Civil War regiments. One evening that fall as we were looking at a contemporary review of Fleharty's history of the 102d that had appeared in the Chicago *Tribune*, we began to discuss the method he had used in developing the book. We were both aware that in his writing Fleharty had relied heavily upon a series of his letters from the field that had appeared in the Rock Island, Illinois, press, and we agreed at that point that it might be interesting to see if a complete run of those letters still existed. With the help of the staff at the Illinois State Historical Library, we determined that the entire series did indeed survive, and were able to procure microfilm copies of all of the letters. As we began to pore over the letters it became increasingly easy to see the potential interest in a modern edition.

For the past two years it has been our privilege, in a very real way, to eat, sleep, and march with Sergeant Major Fleharty and his comrades of the 102d Illinois. It has at times proven to be a trying and frustrating adventure, but altogether one that we would not have missed for anything. We firmly believe that readers of these letters will readily spot those qualities in Fleharty's prose that initially attracted us.

While enjoying the letters, the reader should bear in mind that they originally appeared in print, and consequently had already passed through one editorial process before our work ever began. Fleharty's original manuscript letters to the papers have never surfaced, and most likely no longer exist. The letters we worked with, therefore, were those which the readers of 133 years ago saw, which had been worked on by editors, typesetters, and printers. Any errors in the original printed letters may have been Fleharty's, or they may have been slips of the editorial pen, or even of the weary fingers of a hurried typesetter. There is no way to tell. Where necessary we have corrected misspellings or grammatical errors with appropriate insertions enclosed in brackets, "[]." In other cases, we have indicated the retention of an original error by using *sic* following the occurrence.

Occasionally, the Rock Island editor slipped in his own commentary; the reader will have no difficulty distinguishing his insertions from ours in the context of the letters themselves. There are also several instances of insertions (usually question marks or other punctuation) which are enclosed in parentheses. These belong either to Fleharty himself or to the Rock Island editor. In all cases we have retained the punctuation that originally appeared, supplying periods and commas only when necessary for the sake of clarity, and then always bracketing the addition.

We, of course, owe debts of gratitude to many individuals. First and foremost we must thank Mrs. Sarah E. Glass (great-granddaughter of Fleharty's eldest brother, William) of Warren County, Illinois, for allowing us access to her marvelous collection of Fleharty family papers. We must also thank her husband, Mr. Mack Glass, for tolerating so graciously a number of late-afternoon intrusions into the peace and quiet of his idyllic country home. Their hospitality will remain a very pleasant memory.

Our heartfelt thanks also go to Enid Hanks of Galesburg, Illinois (also William Lane Fleharty's great-granddaughter), for her kindness and generosity in sharing her own excellent collection of family papers and photographs with us, and especially for the constant support and encouragement she gave during the entirety of this project.

Thanks also go to the following individuals for the assistance they freely gave to this endeavor: Rodney O. Davis, professor emeritus of history at Knox College, for reading portions of the manuscript and offering suggestions that added materially to the quality of the final product; Carley Robison, Knox College archivist, and Bonnie Niehus and Kay Vander Meulen of her staff; Laurie Sauer, information-technologies librarian at Knox College, for her willing assistance with assorted technical problems and for gallantly volunteering to prepare our index; Irene Ponce, Mary Lou Gonzales, and Mavis Meadows of the technical-services staff of the Knox College Library; Bob Conklin and Marcia Heise of the Galesburg Public Library; Rex Cherrington of Galesburg, whose expertise in local history and photography was heaven-sent; Andrea I. Faling of the Nebraska State Historical Society in Lincoln; Cheryl Schnirring and Mary Michals of the Illinois State Historical Library in Springfield; Ed Russo of the Lincoln Library in Springfield; Jean Gosebrink of the St. Louis Public Library in Missouri; Janet C. Lu of Nebraska Wesleyan University in Lincoln; Steve Watts of Galesburg; Lucille Simpson of the Rock Island County Historical Library in Moline, Illinois; James Victor Miller of Lebanon, Tennessee; Melvin Simpson of Alexis, Illinois; Ramona Bobbitt of Bowling Green, Kentucky; and Michael M. Nelson of Kent, Ohio.

"Jottings from Dixie"

Introduction

On October 31, 1865, the Chicago *Tribune* announced the publication of a book entitled, *Our Regiment: A History of the 102d Illinois Infantry Volunteers, with Sketches of the Atlanta Campaign, the Georgia Raid, and the Campaign of the Carolinas.*[1] It was one of the earliest histories of an Illinois unit, or of any unit North or South, to appear in print. Indeed, the author of the *Tribune*'s piece noted that it was the first work of its kind he had seen. "It is written in entertaining style," he observed, "often terse, graphic and vivid." It was from works like this, the reviewer continued, that "our future Dumases and Charles Levers will gather the materials for a score of American variations of the 'Forty Guardsmen' and 'Charley O'Malley.'"[2]

The author of the book was Sergeant Major Stephen F. Fleharty of the 102d. In a style resembling Ernie Pyle more than Alexandre Dumas or Charles Lever, Fleharty had put his book together largely from a series of fifty-five of his own letters, written in the field and published over the course of two years in two Rock Island, Illinois, newspapers. It is not certain just when the idea for the book first occurred to Fleharty, but references he makes to it in some of his correspondence indicate that the writing did not take him long.

Unfortunately, little is known of the author's early life. Stephen Francis

---

1. Chicago *Tribune*, October 31, 1865, p. 3. The 192-page book was published in Chicago by Brewster & Hanscom.

2. Alexandre Dumas (1802–70) published *Les Quarante-Cinq* (*The Forty-Five*, or *The Forty-Five Guardsmen*) in 1848, four years after his more famous work, *The Three Musketeers*, first appeared. Charles James Lever (1806–72), an Irish novelist, gained fame for a number of works chronicling the adventures of young army officers. *Charles O'Malley, the Irish Dragoon* was published in 1841.

Fleharty was born in what is now Suez Township, Mercer County, Illinois, on September 6, 1836. He was descended from John Fleharty, who came to America from County Galway, Ireland, in 1702. His great-grandfather, also named Stephen, served from 1775 to 1779 as a corporal in Smallwood's 1st Maryland Regiment, then for the next four years as a sergeant in the 7th Maryland.[3] Fleharty's grandfather, William Fleharty, was a native Marylander with modest holdings on the Eastern Shore near the Choptank River. Both William and his wife were slaveholders who moved their family to Ohio in 1810 to escape the "demoralizing influences" of the peculiar institution. Because it was unlawful to free her slaves in Maryland, Mrs. Fleharty took them with her to Scioto County, Ohio, where the family had settled near Chillicothe, and liberated them. William Fleharty, however, sold his slaves before the move. One of them was the son of the family's housemaid. According to a family historian, the poor woman was so brokenhearted at the loss of her child that she appealed to the Almighty to see that her former master would lose all of his property and find his end in a drunkard's grave. Both of the woman's requests, it is reported, were granted.[4]

From Ohio the family moved again, sixteen years later, to reside for a short while in Sangamon County, Illinois. Here, Fleharty's eldest son, Stephen Withgot, met and married Amelia Kirkpatrick, daughter of Methodist circuit-rider John Kirkpatrick. In 1834 the young couple moved to Mercer County, where Stephen, a lifelong Whig and Republican, farmed and worked as a cabinetmaker. Ten children were born to them, including two sets of twins. Five of the children died very young. Those who survived were all boys, and the youngest was Stephen Francis.[5]

Although the known facts of his early life are sparse, quite an impression of young Fleharty can be formed from a reading of his wartime letters to the Rock Island papers. Even though his education was limited, he presumably was able to attend the common schools of Mercer County before studying briefly at Knox College in Galesburg.[6] From his letters, it is easy to see that

3. George Fleharty, *The Illustrated Life of the Flehartys* (Pleasonton, Nebr., 1920), 46, 49.

4. *History of Mercer County, Together with Biographical Matter, Statistics, etc. . . . Containing Also a Short History of Henderson County* (Chicago, 1882), 803; Fleharty, *Illustrated Life of the Flehartys*, 56–57.

5. *History of Mercer County*, 803–804. Stephen's brothers were William Lane (born 1829), Henry Clay and John Quincy Adams (twins, born 1831), and Jesse Jackson (born 1835).

6. Fleharty's name appears in *Knox Directory: 1837–1963* (Galesburg, Ill., 1963), 50, where

the young man had acquired, from whatever source, more than a passing acquaintance with many of the great and not-so-great literary figures of England and the United States.

Like many young men of the day, after completing his formal education Fleharty taught school for a brief time, but by 1860 he was working as a printer in Galesburg. A year later the Lincoln administration appointed him postmaster of Center Ridge in Mercer County (an office "of no consequence," according to the Rock Island *Argus*). Just what his political connections at this point in his life might have been remains a mystery. Nevertheless, when the war began he still held the position while at the same time clerking in a general store in Berlin.[7]

Early in July 1862, following the bloody battle of Shiloh and McClellan's costly but unsuccessful Peninsula campaign, it became apparent that the war would not be quickly or easily won. Consequently President Lincoln asked the northern governors to supply the Federal service with 300,000 more men. Throughout the loyal states, as Fleharty noted, "the question came home to the hearts of loyal men everywhere, 'is it my duty to go?' and the conviction became universal that the Government would need the services of all."[8]

All over Illinois influential men sought the governor's permission to raise regiments for Federal service. In the northwestern part of the state, former Democratic lieutenant governor William McMurtry of Knox County received authorization to begin recruiting. In Knox, Warren, Mercer, and Rock Island Counties meetings were held at which local political and civic leaders spoke in impassioned tones attempting to appeal to the patriotic impulses of the young men who heard them. Men, some no doubt motivated as much by

---

he is listed as a "special student" from 1857 to 1858. A search of the relevant contemporary college catalogs, which also list students attending the Knox Academy, failed to turn up his name. It must be concluded that Fleharty attended classes only sporadically and for a very brief period.

7. Rock Island *Argus*, July 28, 1861, p. 3. The man he replaced, Almond Shaw, would soon become first lieutenant of Fleharty's company. According to the *Argus*, Shaw was removed because he had circulated secession documents. The "documents" were copies of the New York *Day-Book* which he had delivered to regular subscribers. The Rock Island paper called his dismissal on such a charge "a vile slander upon a better union man than any of those who make it."

8. Stephen F. Fleharty, *Our Regiment: A History of the 102d Illinois Infantry Volunteers, with Sketches of the Atlanta Campaign, the Georgia Raid, and the Campaign of the Carolinas* (Chicago, 1865), 7.

ambition as by patriotism, did their best to find and sign up enough recruits to form the companies that would make up the regiment.

On August 6, 1862, an open letter (dated July 31) appeared in the pages of the Rock Island *Argus*. The letter was signed by Fleharty, his brother Henry, and thirty-four other men of the Berlin neighborhood and was addressed to Joseph B. Danforth, Jr., editor of the *Argus*. The signers told Danforth that they were "sensible of the important service you have rendered as a patriotic supporter of the government" and invited him to address a war meeting in Berlin during the coming week. The meeting was held on Friday, August 8, at Berlin's two-story schoolhouse during the season's most violent thunderstorm. Danforth was the first of seven speakers to address the gathering, which resulted in the enlistment of thirteen more men in the company then being organized in and around Berlin.[9]

The organizer of the company was Frank Shedd, a thirty-seven-year-old New Hampshire native who had been farming in Richland Grove Township in northeastern Mercer County. Shedd began enlisting his company on August 5. Fleharty signed up on the sixth, two days before the Berlin meeting, and was made clerk of the company. By August 21, less than three weeks after he had begun, Shedd's company was full, with eighty-nine men on the roll. Five days later these men gathered at Berlin, climbed aboard wagons and made their way to the fairgrounds at Knoxville, the Knox County seat, where the new regiment was assembling.

It was at this point that Fleharty probably wrote the first of his letters to the Rock Island *Argus*. The letter, which appeared in the August 25 edition, reported on the presentation of a flag to Shedd's company by the ladies of Mercer County twelve days earlier. This letter, signed "Old Flag," and another dated August 28 and signed "Volunteer," are so like Fleharty's known work, both in style and tone, that his identity as their author is almost certain.[10]

The men who would make up what was to become the 102d Illinois Infantry assembled in Knoxville during the last days of August. There the companies (six from Knox County and four from Mercer, with a good number of men from Warren and Rock Island among them) were organized and officers were elected. Frank Shedd's company, of which he was formally elected captain, was

---

9. Rock Island *Argus*, August 6, 1862, p. 1; August 11, 1862, p. 1.
10. *History of Mercer County*, 386. For the text of both letters see Chapter 1.

designated Company C. When the noncommissioned officers were selected, Fleharty was named one of eight corporals.

The 102d was officially mustered into Federal service on September 2, 1862. Company C contained eighty-six men. Mostly they were young—the average age was only 24.8 years. (Fleharty was twenty-six.) The oldest man in the company was forty-four, and the youngest was (officially, at least) only eighteen.[11] Thirty-two were natives of New England or the Middle States, thirty-one were from the states of the Old Northwest, and twenty-three were foreign born. (Most of these, fourteen in number, were from Germany). Fifty-nine of the eighty-six were single, and all but six were farmers. Only thirteen members of the company lived outside of Mercer County.[12]

It was while the regiment remained at Camp McMurtry on the Knoxville fairgrounds that Fleharty's letters began to appear in the *Argus* over his own name. Just how he came to be a regular contributor to the paper is unclear. Perhaps he and editor Danforth had become acquainted at the August 8 meeting in Berlin, or perhaps Danforth was particularly pleased with the two letters that had appeared anonymously just weeks before, or perhaps the influence of an unnamed and unknown third party led to an arrangement for the letters to continue as a regular series. The most likely reason, however, is alluded to by Fleharty at the beginning of his first regular letter which appeared on September 25. In it he proposed to furnish the paper with "occasional notes" from the 102d, "a regiment in which are many of your old subscribers."

Newspapers all over the country published letters from soldiers in the field. It was not uncommon for a single soldier to contribute to the hometown paper on a regular basis for many months, so Fleharty was in very good company. It was rare, however, for the letters to be numbered and published serially as his were. "Jottings from Dixie" continued to appear on a fairly regular basis during the next two years, subject only to the occasional interruptions in northern communications imposed by marauding Confederate cavalry.

11. In computing the average age of the men in Company C, only eighty-five men were considered. The age of one man is not given on the official roster. Privates Major McMullen and Leonard Stark were both forty-four. Actually, Thomas Merryman (a musician) at forty-five and Jacob Robb (a wagoner) at forty-eight were older. McMullen and Stark were, however, the oldest infantrymen.

12. The marital status and the occupation of one of the men is not given on the official roster.

Fleharty, a Mercer County man, and his arrangement with a Rock Island County paper were sharply criticized later in the war, however, by the editor of the Keithsburg *Observer*. After reprinting one of Fleharty's casualty lists from the Rock Island newspaper, the Mercer County editor "respectfully" suggested that the relatives of the men in the 102d were just as interested in their welfare as anyone else, and would hear from them just as soon if he would send his information to the papers in Mercer or Knox counties "as when he sends it to Rock Island, Chicago, New York or London, or any other foreign sea-port town." Then, the editor went on, having done right by his fellow soldiers and their relatives and friends at home, Fleharty could "devote his leisure moments to scribbling 'pomes' and 'jottings' for the more aristocratic city dailies,—*ad libitum et nauseum*."[13]

The 102d Illinois passed the first twenty months of its existence in relative calm. Sergeant Fleharty faithfully reported the regiment's participation in the pursuit of Braxton Bragg's invading Army of Tennessee across Kentucky in October 1862, and the subsequent march to and occupation of Gallatin, Tennessee. Although the duty performed by the regiment in garrisoning towns along the Louisville and Nashville and later the Nashville and Chattanooga Railroads of central Tennessee was crucial to the logistics of the Union army, it did not make for exciting reading. Fleharty compensated for this with his captivating discussion of the South and its people, particularly its black inhabitants. His description of the reaction of a Kentucky slave to the appearance of Union soldiers as she clapped her hands and shouted excitedly, "God bress de union! God bress de union!"[14] conveys something of the common experience of all northern soldiers who spent any length of time in occupied Confederate territory or even in slaveholding border states. Likewise, the account of his encounter with the former slaves of President Andrew Jackson,[15] and their opinion of Lincoln ("he seems to be doing *great things*, but some says *not*, yet I likes him mighty well."), makes the reader appreciate the quiet interludes which allowed him to record such revealing episodes. Fleharty and soldier-correspondents like him served to acquaint the home folks in the North with a people and a culture which most of them had never seen, and which would soon be no more.

13. Keithsburg *Observer*, June 9, 1864, p. 1.
14. Letter No. 4.
15. Letter No. 30.

From the beginning, military life seemed to agree with Fleharty, at least while the regiment was assigned to railroad-guard duty. "Oh! I am so glad that I came into the army!" he wrote to his brother. "Not that I am generally in favor of war; but my health is better than when I entered—I have learned much, and more than all, will have the consciousness that I belonged to the Army of the Cumberland."[16]

When his friend Sgt. Maj. Jacob H. Snyder was promoted to adjutant in March 1863, Fleharty became the regiment's new sergeant major. In that position he was primarily responsible for assisting the adjutant in the performance of his duties. The sergeant major saw to it that the various companies received their daily orders and that they supplied the various details (for guard, fatigue, etc.) required of them each day. In the absence of a principal musician, the sergeant major trained the company musicians. He kept time at headquarters and saw to it that the musician detailed for the purpose sounded the calls at the proper time. As ranking noncommissioned officer of the regiment, he was required to be present at daily guard-mounting and orderly call. He supervised the daily maintenance of the various returns, rolls, and reports required by regulation and kept the regiment's books and records. The sergeant major, noted one authority, "should be a model soldier for the rest of the regiment in his dress and military deportment. His example and punctual requirements of duty go far towards influencing a proper discipline in the regiment."[17]

This was a job that seemed to suit Fleharty's temperament and talent, and he was good at it. In the summer of 1864 he gave some advice to his brother William on the performance of the duties of a first sergeant (which William had recently become), which were somewhat similar to his own duties. The advice he gave permits a look at his own perspective on the art of mastering military paperwork. Although he was sure William would find the orderly sergeant's position "vexatious," still it "affords many advantages." In making out reports, Stephen advised: *"Study the blanks,"* not only when there were actual reports to fill out, but in leisure moments as well. He admonished his

16. Fleharty to John Q. A. Fleharty, July 18, 1863, in possession of Mrs. Sarah E. Glass, Warren Co., Illinois.

17. August V. Kautz, *Customs of Service for Non-Commissioned Officers and Soldiers . . . Enabling Them to Seek Promotion and Distinction in the Service of Their Country* (Philadelphia, 1864), 171–74.

brother to read the printed instructions. Most of them were important and should be *"read* & *re-read* until *thoroughly understood."* He warned William that his adjutant probably knew no more than he did, and that if he were to go to him he would "get confused ideas" of his duties. It was usually better to refer to the army manuals at hand than to ask for help. Although it would occasionally be necessary to ask for assistance, it was generally best to "depend upon one's self."[18]

Although he took very well to army life, Fleharty exerted all the influence he could to keep his brothers from going into the service. He told his brother John not to enlist because the company cooking was "rough" and the fatigue that resulted from all the marching would be too much for him to bear. He relented somewhat when he observed that the army would not be so bad if John could manage to get a commission or an administrative post such as the one he now occupied with the 102d. Otherwise, it was a man's duty to buy himself out of the service if drafted when he knew that army life would be too much for him.[19]

Sergeant Fleharty was particularly emphatic in his warning to his brother to avoid the draft. If it looked as though he would be drafted, he wrote to John in the fall of 1863, he should make up his mind not to enter the service as a conscript. Pay the exemption fee or do anything else that was honorable to avoid conscription.[20]

Although he persuaded John to stay away from the army, Stephen was not so influential with his eldest brother. William enlisted in Company D of the 139th Illinois (a hundred-day unit) in April 1864, and was soon promoted to sergeant. As William's enlistment neared its end that summer, Stephen warned him emphatically *"do not re-enlist."* There would be an effort made to have all "Hundredayers" [*sic*] sign up again, but William should be careful to let no influence induce him to stay in the army. As for himself, Stephen observed, if everything went well he would not regret his own service, but he did not want his brothers going through what he had endured.[21]

18. Fleharty to William Fleharty, July 16, 1864, in possession of Mrs. Sarah E. Glass.

19. Fleharty to John Q. A. Fleharty, August 1, 1863, in possession of Mrs. Sarah E. Glass.

20. Fleharty to John Q. A. Fleharty, December 20, 1863, in possession of Mrs. Sarah E. Glass.

21. Fleharty to William Fleharty, July 16, 1864, in possession of Mrs. Sarah E. Glass; *Report of the Adjutant General of the State of Illinois.* (Springfield, 1901), VII, 129; hereinafter cited as *Adj. Gen. Rep.*

The distractions of military duty, the pleasant excursions into the southern countryside, and the care he felt for his loved ones at home did not interfere with Fleharty's (or any other soldier's) desire or ability to keep up with news from Illinois. Union military setbacks in the spring and summer of 1862 and Lincoln's newly announced emancipation policy had created political tensions throughout the North. The delicate alliance between the administration and pro-Union Democrats was strained in almost every region of the country. Support for Lincoln's efforts to keep the Union intact began to unravel when it appeared that the destruction of slavery had become the more important goal. The soldiers saw this opposition to the administration quite often as a waning of local support for their own often deadly efforts to put down a rebellion. It was this situation, in the early summer of 1863, that caused Fleharty to cease his relationship with the Rock Island *Argus* and to transfer his loyalty and his literary effort to another publication.

As a Democrat, J. B. Danforth had set aside his political differences with the Republicans when the war began.[22] He would support the Lincoln administration in its efforts to suppress the rebellion and restore the Union. But with Lincoln's move toward emancipation in the fall of 1862 and with the issuance of the proclamation on January 1, 1863, Danforth saw that the nature of the war had changed. For him it was no longer "a war for the union and the constitution," but "a war for the negro and not the white man." Shedding the cloak of loyal opposition, Danforth tore into the Republicans: "It is Mr. Lincoln's emancipation policy . . . that we find fault with. And we shall not cease to denounce the miserable and inefficient manner in which the war is carried on, the corruption and imbecility of the administration, the swindling

22. A Vermont newspaperman, Joseph B. Danforth Jr. (1819–96) went to Rock Island in 1851 to open a hardware store. A year later he was back at his old trade as editor of the Rock Island *Republican*. In 1855 the *Republican*, to avoid any confusion with the new political party bearing the same name, became the *Argus*.

Early in his career, Danforth's politics had landed him several patronage positions. President Polk gave him a postmastership in Vermont, Pierce made him U.S. custodian for the island of Rock Island, and Buchanan rewarded his work at the Democratic convention of 1856 with an appointment as a purser in the navy. He had also earlier served on the military staff of the Democratic governor of Illinois with the rank of colonel. See *The Biographical Encyclopedia of Illinois of the Nineteenth Century* (Philadelphia, 1878), 248; and *Portrait and Biographical Album of Rock Island County, Illinois* (Chicago, 1885), 637–38, 713.

of shoddy contractors and cotton generals." For him, after twenty-one months of bloodshed, the fighting was "not a war for the restoration of the union," but for abolitionism.[23] Danforth wrote of himself at the time: "He advocated, with all the earnestness he was capable of, the abandonment of party names and distinctions during the war, and he adhered to that position till forced by the republican party to take sides with the abolitionist or democrats." His enmity for Lincoln's policies resulted in his paper being derisively called the "Secesh" or "Copperhead" *Argus*.[24]

In a March 18 editorial headed "The Secesh Argus," the Rock Island *Weekly Union*, a Republican paper that Danforth would sneeringly refer to as that "poor old nigger-league organ," attacked the Democratic editor for the "Secessionist proclivities" of his paper. The *Union's* editor, J. A. Kuck, felt that Democratic papers like the *Argus* were "secretly and sneakingly endeavoring to cripple the efforts of the Government to preserve the Union" by "finding all manner of fault with the administration." To him, writings like Danforth's reduced "the confidence of our soldiers in their leaders, thereby discouraging them." He saw Danforth exciting "a feeling antagonistical to the great measures adopted by our Government to subdue the rebellion, thereby discouraging enlistments."[25]

The new editor of the *Union*, Myron S. Barnes, formerly colonel of the 37th Illinois Infantry, also resented the attacks of the *Argus* on the Lincoln administration.[26] When the *Argus* "engaged in defaming the administration

23. Rock Island *Argus*, March 10, 1863, p. 2.

24. Ibid., March 13, 1863, p. 2.

25. When editor Thomas Pickett of the Rock Island *Register* resigned to enter the army, the city was left without a Republican paper. Kuck, who had been editing the *Independent* in neighboring Moline, was induced by Rock Island Republicans to move to that city and begin publication of a new party organ. Publication of the Rock Island *Union* began in November 1862. *The Past and Present of Rock Island County, Illinois* (Chicago, 1877), 161–62, 198; Rock Island *Argus*, November 5, 1863, p. 2; Rock Island *Weekly Union*, March 18, 1863, p. 2.

26. Learning the printer's trade as a teenager in his native New York, Myron S. Barnes (1824–89) became a peripatetic newspaperman. By the early 1840s he was in Chicago. At the outbreak of the Mexican War he enlisted in the 2d Illinois Infantry and was wounded at Buena Vista.

After stints with several northwestern papers, Barnes returned to central New York in 1849, and set up shop as owner and editor of the *Independent Watchman* in Ithaca. Initially a Whig, he (and his paper) switched to the new Republican Party; in 1856 he was a delegate to the

and abusing our soldiers in the field," he charged, it was "in the devil's service." By appealing to a "hatred of oppression and to their love of liberty," Barnes felt Democrats like Danforth were hiding their true colors and were not intending to "sustain the administration in putting down the rebellion."[27]

As news from the home front reached the men in the field, they too entered the debate, ensuring that those left behind were aware of their views on the subject. On March 17, 1863, Fleharty's regiment unanimously adopted a series of resolutions "expressive of their true feeling in regard to the war, its conduct, and the acts of the government to carry it on." The men agreed in their resolution that

> the union of our States must and shall be triumphantly sustained and perpetuated to our children; . . . we are . . . citizen soldiers fighting for the best interests of the human race, and against those who upon the destruction of our now free government would establish a tyrannical oligarchy, depending upon force for its maintenance, and fatal to all human freedom, independent of color or race;
>
> . . . there is as much good sense in making the inferior negro help us in our struggle for free government in any way which his capacity will admit of as there is in the rebels using him . . . ;
>
> . . . we utterly repudiate those public presses of the North which persistently vilify officers in the field, and by constant carping at the government seek to

Republican convention that nominated Frémont. Two years later he arrived in Rock Island County and became a partner of Robert H. Graham in the Moline *Independent.* He moved to Rock Island a year later and became one of the editors of the *Register.*

In the summer of 1861 he teamed with Julius White, the Lincoln-appointed customs collector of Chicago, to organize what would become the 37th Illinois Infantry and was elected the regiment's lieutenant colonel. By September, the 37th was involved in the struggle to hold Missouri in the Union and immediately became embroiled in controversy with the Missouri Home Guard over government property and runaway slaves.

Temporarily relieved from railroad-guarding and guerrilla-chasing, the 37th fought at Pea Ridge, where Barnes acquitted himself with distinction. When White was made a brigadier general, Barnes succeeded him as colonel of the 37th. But another run-in with the Home Guard resulted in Barnes's court-martial and dismissal from the service. (It would take two years and the good offices of Illinois congressman Isaac N. Arnold to have the charges overturned.) Barnes then returned to Rock Island and bought the *Union* in May 1863. See James Grant Wilson, *Biographical Sketches of Illinois Officers Engaged in the War Against the Rebellion of 1861* (Chicago, 1862), 32; *Portrait and Biographical Album of Knox County, Illinois* (Chicago, 1886), 782.

27. Rock Island *Weekly Union,* August 3, 1863, p. 2.

weaken its hold upon the affections of the people, and thus injure us more than they could with arms in their hands in open warfare.[28]

Copies of the resolutions were mailed to the Chicago *Times* and *Tribune*, Galesburg *Democrat*, Knox *Republican*, Aledo *Record*, Monmouth *Atlas*, Keithsburg *Observer*, Rock Island *Argus*, and Cambridge *Chronicle*. Danforth did not publish the document, further alienating the soldiers of the 102d.[29]

Uncomfortable and disillusioned with Danforth's editorials, Fleharty elected to terminate his relationship with the *Argus*. In June 1863 his column of "graphic and readable" letters moved to the *Union*. In order to explain the change, Barnes published Fleharty's letter to Danforth. To the colonel, he wrote the following:

> It is the habitual practice of many Northern papers to criticise the war measures of the Administration with much apparent vindictiveness—awakening distrust in the minds of the people, and thus embarrassing the Government in its efforts to suppress the rebellion.
>
> In my opinion, the influence of the *Argus* has long been and still is of this character. . . . and until the storm of bullets is over individuals should sacrifice personal opinions and prejudices for the good of our common country. To do otherwise is to connive at treason.[30]

The rest of Fleharty's work, for the next fifteen months, would appear in the pages of the *Union*.

By the summer of 1863, Fleharty's faith in the administration's course was such that he believed the war would be finished by December and the South would be back in the Union. He did not believe, however, that the institution of slavery or the problems associated with it would be gone. "Now, perhaps more than ever before," he wrote to his brother John, "the wisdom of the Government will be tested. When the rebellion is crushed, our danger will be most imminent. Two strong parties will instantly be formed, one demanding

28. Monmouth *Atlas*, April 3, 1863, p. 2; *History of Knox County, Illinois* (Chicago, 1878), 309–11.

29. Monmouth *Atlas*, April 3, 1863, p. 2. The *Democrat* and *Republican* were Knox County papers; the *Record* and *Observer* in Mercer County; the *Atlas* in Warren; the *Chronicle* in Henry; and the *Argus*, of course, in Rock Island County.

30. Rock Island *Weekly Union*, June 24, 1863, p. 1.

universal emancipation—the other clamoring for a restoration of the Union as it was. The idea of giving freedom to all the negroes of the South, *immediately* is decidedly visionary, and is an exhibition of that *ultra* Republicanism which resulted in the *reinstatement* of a monarchical government in France, at the close of the last century. What we want is *moderation. Civilization* will finally *kill* slavery, and the old constitution and the old government will remain intact. *I would but exact this condition:* 'that slavery shall not be extended.' " [31]

By December, although the war was not finished as he had predicted, he still believed conditions were favorable for an early peace. He was particularly pleased with Lincoln's annual message to Congress and felt it would have a good effect on the rebels, especially the amnesty provisions it put forth. Six months later he was still solidly in Lincoln's corner and was especially cheered by news of the president's renomination. "He is the man to finish up this war. He *must* be elected." No one, he said, could win his vote away from Lincoln with the possible exception of General Grant, and he did not think Grant would run.[32]

But the war dragged on. The 102d Illinois continued to perform duty as railroad guards until the early spring of 1864 when William T. Sherman began to assemble the army that would eventually conquer Atlanta. The last ten of Fleharty's letters to the *Union* deal with Sherman's campaign. They begin on May 8, just days after the Union army set out from its base at Chattanooga, and end September 4, two days after the fall of Atlanta. Their tone is somewhat more sober than that of the previous forty-five. The weather was hot, the

31. Fleharty to John Q. A. Fleharty, July 18, 1863, in possession of Mrs. Sarah E. Glass.

32. Fleharty to John Q. A. Fleharty, December 20, 1863; Fleharty to Stephen W. Fleharty, June 16, 1864; both in possession of Mrs. Sarah E. Glass. Lincoln's annual message for 1863, delivered to Congress on December 8, included a proclamation of amnesty. Lincoln's pardon extended to all persons who had participated "directly or by implication" in the rebellion. A full pardon, restoring all rights of property "except as to slaves," was to be granted on condition the person take and keep a loyalty oath. Exempt from the amnesty provisions were civil or diplomatic officers and agents of the Confederate government; military and naval officers above the rank of colonel and lieutenant (respectively); any person who had left a judicial position, a seat in Congress, or the military service under the U.S. government to aid the rebellion; and anyone who had treated captured Union soldiers and sailors (black or white) as anything other than lawful prisoners of war. See Roy P. Basler, ed., *The Collected Works of Abraham Lincoln* (New Brunswick, N.J., 1953) VII, 36–53, for the text of the annual message, and 53–56 for the text of the amnesty proclamation.

terrain rugged and very difficult, and the fighting desperate and severe. Casualty lists, the names of the wounded and the dead, now began to appear frequently in Fleharty's letters home. Descriptions of sharp encounters with the Confederate army convey the danger that was ever present among the soldiers in the Union lines. The continual rattle of musketry, the explosion of shells, the wounding and killing of comrades, the marching, the exposure to Georgia's heavy summer rains night and day all took their toll on Fleharty and his companions.

Although his letters to the newspaper recounting the regiment's fighting in northern Georgia are full and informative, Fleharty generally neglected many of his personal experiences in the events he described. About his part in the battle at Resaca on May 15, which was one of the two bloodiest days in the regiment's history, he notes only that "I received a slight flesh wound from a musket ball." In a letter to his brothers, however, he reports "standing for a moment at one time with my left side towards the enemy, urging the men to stand their ground when a ball cut through my coat, pants and shirts, almost in the rear of my left thigh[,] and cut a place in my hide about two inches long. It was almost a dishonorable wound but it was honorably received." He remained with some of the men in front of a captured Confederate battery until about eight o'clock in the evening, reporting that he fired his pistol once, a musket once, and a Spencer twice. "A battle," he noted, "is the most horrible thing imaginable."[33]

In the last letter he wrote home before the fall of Atlanta, on August 18, Fleharty was cheerful and confident. He happily noted the onset of cooler weather and looked forward to a trip to Iowa with his brother when the war was over. Although he was unsure of the exact course Sherman's army would take in the near future, he observed an optimism among the men. "The army *intends* to have Atlanta. There is no thought of retrograde movement. Yet Sherman has a difficult task to perform. It is next to impossible to take their works by assault, and it seems that they have been quite largely re-enforced. If this is so flank movements will be less practicable than heretofore. But then we think 'Old Billy' will *'oust'* them in some way."[34]

---

33. See letter No. 47. Fleharty to Henry C. and John Q. A. Fleharty, May 22, 1864, in possession of Mrs. Sarah E. Glass.

34. Fleharty to William Fleharty, August 16, 1864, in possession of Mrs. Sarah E. Glass.

It is apparent from his last letter to the papers, written September 4, 1864, that many of the men expected Sherman's campaign to end with the fall of Atlanta. Although the flag of the Union could be seen floating over the city, still "it does not appear that the campaign is ended. One of our men remarked when he heard of Sherman making his onward movement, that 'he is a glorious General, but don't know when to close his campaign.'" The war would continue for another seven months. The men, including Fleharty, were getting tired. There is a very real tone of disappointment in the last letter, as it becomes finally clear that the fighting will continue. Perhaps this is the reason Fleharty chose to stop sending his letters to the *Union*. He does not clearly say. In the last paragraph he wrote, Fleharty cryptically announced to his readers: "With the apparent close of the campaign, I conclude my series of letters to the UNION. If any of your readers are inquisitive and wish to know why I discontinue the correspondence, I will tell them that my reasons are weighty and most decidedly confidential. I may assure them that I remain on the best of terms with the UNION, and I trust also, that I have the good will of those who have read my rambling productions." With that "Jottings from Dixie" came to an end.

After the fall of Atlanta, the 102d went into camp on the Chattahoochee River where it remained until November 15, when Sherman's army set out on the "March to the Sea." In the intervening days, two of the most important preoccupations in Fleharty's life were elections; one for regimental chaplain and the other for president of the United States.

On September 12 Fleharty wrote his brother that "the *Chaplain has at last tendered his resignation.*" The chaplain, not particularly noted for his spiritual qualities, would mostly be missed because he was reputedly the best card-player in the regiment—a talent "learnt on Sunday," speculated one soldier.[35]

35. Fleharty to Jesse J. Fleharty, September 12, 1864, in possession of Mrs. Sarah E. Glass; William F. Cochran to "Kind Friend," September 22, 1864, William F. Cochran Papers, Illinois State Historical Library, Springfield. The chaplain was Jesse E. Huston, a farmer from Eliza Township, Mercer County. He was originally a corporal in Co. K, was promoted to sergeant, and became chaplain in December 1862 when Amos K. Tullis resigned the position. In recommending the commissioning of Huston, Colonel Smith had called him "a most worthy young man" and pointed out that he had been a regular minister in the Universalist Church for five years. See *Adj. Gen. Rep.*, V, 593, 611; "Descriptive List of Company K," and Smith to Gov. Richard Yates, December 27, 1862, Record Group 301, Illinois State Archives.

Seeing an opportunity, Fleharty approached Col. Franklin C. Smith to explore the possibility of the selection of his brother Jesse to fill the vacancy. Smith was receptive and said that if Jesse were interested in the spot he should "drop us a line" so indicating, and an election would be held immediately. If Jesse prevailed, Smith promised to recommend him for the appointment. Fleharty predicted to Jesse that he would certainly win the election and promised to speak to every officer in the regiment on his behalf. He did not wish to influence Jesse in either direction and suggested that maybe he had better not accept *"unless you have been drafted!"*[36]

The issue, however, was not quickly decided. By the end of October the regiment's officers had taken a vote on the subject, and of those voting thirteen were for Jesse and two were for Rev. Cornelius M. Wright, the only other candidate for the office.[37] One of the officers had then moved that the position not be filled at all and the motion had carried. The men, however, wanted a chaplain, and a petition was circulated on behalf of Wright. It was signed by two-thirds of the men of the regiment and submitted to the officers, who then agreed to allow the men to vote on their choice. Those who had signed Wright's petition, Fleharty complained, now felt obliged to support him in the election. The whole affair only proved, he concluded, that "there are fools & blockheads and sinners in the army as well as in other places." Wright won the election and served as the regiment's spiritual leader until it was mustered out.[38]

The upcoming presidential election proved to be a cause for some anguish to Fleharty. His political opinions and his adherence to the tenets of the "old constitution," at least as he interpreted it, were beginning to get Fleharty into trouble back home. In a lengthy and powerful letter to his father, the young man set forth his political principles in a manifesto worthy of any politician.

His political sentiments, he declared, had not changed since the war began. He still believed that slavery was wrong, but it was a matter for local and state legislation. The North had no more business interfering with slavery than it had going around the world righting all its wrongs. If slavery were to receive

36. Fleharty to Jesse J. Fleharty, September 12, 1864, in possession of Mrs. Sarah E. Glass.

37. The Rev. Mr. Wright was a Methodist clergyman from Keithsburg in Mercer County.

38. Fleharty to Stephen W. Fleharty, October 24, 1864; and Fleharty to "Brother," November 7, 1864, both in possession of Mrs. Sarah E. Glass.

such a blow in the war that it could never recover, Fleharty observed, "I would be highly gratified." But the president's responsibility in the conflict extended no further than the restoration of the Union with as little loss in blood and money as possible. If the "Ultra men" of the North found it impossible to reunite with a South that tolerated slavery, they should have rejoiced at secession. If they now felt it their duty to abolish slavery by force, then John Brown had not been wrong when he had attempted the same thing.

He differed, he said, from the ultras of both regions in this: *"I believe the government*—(the Union)—may exist upon the basis that our fathers gave it—the Constitution." If the government attempted to restore the Union on any but this constitutional basis it was being false to its promises, not only to Union men in the South, but to the whole world.

Nothing but "intolerable oppression," he believed, would have given the South cause for rebellion, and that condition had never existed. The Federal government, therefore, was well within its rights to use the bayonet to restore the Union. But once that restoration had taken place the power of the bayonet should cease. The president could justify an antislavery crusade only on the basis that he was divinely appointed for that purpose.

Fleharty recognized that many in the country were saying that sound policy dictated universal emancipation and the arming of the slaves to aid in suppressing the rebellion. In his experience, he noted, he had seen enough of the black man to convince him that "he is incapable of decent self-government." He believed blacks could never be educated to be the equal of whites and that they would forever occupy an inferior position. He went even further by saying that blacks had more of an "animal nature" than did whites, and seemed to be most happy in the gratification of their "animal desires." Without help the black man would never attain intellectual improvement. "Are such men," he asked, "fit for Soldiers?" He did not think it right to arm blacks as soldiers unless they were also accorded the privileges of citizenship. But was the white American population ready to make the black a citizen? He did not think so. The arming of blacks had united the South and divided the North and was bad policy. There were, he conceded, many brave black men, but as a class they could not be depended on in the field.

Emancipation, he noted, had been embraced by Lincoln as a necessary war measure; a position with which he heartily disagreed. When the object of the war was achieved (the restoration of the Union), the emancipation movement should be forgotten. Fleharty feared, however, that universal emancipation would then become a "necessary peace measure." He had differed with Lincoln on other questions before emancipation, but the proclamation had "widened the gulf." Fleharty never doubted the honesty of Lincoln's intentions, and believed the president possessed many noble qualities. But Lincoln was, he felt, "imbued with the delusive idea that he is a heaven-appointed instrument to abolish slavery." When rulers had such ideas, he warned, "they override constitutions and laws and appeal to a 'higher law' for justification." At this crucial point in the country's history, "sober counsels should prevail. We want no experiments. We want straight-forward, out-spoken, and unvascillating [sic] statesmanship."

Lincoln's Democratic opponent, General George B. McClellan, would be less trustworthy, but Fleharty felt that the Democratic candidate would "vigorously prosecute" the war for the sole purpose of restoring the Union. He did not have the same confidence in McClellan's *"moral integrity"* as he had in Lincoln, but he noted that the Democrat's letter of acceptance "suits me precisely." He did not share the same feelings about the Democratic Party's 1864 platform, calling it the "most sneaking[,] treasonable, contemptable [sic] document that has ever been made the basis of a great party." Most of the men who framed it, he said, were traitors. If McClellan endorsed it, it would likely kill his candidacy.[39]

His opinions, he noted, were not given in a "dictatorial style." It was, after all, "human to err." He believed in freedom of thought ("it is about all the liberty I have left"), and wished for others to exercise "unlimited" liberty in their political words and actions, as long as "they are loyal to the Government." Having endured so much in the service, he felt he was entitled "to the credit for being a loyal man." The opinions of others, however, would not change his political ideas. *"Through a rough school of experience I am learning to think for myself."*[40]

39. General McClellan's candidacy was effectively torpedoed by the insertion of a "peace at any price" plank (a feat engineered by Clement Vallandigham) in the platform adopted in August at Chicago. In his letter of acceptance, which went through six drafts, McClellan clearly stated: "The Union is the one condition of peace." He made no mention at all of slavery. See Stephen W. Sears, *George B. McClellan: The Young Napoleon* (New York, 1988), 372–76. For the text of the Democratic platform, see Donald Bruce Johnson and Kirk H. Porter, comps., *National Party Platforms, 1840–1972.* (5th ed., Urbana, 1973), 34–35. For the text of McClellan's letter of acceptance see Stephen W. Sears, ed., *The Civil War Papers of George B. McClellan: Selected Correspondence, 1860–1865* (New York, 1989), 590–92.

40. Fleharty to Stephen W. Fleharty, September 18, 1864, in possession of Mrs. Sarah E. Glass.

By November 4 Fleharty's views on the presidential contest had been somewhat refined. Although he had not altered his opinion of Lincoln's emancipation policy at all, he reiterated his previous statement that he could not support
McClellan as long as he ran on the Democratic platform. If he were home
on election day, he concluded, he would vote for Lincoln. "A true Union
Conservative man on an unconditional Union platform would have suited me
better, but there is no alternative. It is better to risk the interests of the country
in the hands of Lincoln, with his conditional Union policy, than in the hands
of a man of *doubtful integrity,* who is also *conditionally Union.* "[41]

On November 15, one week after Lincoln won his second term, Sherman's
army set out on its memorable march to the sea through some of the richest
agricultural land in the South. To assure his success, Sherman cut all communication between his army and the North. Nothing was heard from Sgt. Maj.
Fleharty by family or friends until the city of Savannah was under siege of the
Yankee army a month later. In his first letter home it was apparent to all that
Stephen was in fine spirits. He could never have envisioned when he enlisted,
he said, that he would "drift away down to this place." He had written a long
account of the march in a diary which he had kept "in camp at evening,
sometimes; and often by the roadside when the column had halted to rest." It
was not, he noted, half as full as it might have been. In keeping with his
penchant for journalism, he had sent it not to his family but to the editor of
the Galesburg *Free Democrat* for publication in that paper.[42]

The young man's exuberance over this great adventure was not in the least
restrained. He described for his father some of the sights he had seen:

> Oh! what a time we have had! No other raid ever equalled the one we have just
> made! How we lived like kings! Yea on the fat of a fat land; but I cannot tell
> you half. We were turned loose in a plentiful country and I believe there is or
> was a greater variety of provisions in the country through which we passed than
> we could find in passing through the heart of Illinois. Yams, yams, yams! there

41. Fleharty to Stephen W. Fleharty, November 4, 1864, in possession of Mrs. Sarah E.
Glass. At a regimental election held September 28, Lincoln had defeated McClellan 236 to 136.
See Keithsburg *Observer,* October 20, 1864, p. 1.

42. Fleharty to Stephen W. Fleharty, December 17, 1864, in possession of Mrs. Sarah E.
Glass. Unfortunately, it has proven impossible to locate any existing copies of the *Free Democrat*
from this period to determine whether the diary was ever published. The diary itself has not
been found.

was no end of them. Fresh pork[,] molasses, always, and often preserves, honey butter (and once I had sausage, and once a good heavy horn of 'Old Madeira Wine,' perhaps forty years old!)[43]

He could have gotten rich, he observed, if he had resorted to pillage as had so many of his comrades. He noted that many of the Georgians in the path of Sherman's legions had buried their valuables, but to no avail, as the "keen scented Yankees soon found them." The army had camped one night near the plantation of former U.S. senator Herschel V. Johnson (who had been the running mate of Stephen A. Douglas in 1860). Everything of value on the place had been buried, and even though Col. Smith had said that Johnson was a Union man, the Federal troops "just *waded in* there."

The looting was so pervasive, Fleharty explained, that if an invading army "should take from Illinois as many coverlets[,] quilts & blankets as our army took by the way, the people would certainly suffer with cold." At Milledgeville, the Georgia state capital, many of the books in the state library were thrown into the street and trampled by Union troops and horses. One soldier brought a large book from the library back to camp which Fleharty thought his father would like. He figured the soldier would probably have left the book behind, and that "under the circumstances there would be no wrong in sending it where it would be appreciated." So he took it along and promised to send it home as soon as he could. He also managed to get a cutlass from the state arsenal and was sending it home, along with some old Georgia state seals made of wax.

"You could hardly overestimate," he wrote, "the aggregate value of the property destroyed." He did not think an hour had gone by from November 14 to December 10 in which the smoke of burning Rebel property could not be seen. "I tell you we were death on cotton and railroads." Such work had indeed turned the Confederacy into a shell. But, Fleharty warned, the shell was still "pretty hard in some places." He thought that it was very likely the Rebel army under Lee in Virginia could still be supplied from the country between Sherman and Richmond, but still "this army has dealt the Confederacy a heavy blow."[44]

By the end of December, General Sherman had presented the city of Savannah to President Lincoln as a Christmas gift and it was rumored that the army

43. Ibid.
44. Ibid.

was about to embark on another campaign. Then, Fleharty wrote, "look out ye *Rattlesnakes!* for I think we will cross over to the 'sacred soil' of South Carolina." Although he would just as soon remain in camp for a while longer, if there must be another campaign right away then "let it be by all means into South Carolina."

The army was more than ready, and confidence in the commanding general was stronger than ever. "Gen. Sherman is the man to lead us," Fleharty wrote his father. "He commands an army which thinks he can go where he pleases in the Confederacy. We are all proud of our noble General. I wish his subordinates were as much entitled to our esteem and confidence."[45]

After Savannah's capitulation on December 21, the men began laying out a permanent camp and constructing "board quarters." But Sherman, who kept a tight lip about his plans, was halting in Savannah just long enough for the army to catch its breath and refit. There would be no winter quarters this year. Supply ships arrived by previous arrangement to meet the army, bringing needed clothing, shoes, ammunition, other necessary equipment, and (just as important) mail from home.[46]

On December 30 Sherman reviewed the 20th Corps, and the next day with the 102d leading the advance, the 3d Division crossed the Savannah River into South Carolina. New Year's Day found the men camped on the premises of Langdon Cheves, "once a prominent South Carolina secessionist." In a letter to his father, Fleharty enclosed a printed copy of a speech found in Cheves's papers. In the 1850 address, Cheves had asked a Nashville audience what course the Yankees could pursue if the South seceded: "Will they invade us? Where is their army?" Fleharty proudly told his father: "It is enough for me to say that our army camps now upon his plantation." When the 102d left Cheves's plantation three days later, the beautiful grounds and "once peaceful home" had been destroyed.[47]

Setting foot on the soil where secession was born and reared, Sherman's

45. Fleharty to Stephen W. Fleharty, December 28, 1864, in possession of Mrs. Sarah E. Glass.

46. Fleharty, *Our Regiment*, 128.

47. Ibid., 128, 130; Fleharty to Stephen W. Fleharty, January 5, 1865, in possession of Mrs. Sarah E. Glass. Langdon Cheves (1776–1857) had been a member of the U.S. House of Representatives from 1811 to 1815 (serving as Speaker in 1814–15). After two years on the South Carolina Court of Appeals, he became president of the Second Bank of the United States.

"high privates" instantly began settling the score for the sundering of the Union and more than three years of war. Having been plucked from their homes, endured privations beyond description, and forced to see so many of their friends and comrades dead or maimed, the Federal soldiers began to balance the account with fire and destruction.

Fleharty described what became a common occurrence. When the men would come to "a charming palatial residence," they began ransacking where "the richest of carpets covered the floors; splendidly bound books ornamented the library ... [and] a sweet-toned piano was in the parlor." Then, he explained, "[i]n accordance with orders received *from a proper source*, the building was burned." Each day as the men marched through South Carolina the burning continued, always "according to orders." After visiting the ruins of another grand old southern home, Stephen wrote his brother that the men were "destroying everything as they go. Nearly every fine dwelling is burned." All that remained of the great mansions "as monuments of departed glory," he noted, were the chimneys and the steps.[48]

A month into the campaign, Fleharty wrote home saying that the army was about forty miles from Savannah and about four miles from the Savannah River, but that the men did not know their "final Objective Point." Having no idea of their commander's plan, Sherman's men continued with their own work, which was to destroy all the property in their path. "On the right, on the left, and in front, dark columns of smoke rolled up, as the great army, with its flankers, the foragers, pressed forward."[49]

As he had done during his march through Georgia, Sherman severed his supply and communication link with the North. To feed the army, foragers spread out to commandeer food for the marching columns. Fleharty took his turn with the regimental foraging parties, sharing the adventures and close calls that invariably occurred when the men were away from the main column. On one early foraging expedition, he returned with a sheep and "thought then it was a rich prize." But it was not long before he could "hardly look at mutton." After that the foragers returned regularly with "Hams—nice—half-cured rich hams."[50]

48. Fleharty, *Our Regiment*, 134; Fleharty to William L. Fleharty, February 1, 1865, in possession of Mrs. Sarah E. Glass.

49. Fleharty to William L. Fleharty, February 1, 1865, in possession of Mrs. Sarah E. Glass; Fleharty, *Our Regiment*, 135.

50. Fleharty to William L. Fleharty, March 3, 1865, in possession of Mrs. Sarah E. Glass.

"It would be difficult," he wrote to his brother, "to give you an adequate idea of the manner in which this foraging business is conducted." In an attempt to explain, he constructed the hypothetical case of a division marching from Galesburg to Rock Island. To make his points clear, his account made use of towns and families familiar to the home folk. He told how friends and relatives would have their crops and food stores taken while soldiers rummaged through the house looking for anything of value. It was a rough side of the war that obviously troubled him. He did not want to be seen as a marauder and a thief, and he wanted his family to know the difference. *"Not all* of the *foragers* would steal. *All* were ordered to take provisions. I felt that provisions[,] fodder &c belonged to me (except when in the possession of the poor)[.]"[51]

For three days beginning February 8, the bulk of Sherman's army was engaged in destroying the Charleston and Augusta Railroad. "The smoke of the burning ties," Fleharty observed, "rising mile after mile, and mingling with the smoke of burning buildings, burning fences and burning cotton, enveloped the whole country."[52]

In general, the Confederate army offered little resistance as Sherman moved northward. The fighting was left mainly to the foraging parties who periodically came in contact with Joe Wheeler's cavalry. On occasion, the rebels would make a stand that called for the regiment or the brigade to form a battle line. Fleharty participated in one of those skirmishes ("where the bullets whistled around quite wickedly") near Lawtonville on February 2. The Federal advance had come upon a rebel force that determined to stand its ground and put up a stiff fight. Fleharty's brigade deployed and a brisk struggle ensued. "I was riding along the line, about to give my horse into the hands of a man until the fight was over, when a ball struck a man [Cpl. William Siverts] in Co. E almost directly in front of me and instantly killed him. The same ball wounded another man [James C. Simpson]." War was a deadly business no matter how large the action.[53]

On March 4 the 102d crossed into North Carolina, where the destruction was now limited to military objectives such as "burning stores of rosin." By

51. Ibid.

52. Fleharty, *Our Regiment,* 136.

53. Ibid., 136; Fleharty to William L. Fleharty, March 27, 1865, in possession of Mrs. Sarah E. Glass; *Adj. Gen. Rep.,* V, 603; Thomas Simpson Diary, February 2, 1865, in possession of Melvin Simpson, Alexis, Ill. (James C. Simpson, Thomas Simpson's brother, died of the wound received at Fayetteville, N.C., on March 14, 1865.)

the eleventh the regiment was encamped at Fayetteville. Here the men were allowed to send letters home, having been "cut loose from communications 37 days." It was a short rest. On the thirteenth the brigade marched in review before Sherman as it left the city.[54]

After having been unable to mount a credible defense for several months, the Confederate command had finally concentrated a significant force in North Carolina and prepared once again to oppose Sherman. Gen. Joseph E. Johnston, Sherman's old nemesis in Georgia, had scraped together about twenty thousand men. Uncharacteristically, Johnston took the offensive with a plan to ambush a wing of Sherman's army, hoping to halt the Federal advance toward Goldsboro.

While Johnston organized his army, a force under Gen. William J. Hardee fought a delaying action south of Averysboro on March 16. Here advancing Federal troops found their way blocked by rebel infantry protected by breastworks. Sherman, writing after the war, recalled: "Coming up, I advised that a brigade should make a wide circuit by the left, and, if possible, catch this line in flank." The brigade in position to carry out Sherman's order was Fleharty's.[55]

Maneuvering to the left, the brigade halted within 125 yards of the rebel flank and rear. Having "come to the position by a circuitous route," the Union line hesitated momentarily to be sure it was actually the enemy in its front. "At length all became satisfied that they were Rebels—a terrific yell was raised—we rushed upon them yelling like demons," Stephen wrote his brother, "and oh! It would have done you good to see them run!" The charging Federals captured three guns of Macbeth's Charleston Battery and 217 prisoners, who were caught "in the trench behind their works holding up white handkerchiefs." The fleeing rebels left behind a field strewn with "all sorts of rebel property" and a number of killed and wounded.

The retreating Confederates re-formed at a second line of works, but the

---

54. Fleharty to William L. Fleharty, March 27, 1865, in possession of Mrs. Sarah E. Glass; Fleharty, *Our Regiment*, 156.

55. Joseph T. Glatthaar, *The March to the Sea and Beyond: Sherman's Troops in the Savannah and Carolinas Campaigns* (New York, 1985), 167; James M. McPherson, *Battle Cry of Freedom: The Civil War Era* (New York, 1988), 830; Mark M. Boatner III, *The Civil War Dictionary* (New York, 1959), 35; E. B. Long, *The Civil War Day by Day: An Almanac, 1861–1865* (Garden City, N.Y., 1971), 652–53; William T. Sherman, *Memoirs of Gen. W. T. Sherman* (4th ed.; New York, 1891), II, 301.

arrival of the rest of the Federal column and a general advance forced the rebels back to a third position. At this point the Union attack ground to a halt. "We went as close [as] 150 yds of their artillery and were under a desperate fire until dark." With little cover and the "grape shot . . . rattling around like hail," the Federal soldiers "threw up some light breastworks" and awaited darkness. With the coming of dawn it became evident that the Confederates had retired during the night. [56]

Three days later at Bentonville, Johnston attacked Sherman's left flank with everything he had. The rebel trap caught portions of the advancing 14th and 20th Corps off guard. Although initially thrown back in disorder, Sherman's veteran troops rallied and withstood several assaults. Ward's 3d Division of the 20th Corps (including the 102d) was guarding a wagon train when ordered into action. The men hurried forward, formed on the extreme left, and quickly threw up breastworks. The 102d, however, did not become engaged. By March 21, the rest of the Union army was on the field. Johnston withdrew the next day allowing Sherman an unblocked route to Goldsboro.[57]

Writing to his brother Jesse from Goldsboro on March 31, Stephen reflected on his good fortune thus far. "I am thankful that through so many dangers I have escaped unhurt. And I have felt that many better boys have fallen—victims of disease and the fatal bullet. Certainly I am not permitted to live on account of any worth or goodness in me." He went on to say that there was a rumor in camp that Richmond had fallen. "Perhaps it is true," he hoped. It was not.[58]

By April 9, however, things had changed. He wrote his father that the

56. Fleharty to William L. Fleharty, March 27, 1865, in possession of Mrs. Sarah E. Glass; Fleharty, *Our Regiment,* 157–59; Henry W. Slocum, "Sherman's March from Savannah to Bentonville," in Robert U. Johnson et al., eds., *Battles and Leaders of the Civil War* (New York, 1888), IV, 691; *The War of the Rebellion: A Compilation of the Official Records of the Union and Confederate Armies* (Washington, D.C., 1880–1901), Ser. I, Vol. XXXVII, Pt. 1, pp. 789–90, 794–95, 798–801 [hereinafter cited as *OR.* Unless otherwise noted, all citations are to Series I]. See esp. the report of Maj. Hiland H. Clay of the 102d on pages 794–95. The 102d lost two men killed and seventeen wounded at Averysboro.

57. Fleharty, *Our Regiment,* 101; Glatthaar, *March to the Sea,* 169–72; McPherson, *Battle Cry of Freedom,* 830; Boatner, *Civil War Dictionary,* 61; and Long, *Civil War Almanac,* 654–55. For the most recent scholarship on Bentonville, see Nathaniel C. Hughes, *Bentonville: The Final Battle of Sherman and Johnston* (Chapel Hill, 1996).

58. Fleharty to Jesse J. Fleharty, March 31, 1865, in possession of Mrs. Sarah E. Glass.

army was preparing to chase Johnston toward Raleigh. News had arrived, he announced, of the fall of the Confederate capital. "Richmond is at last ours[,] thank God! I hope the day of Peace is now not far distant." Five days later he wrote from Raleigh of the long-awaited news of Lee's surrender that had finally reached Sherman's camps. "Oh! Happy day for our country! *Peace is at hand! It is now inevitable!*" On the fifteenth he reported that it *"is strongly rumored that Johnston* is surrendering to-day." The rumor was false.[59]

The morning of April 16 dawned rainy. Fleharty was ill, but breakfasted on hard tack and coffee as the regiment prepared to join the pursuit of Johnston's army. Before the 102d could join the line, however, the marching column was halted and sent back to camp. Johnston had sent a courier to Sherman to ask for terms. The hope that this development had brought to the army was seriously dampened the next day when word reached the Union camp of the assassination of President Lincoln. "It seemed," wrote Fleharty, "that the army had lost a father. I did not know that I myself had thought so much of Lincoln. And I did not know that the army loved him so well."[60]

By April 21, Sherman's men knew that he and Johnston had reached an understanding and come to terms that "will secure peace from the Potomac to the Rio Grande provided the agreement is approved at Washington." The men were sure that "Uncle Billy" would accede to nothing that was not "all right."[61]

But the terms were not acceptable to the government at Washington, and on April 25 the army took up its pursuit of Johnston once again. Fleharty was ill again that morning, but "determined to go as long as I could." During the day the army marched from Raleigh about fifteen miles in the direction of Goldsboro. "I thought many times during the day," Fleharty reported, "that I could not possibly stand it until night." With help from the regiment's new chaplain, Fleharty made it to camp. For the next two days he was down with fever, and during that time, on April 26, Johnston surrendered his army to Sherman.

The day following the surrender, the 102d was ordered back to Raleigh,

---

59. Fleharty to Stephen W. Fleharty, April 9, 1865; to Jesse J. Fleharty, April 14, 1865; and to "Dear Brothers," April 15, 1865, all in possession of Mrs. Sarah E. Glass.

60. Fleharty to Stephen W. Fleharty, April 21, 1865, in possession of Mrs. Sarah E. Glass.

61. Ibid.

and Fleharty was forced to make the trip in an ambulance. It was "the first ambulance ride that I ever had," he noted. Orders then came to send all men unable to march to the convalescent camp at Alexandria, Virginia. Fleharty desperately attempted to procure a horse for the journey. When he was unable to find one, Colonel Smith strongly advised him to make the trip by boat, as it was evident that he could not march.

Consequently, on May 3, Fleharty boarded a transport at New Bern; it sailed down Pamlico Sound, through Hatteras Inlet, and into the Atlantic Ocean. The ship reached the Atlantic about noon on the fourth, and within five minutes Fleharty became dizzy and was forced to take to his bunk, "lest I should be the first to heave up Jonah." It did not take him long, however, to find his sea legs, and he made the rest of the trip in relative comfort.[62]

On May 5 Fleharty and his companions entered Chesapeake Bay and by evening had steamed into the mouth of the Potomac River. Fleharty wrote to his father that he had taken up a position on the starboard side of the ship to get a good view of that part of Maryland in which his ancestors had settled. He was, he thought, probably the first of the family to see it in many years. He apparently did not know that Dorchester County and the mouth of the Choptank River were still nearly fifty miles to the north, and that his ship had turned in to the Potomac long before reaching that point.

The next day, after sailing past Mount Vernon, Fleharty caught sight of the capitol dome ("the proud Capitol of the proudest nation of the earth"). The transport landed at Alexandria, and Fleharty made his way to the camp, where he was soon put in charge of about a hundred convalescent soldiers. "The duty is light," he noted, "& may help me to pass off the time until the Regt comes up."[63]

While waiting for the regiment to come up, Fleharty took an opportunity to do some sightseeing in the capital. On May 16 he and a friend spent six hours touring the capitol, the White House and the Smithsonian Institute, which he called "one of the pro[u]dest evidences of our nation's greatness." The variety of plants and animals he saw there would provide "material for a life-time of study."[64]

62. Fleharty to Stephen W. Fleharty, May 9, 1865, in possession of Mrs. Sarah E. Glass.
63. Ibid.
64. Fleharty to [?], May 17, 1865, in possession of Mrs. Sarah E. Glass. On the same day that he visited the Smithsonian, a tragedy befell Fleharty and the 102d. As the regiment lay in

The regiment did not reach Alexandria until May 19. Five days were then spent preparing for the grand review of the Union armies that would display the military might that had overcome the Confederacy. At 9:00 A.M. on May 24, the 102d crossed the Long Bridge over the Potomac with the rest of Sherman's army and headed for the capitol building. From there the procession continued up Pennsylvania Avenue to the White House where the regiment "'dipped' the old flag to the President, Grant, Sherman, and a brilliant galaxy of other distinguished men of our own and other lands." From there it was back to camp, where the officers made out the regiment's rolls in preparation for its separation from the Federal service. On June 6, Fleharty noted, "we ceased in reality to be soldiers of the Union army—and became as the men expressed it, *brevet* citizens."[65]

At four o'clock that morning the regiment marched away from the brigade encampment to the accompaniment of the band of the 79th Ohio. They stopped briefly at brigade headquarters to give three cheers for Colonel Harrison, then again at division headquarters where they did the same for old General Ward. By nine o'clock the 102d had boarded a train in Washington and begun its journey home. The route took the men through Baltimore; through York and Johnstown, Pennsylvania; and into Pittsburgh, where they were serenaded and treated to a great breakfast on the morning of June 8. Then it was on through Ohio and Indiana until, at last, the train pulled into Chicago on the morning of the ninth. The 102d was assigned quarters at Camp Fry where it received final pay and discharge five days later. Each man then boarded the first available train and made his way home.[66]

Fleharty returned to Galesburg, but was soon back in Chicago to work with the printers on the publication of his regimental history. Work on the book must have begun no later than late April or early May. He had written to Jesse

---

camp near the old Chancellorsville battlefield, Adjutant Snyder and his orderly, Pvt. William Jones of Company I, set out on the morning of the sixteenth to explore the battleground. They were last seen two miles from the regiment asking directions from a group of former rebels. When they failed to return, Lieutenant Trego and a squad went in search of the missing men. The search party returned, however, without a clue as to their fate. Suspecting foul play, the men of the 102d concluded that Snyder and Jones had been bushwhacked and murdered. Fleharty, *Our Regiment*, 171; *History of Mercer County*, 422.

65. Fleharty, *Our Regiment*, 172–73, 177.

66. Ibid., 177–80.

in late April: "I am now thinking strongly of writing the History of the Regt. If I do I will have the financial part of the work arranged before the Regt separates. Probably will obtain about twenty subscribers who will furnish $20 each. Their pay to be taken in books—perhaps—or money as soon as realized. I would also inform all the boys that they could o[b]tain the books by sending to Galesburg. I think I could make it *safe* & *make it pay*. Had not thought so strongly of it until I received your letter."[67]

Jesse in turn responded, "I think your plan for the publication of your regimental history would be very fine indeed—but what you do must be done very quickly." He advised Stephen that the first volume of Dr. Thomas M. Eddy's *Patriotism of Illinois* was to appear later that same month, and that if he could publish his history before the second volume appeared "many facts might be permanently bound up in this great book of Illinois patriotism—as the Chicago press speaks of it as a 'master piece.'"[68]

In addition to consulting his own letters and notes, Fleharty used the diaries of at least three other members of the 102d, and he corresponded with other comrades to obtain their recollections and contributions while the events being described were fresh in their minds. By June he had had circulars printed announcing the book, and early in July 1865 he advertised the prospective publication of the book in the press. "It will be well bound," he promised, "and will contain over 200 pages." To ensure the availability of copies, he advised readers to have their orders in by September 1. The price was $1.25 plus an additional .15 if sent through the mail.[69]

Once the book had been published and he had returned to Mercer County, Fleharty combined book promotion with his search for a peacetime career.

67. Fleharty to Jesse J. Fleharty, April 21, 1865, in possession of Mrs. Sarah E. Glass.

68. Jesse J. Fleharty to Fleharty, May 8, August 28, 1865, in possession of Mrs. Sarah E. Glass. Eddy's book, *The Patriotism of Illinois: A Record of the Civil and Military History of the State in the War for the Union, with a History of the Campaigns in which Illinois Soldiers Have Been Conspicuous, Sketches of Distinguished Officers, the Roll of the Illustrious Dead, Movements of the Sanitary and Christian Commissions* (Chicago, 1865), contains a one and one-half page sketch of the 102d in II, 390–91. There is no hint that Eddy made use of Fleharty's work.

69. He used the diaries of Capt. James Y. Merritt (Co. K), Lt. Byron Jordan (Co. C), and Sgt. Thomas M. Bell (Co. D). Fleharty, *Our Regiment*, 5. See also letters to Fleharty from Capt. Dan W. Sedwick, August 4, 1865, and Lt. Col. Isaac McManus, June 23, 1865, in possession of Mrs. Sarah E. Glass; and from McManus, August 21, 1865, in Stephen F. Fleharty Papers, Henry M. Seymour Library, Knox College; Keithsburg *Observer*, July 6, 1865, p. 1.

He sent complimentary copies of *Our Regiment* to persons of authority, accompanied by a request for a job. Governor Richard J. Oglesby called the book "well written" and "logically arranged" but regretted that he had no vacancies to fill.[70]

Fleharty even sent a copy to his old commander, General Sherman. Writing from his St. Louis headquarters, Sherman politely acknowledged receipt of the book, but went on to share his opinion of the genre in which Fleharty had chosen to work: "I regret that you make a mistake so natural, for the Book which I have read must certainly be most welcome to all members of the 102nd Ills. as well as the friends of it. But the outside world cannot afford to read Regimental Histories because we had so many of them, that in detail they are too voluminous and can be condensed into histories of great Armies or Campaigns." As far as a job was concerned, Sherman assured Fleharty that he had not a single office at his disposal and that he ran his headquarters with but a few soldier-clerks. However, he concluded, "I will do the best that I can which is to send you $3 for the Copy you sent me [more than twice its price] which I repeat interested me very much and is now a part of my War Library."[71]

Fleharty also participated in the public life of Mercer County. In 1866 he was elected justice of the peace. Then, on September 14, 1870, he announced his candidacy for the seat from the Seventy-first District (which included only Mercer County) in the Illinois House of Representatives. The local Republican press ran a typically negative campaign, giving far more attention to the faults and foibles of Fleharty's opponent, Democratic editor John Geiger, than it gave to its own man. In the end, however, Fleharty won the election with almost 56 percent of the vote, carrying ten of the county's fourteen townships.[72]

70. Richard J. Oglesby to Fleharty, May 21, 1866, in possession of Mrs. Sarah E. Glass.

71. William T. Sherman to Fleharty, June 25, 1866, in possession of Mrs. Sarah E. Glass. More than two and a half years later, on December 28, 1868, Fleharty returned Sherman's $3 and sent him the manuscript of a play he had written, asking for his thoughts. Sherman noted the receipt of the $3 ("I am glad you do not need it") and reluctantly commented on the play. "I do not like to act as a critic of Literary matter," he said, "as that is not my vocation. I prefer you should submit it to the judgment of a more competent person. It hardly seems to me suited to the modern stage and is somewhat allegorical." He returned the manuscript, which has since disappeared. Sherman to Fleharty, January 2, 1869, in possession of Mrs. Sarah E. Glass.

72. Aledo *Weekly Record*, September 14, 1870, p. 3; October 26, 1870, p. 2; and November 16, 1870, p. 2. In the election Fleharty received a total of 1,259 votes to Geiger's 997.

The Twenty-seventh General Assembly (1870–1872), to which he had been elected, held four sessions (one regular, two special, and one adjourned). It was the first legislature to meet since the adoption of the state's new constitution; hence much of its time and legislative activity was occupied in crafting new laws that would put the document into operation and in adapting laws already on the books to its requirements. The first special session called by Gov. John M. Palmer was required to make additional appropriations for government expenses and for work on the new statehouse. (During Fleharty's term the House was forced to meet in Springfield's Second Presbyterian Church.) The second extra session was called in October to attempt to provide some financial relief for the city of Chicago, which was suffering the devastating effects of the famous fire of October 9, 1871. This was also the general assembly that put former general John A. "Black Jack" Logan into the United States Senate. In all the Twenty-seventh General Assembly met for 293 days, far longer than any of its twenty-six predecessors.[73]

More public attention, however, was paid to a single letter written by Fleharty than to any of his other legislative activities. The letter was written, characteristically, to a newspaper (the Chicago *Tribune*) less than two months before the legislature adjourned for the final time; it concerned the candidacy of President Ulysses S. Grant for a second term.

Fleharty was not, he wrote, "unconditionally, and without qualification" opposed to Grant's renomination, but he had three major objections to it. First, he was in favor of the "one term principle." Second, as a rule, he thought it best to choose the presidential candidate from civilian life. He thought the exercise of military power to be "arbitrary" in nature and contrary to the "spirit of our Government." Finally, although he considered the Grant administration a success financially, it was a diplomatic failure, "too good to be called bad, and too bad to be called good."

If Grant won the Republican nomination, however, Fleharty expected to support him. He felt the one tie that bound the Republican Party together was its support of the principle of "equal civil rights" for men of all races, a

73. The first regular session of the legislature met from January 4 to April 17, 1871; the first special session from May 24 to June 22; the second special session from October 13–21; and the adjourned session from November 15, 1871, to April 9, 1872. Before this, the record for legislative longevity had been held by the 11th General Assembly (1838–40) which met for 149 days.

position he felt to be the "true and only basis of a Republican or Democratic form of Government." The Republican platform that would be adopted at the party's convention in Philadelphia would provide the surest means of seeing this principle upheld by the government. For that reason he would feel compelled to support the party's nominee. Fleharty was "so much in favor of the Republican party" that he felt he could not be in favor of Grant's candidacy before he was actually nominated, and he was so opposed to the democratic stand that did not back an equality position that he would "hardly be able to find a plank to stand upon in opposition to him [Grant] afterwards."[74]

If the party could unite on any other candidate at all, Fleharty wrote, it would be a great mistake to nominate Grant. In 1868 the Republicans had needed Grant to be sure of victory at the polls, but in 1872 it was Grant who needed them. The party would be better off to drop the president if he failed to step aside, and to settle upon another candidate (Supreme Court justice David Davis, for example) who would be acceptable to all.[75]

Party reaction to the letter was not long in coming. If Fleharty spoke only for himself, shot back a local Republican organ, all right then. But if he pretended to represent the opinion of Mercer County Republicans, or even a significant number of them, "we decidedly object." Mercer County Republicans, the editor continued, believed it would be "hazardous" to change candidates now. If Fleharty was interested in settling the question of the nominee within Republican ranks, that was one thing. But "it strikes us as rather strange, that those Republicans who oppose the renomination of Gen. Grant, invariably propose men who are named for the same office by Democratic wire workers."[76]

---

74. The liberalization of Fleharty's attitude toward blacks since 1864 is a mystery. There are some clues to the change in a July 28, 1865, letter to Stephen from his brother Jesse. In it he warns Stephen that if he hopes to succeed in the newspaper business in northwestern Illinois after the war he will have to support black suffrage. "I know of no paper opposed to it but 'copperheads,'" he wrote. He went on to express his astonishment at Stephen's "'drift' into this Semi-*Southern* view of this subject." The letter went on at length on the political necessity for black participation in the electoral process if the influence of former rebels in the government was to be curbed. Apparently Stephen heeded the advice. Letter in possession of Mrs. Sarah E. Glass.

75. Chicago *Tribune*, February 14, 1872, p. 4. Fleharty's letter was dated February 11.

76. Aledo *Weekly Record*, February 21, 1872, p. 2.

In the end, Fleharty found himself backing President Grant. Horace Greeley, candidate on both the Liberal Republican and Democratic tickets, was completely unacceptable to him because of his lenient attitude toward former rebels. In a letter to a former Union officer, Fleharty wrote that the result of the Greeley movement was a "mongrel party" much like the old pre-war Democratic organization. He did not like the Grant administration, he said, but "principles for which you and I fought would be safer under Grant and [Vice President Henry] Wilson" and men they had fought beside, than they would be under Greeley backed by the very men they had fought against.[77]

More important, and probably much more satisfying, than his brief foray into politics was Fleharty's continued involvement with journalism. Even before the war ended, he had corresponded with his brother about a possible future in the newspaper business. The establishment of a daily paper in Galesburg was one possibility they discussed. If the times continued "good" and the source of news did not dry up when the war ended, Jesse thought the prospects for such an enterprise were favorable. He advised Stephen that it might be a good idea to learn shorthand "so as to be able to take down addresses—the time of war will probably be succeeded by a season of speaking [at] great occasions—'reviews' etc etc." At one point, he suggested that Stephen buy the Galesburg *Free Democrat,* where he would be able to "Edit for a reputation—and do job-work for a *living.*"[78]

Not until the end of his legislative career, however, was Fleharty able to find a place in the world of journalism. Late in 1872 he proposed to the board of directors of the Galesburg *Republican and Register* that he would write three letters a week from Springfield during the upcoming legislative session. The letters would average a half column in length, for which he asked $4.00 a week. He would, he promised, "try to make them what you want—racy & readable." The paper countered by offering him $1.00 apiece for three letters a week, provided he could "get them up in such a manner that they would not be identified as emanating from the source that produced other letters which

77. Fleharty to Capt. Eric Johnson, July 17, 1872, Fleharty Papers, Knox College. Captain Johnson had commanded Company D of the 57th Illinois Infantry.

78. Jesse J. Fleharty to Fleharty, May 8, July 11, 28, 1865, in possession of Mrs. Sarah E. Glass. The *Free Democrat* had been an antislavery paper; it was sold in 1865 to Bailey and McClelland, who changed its name to the *Free Press.* They in turn sold the paper in 1872 to none other than Col. Myron S. Barnes.

would appear in other papers in this part of the country." Other letters written by Fleharty did indeed appear in other papers in the region; he reported on legislative activity for more than twenty papers and made daily reports to the Springfield *Journal*, the St. Louis *Democrat*, and the Quincy *Whig*. In the spring of 1874 he even traveled to Washington, where he briefly covered Congress for the Quincy paper.[79]

His personal life was not quite so happy or successful. Fleharty never married, although it was apparently not for lack of effort. Evidence of a romantic disappointment is clear in a letter he wrote (and very likely never sent) in the summer of 1866 to Jennie C. Trego, a woman with whom he was obviously quite smitten.[80] "Is it a *fault* of mine," he began, "that *I love you so madly?*" The "excentric [*sic*] conduct" of which he had lately been guilty he attributed to a love that "*absorbs* every other thought—every other feeling!" Miss Trego apparently did not return Fleharty's affection and quite likely was keeping company with another young man. Fleharty jealously wondered whether he was "unworthy one moments['] attention," pointing out to her that he had asked only for "the place of a friend" in her life, a favor that had been granted to unnamed "others." She was, he was certain, quite unaware that she could have "relieved and enlivened many weary hours without being to me, practically, more than a friend."

A letter he had sent her a week earlier asking her for "the *privileges of a friend*" had gone unanswered, and Fleharty now found himself in a quandary. He at first despaired of his future, wondering what was left for him: "*blackness?*

79. Fleharty to "Gentlemen," December 18, 1872; and John D. Devin to Fleharty, December 19, 1872, in possession of Mrs. Sarah E. Glass; Fleharty to Stephen W. Fleharty, January 30, 1874; and Sen. John A. Logan to the Departments of the Government, April 26, 1874, both in Fleharty Papers, Knox College. Fleharty's coverage of the first session of the 28th General Assembly first appeared in the January 18, 1873, edition of the *Republican and Register* (p. 8) under the name "Frank," and continued through May 8, 1873 (p. 7). His coverage of the adjourned first session (under his own initials, S. F. F.) began January 17, 1874 (p. 8), and ended April 4, 1874 (p. 2).

80. Fleharty to Jennie C. Trego, August 18, 1866, Fleharty Papers, Knox College. Jennie (Clark) Trego was the widow of Capt. Edgar P. Trego of the 8th Kansas Infantry, to whom she had been married in 1861, and who had been killed at Chickamauga two years later. In February 1869 Mrs. Trego married Dr. J. M. Ansley of Swedona, Mercer County. They had two children, Clark F. and Charley. Mrs. Ansley died in 1873. See Jane (Shaull) Lutz, *A Historical Account of the Trago/Trego Family* (Grand Rapids, Mich., 1983), 22; *History of Mercer County*, 738–39.

darkness? despair? death?" His soul must "suffer eternal anguish," he mourned, then brightening a bit, continued, "but I feel that the true spirit of manhood will yet rule my life. *Jennie, I will live a life not unworthy of you.*" He concluded by asking her to remember him when he was no more by scattering some of the flowers she loved so well on his final resting place.

One could almost conclude that Fleharty was engaged in nothing more than a childish game, but he was almost thirty years old, well past the usual age for such behavior. Then there was a note he scribbled at the top of his letter to Miss Trego. The note is dated September 24, 1871, some five years after the letter was originally written and while he was a member of the general assembly. It indicates not only the seriousness of his feelings for Jennie Trego in 1866, but also for another who came after her. He wrote, apparently to himself:

> This love is all in the past. She was forgotten long ago—and I meet her often now—and play with her little boy. She is the wife of another. I wonder at myself—
>
> But I love another—and have for years. She is good and true and pure. I do not know that she will ever love me. O God! give me a *nobler*[,] better nature— a truer heart. Let me see my own fickleness—my own weakness.
>
> If the one I love should return that love[,] O! let me be a true man. And let my love be calm & pure.

Whoever this mystery woman was, she apparently did not return Fleharty's feelings any more than Jennie Trego had.

Even as early as his army days, Fleharty had written to his family of the great good fortune that would be found in the West after the war. By late 1874, his brother John (who, like Jesse, was a Methodist minister) had been appointed to a position in Iron Bluffs, Nebraska. In his letters home he talked up the opportunities to be found in the new state, even going so far as to say that he wanted Stephen to come out and run for Congress ("you can *'win'* easily enough I think"). He pointed out the money to be made in land speculation and reminded Stephen that he could obtain recommendations from his political friends in Springfield and Washington and thereby win the confidence of eastern speculators. He did not think it would take much capital to get started in the business, and Stephen could gain valuable knowledge of the lands available enabling him to secure "valuable bargains" for himself. "[B]esides," he continued, "you could undoubtedly have office if you wished it, Senator or Congressman[,] I don't see anything in the way of your success in that direction."[81] Whether it was the prospect of financial success and political preferment or just the desire for a change, Fleharty did move to Nebraska sometime shortly after his eldest brother William died at the age of forty-six in October 1875. By the following January, Fleharty was editing and publishing the Osceola *Homesteader* (later the Osceola *Record*) in Polk County, about eighty-five miles west of Omaha.

In his maiden editorial, Fleharty announced that the *Homesteader* would be Republican in its politics but would always attempt to give the other side a "fair hearing." "Beyond this," he went on, "it is not necessary to lay down our platform, except perhaps to say in general terms that we are opposed to the 'broad road' that don't lead to heaven, and in favor of the narrow gauge railroad to Omaha."[82] The paper's office was located on the second floor of a frame building on the west side of the town square. Downstairs was a combined store and post office, which, along with a blacksmith shop, constituted the "business part of the town." One old-timer commented that it was here that Fleharty and others of his kind "exercised their gray matter by grinding out of their exuberant and sometimes lurid imaginations original local items and weighty editorials." Fleharty maintained his interest in Osceola's journalistic establishment until at least the late fall of 1880.[83]

For a time he and his brothers John and Henry were helping Jesse promote a fledgling Methodist college in Osceola. The first classes were held in September 1879, with eleven students and four teachers present. Jesse served as president of "Nebraska Wesleyan University," but his enterprise was on very shaky ground. The Methodist hierarchy in Nebraska favored a seminary, not a college, and the school's financial situation was precarious. By June 1881, with Jesse still heavily involved, the school was forced to move to Fullerton.[84]

81. John Q. A. Fleharty to Fleharty, October 9, 21, 1874, in possession of Mrs. Sarah E. Glass.

82. Osceola *Homesteader,* January 5, 1876, p. 2.

83. Calmar McCune, "Early Days in Polk County," *Collection of Nebraska Pioneer Reminiscences* (N.p., 1916), 248. On December 1, 1880, Fleharty announced the sale of his interest in the Osceola *Home News,* a publication still in its first year. It is unclear just when Fleharty's interest in the *Record* ended and when or how his interest in the *Home News* began. See Osceola *Home News,* December 1, 1880, p. 2.

84. David H. Mickey, *Of Sunflowers, Coyotes, and Plainsmen* (Lincoln, Nebr., 1992), 5.

Stephen also engaged in land speculation. Although he was not elected to high office, in 1881 he was appointed private secretary to Nebraska governor Albinus Nance, and two years later he was reappointed by Nance's successor, James W. Dawes. But by that time a worsening case of tuberculosis forced him to move to Tampa, Florida.[85]

While there he continued to work in the real-estate business and secured a position in the Tampa post office. Late in 1883, however, word reached him of the serious illness of his brother Jesse, who was still ministering in Nebraska. Jesse's ailment was similar to his own, so Stephen telegraphed him to bring his wife and come to Florida. Although he had only been in Tampa for a short time, he said, he was already "well acquainted" and had "quite a number of good friends." Fleharty planned to hire a cottage for four or five months where Jesse and his wife could keep house and they all could board together. He believed that the extremes of weather in Nebraska were responsible for his brother's condition. He felt sure that several months in the mild Florida climate would do Jesse as much good as it had done him. He had not felt so well in ten years, he boasted.[86]

Jesse and his wife did come to Tampa, and Stephen did everything he could to make his brother comfortable, even going so far as to give up his position with the post office. But Jesse's condition did not improve, and he died on May 2, 1884.

Stephen remained in Florida until 1896, when he moved to North Carolina. He located first in Dillsboro, Jackson County, in the extreme western end of the state. Two years later he moved to Waynesville, Haywood County (about twenty miles northeast of Dillsboro), where he was employed as secretary of the National Abrasive Manufacturing Company. He was happy there and described Waynesville as "the most charming place" he had ever lived. The Smoky Mountains, he wrote home, "loom up . . . on every side of the 'city.'" The scenery was "wonderfully beautiful," and the air at that altitude was "most of the time delicious." The mountain streams and springs supplied the "purest water," and he felt that he was slowly but continually gaining health and strength there.[87]

---

85. Nance was governor of Nebraska from 1879 to 1883, and Dawes from 1883 to 1887.

86. Fleharty to Jesse J. Fleharty, December 20, 1883, and John Q. A. Fleharty to Fleharty, March 15, 1884, both in possession of Mrs. Sarah E. Glass.

87. Fleharty to John Q. A. Fleharty, June 19, 1898, in possession of Mrs. Sarah E. Glass.

He was not quite so happy with his situation at the manufacturing company. The business controlled large deposits of corundum in the United States and mined, processed, and then marketed the substance for its abrasive properties. The company had recently built a large finishing mill in Waynesville and was about to begin operations in it. Fleharty had hoped to be able to invest more heavily in the enterprise than circumstances had allowed. *"Capital,"* he complained, "is greedy, and a fellow *without it* has to *put up with what he can get."* What he was able to get was a $50-a-month position in which he was "to look after their books and accts . . . and attend to the correspondence of the Gen'l Manager."[88]

By early 1899 Fleharty had contracted pneumonia and had become very frail. In a curious letter to Fleharty's niece, Stephen A. Jones (general manager of the National Abrasive Manufacturing Company), noted that although frail, Fleharty did not feel "far away from home among strangers" in Waynesville. Fleharty had, he continued, been "my brother for over fifteen years. My house has been his home just as much as it has been the home of one of my children[.] Where ever we have lived here allso [*sic*] he has lived for over 15 years." Although Fleharty had never joined a church, Jones noted that he continued to be a believer and was a regular attendant at the family's church services and at prayer meetings on those evenings when it was Jones's turn to lead.[89]

But Fleharty himself, in the last letter he wrote, seemed bitter and felt anything but part of a family circle in Waynesville. "You have not the least conception," he told his brother, "of the hard battle for life I have had. The impression went North that I was having every possible attention. The first week or two I had very good attention. After that the personal friendship business played out, as it naturally would and I had to come down to cold cash and hired help—and such help as it was! . . . I have paid out about $65 or $70 for nurses, and have had to *guide them* every minute. This is the heaven I have been in. . . . The rasping conditions have nearly driven me into regular consumption, but I still hope to escape it."[90]

88. Ibid.

89. Stephen A. Jones to Clara Viola Fleharty, February 15, 1899, in possession of Mrs. Sarah E. Glass.

90. Fleharty to John Q. A. Fleharty, May 2, 1899, in possession of Mrs. Sarah E. Glass. Characteristically, in his last letter Fleharty had a bone to pick with his brother. Ever since his service in the Illinois General Assembly, more than twenty-five years earlier, his family members

But he could not escape. On April 29, 1899, for the first time in his life, Fleharty applied for a government pension owing to the disability resulting from his tubercular condition. But he did not live to receive any benefits. His pneumonia worsened, and he died in Waynesville on May 9, 1899, at the age of sixty-two.[91]

---

had continued to address him as "Hon. Stephen F. Fleharty." In a postscript to his letter, Fleharty admonished his brother, "Soon after I was taken sick scores of family letters came in all addressed to 'Hon' S. F. Fleharty,—the effect was ludicrous as all other letters except one ignored the 'Hon[.]' I wrote to my folks to drop it. All have done so but you. It will be a *special favor* if you do. Your title [Rev.] is a *live* title. Mine *is not.*"

91. Unidentified newspaper clipping in possession of Mrs. Sarah E. Glass; Fleharty to Commissioner of Pensions, April 17, 1899; and Declaration for Invalid Pension, April 29, 1899, both in Records of the Record and Pension Office of the War Department, Record Group 94.12, National Archives, Washington, D.C.

CHAPTER 1

"The Crude Material of a Regiment"

FLAG PRESENTATION.[1]—The ladies of Rock Island and Mercer counties, residing in Coal Valley, Preemption, Berlin, Richland Grove and vicinity, have presented captain Shedd's company, with a beautiful flag. A large public meeting was held at Dr. Rathbun's, at Richland Grove, on Wednesday, the 13th inst., for the purpose of presenting the flag to the company, and a bountiful dinner was provided for all. Joseph McLane, of Coal Valley, acted as marshal of the day, and Capt. John A. Jordan, of Coal Valley, as chairman. The presentation of the flag was made by—[we have done our best to make something out of that name, but we give it up. People who write communications for the papers should always use extraordinary care in writing names plainly.—ED. ARGUS.]—In a very appropriate speech. The flag was received on the part of the company, by Mr. Snyder, who paid a high compliment to the ladies of Rock Island and Mercer counties for the taste they had displayed in getting up the flag, and for their patriotic devotion to the cause of the union. Speeches were also made by Mr. Roberts and by Jos. McLane.[2]

Several recruits were sworn into the company on that day. The company now is about full, and, it is expected, will join Col. McMurtry's regiment at Galesburg.

Yours truly,

Old Flag.

(Rock Island *Argus,* August 25, 1862, p. 3)

1. This letter and the one following, although not signed by Fleharty, are almost certainly the product of his pen.

2. Dr. John B. Rathbun was a physician from Richland Grove in Mercer County. The identity of the other speakers is unclear.

Camp McMurtry, Knox Co., Ill.,
August 28th, 1862.

Mr. Editor: Supposing your readers would like to hear something in connection with the organization of the 102d regiment of Illinois volunteers, I will occupy a few moments in giving them a short account of it. I was on the ground on Tuesday evening the 26th, in connection with Capt. Shedd's company, of Richland Grove, Mercer county.—we marched into camp about 5 o'clock p. m. of the same evening, under the command of Capt. John Jordan, of Rock Island county, who, by the way, is considered one of the best drill masters at the camp. Our company was, up to that time, the eighth company reporting itself at the camp. Halting in front of headquarters, we was [*sic*] received by Ex-Lt. Gov. McMurtry, as one of the best looking companies of men the sun ever shown [*sic*] upon. In a short time after, Capt. Mannon's company, from Aledo, Mercer county, was marched into camp—a very fine company also. As the camp occupies the Knox county fair ground, we were all quartered in the buildings connected therewith, the first night.[1] The next morning the last company arrived, by railway, from the western part of Mercer county, and was received in camp with military honors by the nine preceeding [*sic*] companies. The regiment being full, order No. 7 was posted, notifying the companies comprizing [*sic*] the 102d regiment that they were to form around the speaker's stand the next day at 3 o'clock p. m., for the purpose of electing their colonel, after which the commissioned officers of the regiment would meet in the dining room and elect the lieutenant colonel and major.[2] At the appointed time the companies were formed according to order, and elected Ex-Lt. Gov. McMurtry, of Knox county, colonel. The result of the election at the dining room, was as follows:—Frank Smith, of Knox county, lieutenant colonel, and James M. Mannon, of Mercer Co., major.[3] The meeting also voted, unanimously, in favor of a resolution authorizing the colonel, elect, to appoint the adjutant. Upon whom the appointment will rest, is, not publicly known, as yet. Thus passed the election at Camp McMurtry, amidst log-rolling and wire-pulling, such as would do honor to a presidential campaign.

Following the election the colonel re-appeared at the speaker's stand, and gave the boys a fine little speech, in which he told them that he was proud of the honor and respect they had manifested towards him in their selection of colonel. He hoped they never would have occasion to regret their choice—

that they never would have less confidence in him than they have; and that he would lead them to Dixie and to glory. In conclusion he introduced to the boys their newly elected lieutenant colonel, who gave them a short speech, and then introduced to them their newly elected major, who made his bow, and the crowd disappeared.

Volunteer.

[We "reckon" about the same "log-rolling," and "horseshedding" takes place in every regiment, and that men who did not consider themselves fit for 2d lieutenant, when they left home, have suddenly found out that they ought to be colonels—or ought to ride a horse, anyhow. The selfishness and ingratitude displayed by some captains and lieutenants, when they get into camp, is a subject of general remark. When they have once secured a position, for them-selves, instead of being satisfied, and trying to help their friends who aided them in raising their companies, their only object seems to be to secure some higher place for themselves, before they have even shown the ability to fill the place they now occupy.—ED. ARGUS.]
(Rock Island *Argus*, September 3, 1862, p. 2)

1. The fairgrounds were in the northwestern corner of the corporate limits of the city of Knoxville (in the NE quarter of Section 29 in Knox Township).

2. By August 1862 the method for forming regiments had, with some exceptions, become standardized. Men authorized by the governor to recruit and organize companies were normally elected field officers; the vote was usually a mere formality. They in turn appointed the noncommissioned officers. With the arrival of all the companies at a rendezvous camp, the regiment was formed. The company officers would then meet to elect the field officers.

The election of field officers for the 102d, however, stirred a controversy that reverberated all the way to Springfield. At the center of the dispute was P. R. Kendall, president of Lombard University. Involved in raising several regiments, the Galesburg Republican expected a field officer's commission in the 102d. An open vote for colonel was held on August 28, and former lieutenant governor William McMurtry, a Democrat, was elected. The commissioned officers then met and selected Franklin C. Smith, another Knox County Democrat, to be lieutenant colonel, and James M. Mannon, a Mercer County Republican, major.

Rankled Kendall supporters quickly fired off letters to Governor Richard Yates, voicing dissatisfaction with the election's outcome. One writer protested that "Kendall is a Republican who believes in fighting rebels . . . his opponent [Smith] was a new Constitution man—& would like to kill our state & national administration." Another wrote: "To explain why Kendall was not voted for Lt. Col.—*pretended* friends went to him & told him that he could not be elected Lt. Col.; but if he would be a candidate for Major & let Capt. Smith be elected Lt.

Col. that they would elect him (K.) Major. To this Kendall consented, believing it was intended in good faith. To his utter surprise however, & the utter surprise of all who were not in the plot, Kendall was defeated." He further entreated: "Will you not order that the *regiment*, not the line officers, by ballot, choose their own field officers[?]"

In a letter to the *Aledo Weekly Record*, a soldier using the pseudonym "High Private" explained the issue's resolution: "Mannon was fairly and honestly elected, but his opponent (Kendall), by pretty good engineering, got the Governor to call a new election, which resulted in electing Mannon again by a majority of only 37." The final tally was 410 for Mannon and 373 for Kendall.

Bell Irvin Wiley, *The Life of Billy Yank: The Common Soldier of the Union* (Garden City, N.Y., 1971), 24; Letter to Gov. Yates with illegible signature, dated September 1, 1862, Record Group 301, Illinois State Archives; Elisha Miles to Governor Yates, August 30, 1862, Record Group 301, Illinois State Archives; and "High Private," Aledo *Weekly Record*, September 23, 1862, p. 1.

3. Franklin C. Smith (1824–91) was born in Portageville, New York. He attended Hamilton College for a year, read law, and was admitted to the bar. Instead of practicing law he engaged in engineering and contracting until moving to Illinois in 1859, and locating in Knox County. Galesburg *Republican-Register,* September 5, 1891, p. 6.

James M. Mannon (1823–1901) was a native of Wayne County, Indiana, where he lived until moving with his parents to Mercer County at the age of thirteen. He farmed there until being elected sheriff on the Republican ticket in 1856. At the end of his term two years later, he was elected circuit clerk and recorder of Mercer County, in which capacity he served until 1860. *History of Mercer County,* 96–97.

William McMurtry (1801–75) was a native of Mercer County, Kentucky, but moved early in life to Crawford County, Indiana. By 1829 he had arrived in Knox County, Illinois, as one of the first permanent white settlers. McMurtry immediately took a leading role in the life of the community. His public service included terms as a justice of the peace, school commissioner, captain of a company of mounted rangers in the Black Hawk War, and colonel in the state militia. He was elected to one term in the Illinois House of Representatives (where he served with Abraham Lincoln), and to one in the state senate. A lifelong Democrat, McMurtry capped his political career by being elected lieutenant governor of Illinois, an office he filled from 1849 to 1853. A year later he was the unsuccessful Democratic candidate for Congress.

ᳵ No. 1 ᳵ

Camp McMurtry
Knoxville, Ill., Sept. 17, 1862

Col. Danforth—With your permission, I propose furnishing the readers of the *Argus* with occasional notes from the "102" a regiment in which are many of your old subscribers. I promise you, Mr. Editor, in the outset, that I will *endeavor* to be brief—interpreting that word contrary to its clerical construction, in which sense it is usually ominous of a long sermon.

You have doubtless received and published the roster of our regiment, and I presume will agree with me in the opinion that it presents an array of good names. Col. McMurtry, a "rough and ready" pioneer settler—a man of large soul and true patriotism—is well fitted to lead our "sturdy sons of toil" against the rebel foe. The Colonel has figured quite prominently in the political history of Illinois, and has been denominated the "old war horse" of the democracy. In his new sphere I predict he will win brighter laurels. The boys look upon him not only as a leader, but as a protector, and woe betide the wretch who attempts to practise any imposition upon his men. If no actual punishment is visited upon the offender, a string of hearty "blessings" hardly suitable for ears polite together with an expression of countenance that would seem to indicate the presence of an incipient thunder-storm, makes him tremble in his boots, if his nerves are not made of steel. In this connection I may state that the Colonel has invoked the most withering anathemas upon the tight-fisted, lean-hearted action of the Mercer county board of supervisors, in reference to bounties for volunteers. It is indeed a burning shame—a stigma upon the character of the county that years will not obliterate. While the recruits from Knox county are receiving $50 each, we are compelled to admit, when asked what Mercer county has done, that we have received nothing. I was born in old Mercer, and love her rolling prairies, her winding streams, her beautiful valleys, and her *many* good people, and for them feel proudly willing to fight, but if there were in Mercer county nothing nobler to defend than her cold-hearted batch of supervisors, I *would hardly own my birth place.* There are men possessing all the appliances of wealth, who are too cowardly, or who think too much of their precious selves to enlist, and while their brave fellow citizens are battling in defense of *their* lives, *their* homes, *their* property, *they* withhold the ample means at their command, which should cheer the soldier in his arduous duties. Alas, that Mercer county should be burdened with such men! But enough of this—we did not enlist for money, and feel that we would rather be penniless, and doing our duty in the service of our country, than to be rolling in wealth and dead to all patriotism and magnanimity.[1]

The commissioned officers in company C (in which the writer holds an humble position) are Capt. Frank Shedd; 1st Lieut. Almond Shaw; 2d Lieut. Watson C. Trego—all good men and true; and who have friends in the company may rest assured that the "dear absent ones," will not suffer through any direliction [*sic*] of duty on their part.[2]

The men are generally in good health, and the crude material of a regiment, gathered from the farms and the workshops, is gradually being moulded into the form of a disciplined army. Yet it takes time to learn to be a machine! I think, however, I am slowly approaching perfection in this line.—shut up in the fair-ground enclosure, we feel some of the restraints of prison-life. Then to eat by rule, sleep by rule, roll out of bed according to military rule, walk by rule, and refrain from brushing an impertinent fly from your face (according to military rule) when in line, on dress parade, seems like a slight infringement on the natural freedom of man. Its [*sic*] all well, however, and the end justifies the means.

But I have written enough for letter No. 1, and will close with a few data.

We came into camp on the 26th ult., were mustered into the service on the 2d inst., have received our bounty ($25) and one month's pay; also our uniforms. To morrow and next day we will be transferred to Peoria, where I will write again.

S. F. F.

(Rock Island *Argus,* September 25, 1862, p. 2)

1. At the September 1862 session of the county board, a tax of five cents on every $100 was levied for the benefit of volunteers and their families. It was also ordered that $25 out of the military fund should be paid to each supervisor to buy "necessaries to the families of volunteers who might be destitute." In light of an $8,000 deficit being run by the county as late as November 1861, the board's war-relief measures were perhaps not as stingy as Fleharty suggested. See Isaac Newton Bassett, *Past and Present of Mercer County, Illinois* (Chicago, 1914) I, 69, 114.

2. Capt. Frank Shedd was from Richland Grove, 1st Lt. Almond Shaw from Berlin, and 2d Lt. Watson C. Trego from Preemption, all in Mercer County. All had been farmers before the war. "Descriptive List of Co. C," Record Group 301, Illinois State Archives.

∾— No. 2 —∾

Camp Peoria,
Sept. 23, 1862.

My last letter was written under the impression that at the end of a few intervening hours we would be landed in Peoria; but the time came—our clothes, camp equippage [*sic*], &c. were all packed—when, to our intense mortification the military machine stopped—the order to move was counter-manded. Faces that were a moment before brightened by the anticipated change, suddenly became elongated. When we would go, no one knew.

En passant, I will give you a little episode showing the jovial, perhaps I should say war-like nature of the boys, during the time they were awaiting the momentarily expected "marching order." A large lot of bread had become mouldy and useless, whereupon "Young America"[1] (an element that is pretty well represented in the regiment in spirit, if not in years) commenced an indiscriminate battle—the huge loaves and fragments of loaves, as they flew in every direction, reminding one of Milton's account of the contest between Lucifer and the Arch-Angel.[2]

Another day brought the cheering order for five companies, including ours, to prepare two days cooked rations and be ready to start for Peoria on the morning of the 22d inst. At the appointed time we were marched on board a train of passenger cars, and waving a long adieu to visiting friends and specta-tors, moved rapidly away over a rich and varied country to this place.

We have a beautiful camping ground, about two hundred yards from, and in full view of, Peoria Lake, and about the same distance from the immense Peoria pottery works. The Henry county regiment is encamped on the fair ground, about a mile distant. There are now five regiments here, all under the command of Col. Bryner, formerly of the 47th Illinois. The 108th, encamped here, has marching orders, and will leave in a day or two for Dixie.[3]

In company with a friend I scaled the bluff in rear of our camp this morning, where we had a fine view of the camping ground and Peoria Lake. It is a lovely scene—in the foreground and to the left are the regimental encampments— long and sharp-roofed (all roof) board quarters, and groups of cloth tents— beyond these the placid lake, and in the back ground a dense body of timber crowning the opposite bluffs. All the varied occupations connected with camp life are in full blast—soldiers not on duty, promenading here and there; compa-nies drilling; guards walking their tedious "beat," while from many company kitchens may be heard the "busy notes of preparation" for dinner.

The left wing of our regiment arrived this afternoon—tired, hungry and dirty, the march from the depot to camp being mainly between walls of stone and brick, where street sprinklers appear to be unknown. They were welcomed by their comrades with hearty cheers and full buckets of water, with which to slake their thirst. The colonel was on the ground, and incidentally speaking of the manner in which our regiment had been fitted out, in comparison with others, some one remarked that he (the colonel) had performed all that he had promised. In reply the colonel said, "Boys, I will promise you more—I intend to take my chances with you; and by the gods, I'm going to board with you!" Hats flew off, and three hearty cheers followed the old veteran as he left the crowd.

The mania for *confiscating* seems to be growing among us.[4] I noticed just now, thro' an open space in our quarters, that two or three of the boys were quietly milking as many cows, that had strayed into our camping ground. The gentle animals submitted to the operation with apparent satisfaction, and were doubtless proud of the privilege of being *pressed* into the service of "Uncle Sam." We will probably have cream for our coffee in the morning.

Since arriving in camp we have received the following compliment from the "local" of the Peoria *Transcript*, who was visiting the camp at the time we came in. He says:

"As we were about to return we were met by five companies of Col. McMurtry's regiment, the 102, which were just coming out to their quarters. Though nearly covered with dust, they were nevertheless discernable.—they are some of the best men that the state affords, and their colonel, though well advanced in years, is known to be a fighting man and one that will lead instead of going behind. The rest of the regiment is expected in to-day."

But my letter is long enough, and I will bid you good bye for to-day.

Ever yours,

S. F. F.

(Rock Island *Argus*, October 1, 1862, p. 2)

1. Fleharty undoubtedly alludes to that faction of the Democratic Party that flourished in the first half of the 1850s under the leadership of George Henry Evans and his *Democratic Review*. Evans and his followers sought to unite the party around a number of issues (*e.g.*, free trade) that transcended the sectional discord that was then developing over slavery. It supported the ideals of service and duty to country, assistance to democrats around the world, and the election of Stephen A. Douglas as president. The movement met with limited success. See Merle E. Curti, "Young America," *American Historical Review* XXXII (October, 1926), 34–55.

2. See *Paradise Lost*, Book VI, for Milton's account of the war in Heaven.

3. In the summer of 1862, Peoria was designated one of several rendezvous camps for regiments organizing in Illinois. The first regiment to arrive (the 102d) occupied the county fairgrounds (known as Camp Lyon), while later arrivals camped on ground in the northeastern quarter of the city. Both sites were collectively known as Camp Peoria. At the time of the stay of the 102d, four other regiments also occupied Camp Peoria: the 77th, 103d, 108th, and

112th ("the Henry County regiment"). The commandant of the post of Peoria at that time was Col. John Bryner (1820–65), late of the 47th Illinois Infantry.

4. The rendezvous camps were thrown up almost overnight in the haste to organize, equip, and teach the basics of soldiering to the Union recruits. Consequently they were often short of food. From the beginning, Union soldiers became ingenious and resourceful in supplementing their meager diet of coffee, bacon, and hardtack.

⌁ No. 3 ⌁

Louisville, Ky.,
Oct. 3, 1862.

Mr. Editor:

The life of the soldier is indeed a mutable one. My last letter had scarcely been mailed when an order was read to the regiment directing us to prepare three days rations and be ready to start for Louisville on Monday the 29th ult.[1] We were in quite comfortable quarters, and expected to be put through the rudiments of the soldier's drill before going farther, but the order was received cheerfully, though calmly, by men who were ready to be marched anywhere, even

> Into the jaws of death—
> Into the valley of hell,[2]

in defense of a beloved country. We did not start however at the appointed time.

On Tuesday morning the 30th, we were marched to the depot in a drizzling rain, which increased to a steady "pour" as we waited for the train. About midday we went on board a mixed train of passengers, baggage and freight cars, at the depot of the Peoria, Burlington and Logansport railroad, and were soon sweeping over the grand prairies that lie to the east of the Illinois river.

Though a "Sucker boy,"[3] I was surprised at the boundless sea of prairie. The eye grows weary scanning the wide expanse. As mile after mile we flew along, the sun sinking low in the west, lighted up the horizon with a golden lustre—picturing in our imagination what we have often read, and what you have so often seen, of the glorious sunsets at sea. As the shadows of night close around us, occasional lights from quiet cottage homes would flit for a moment before the vision, and then we would think of our own dear homes and the loved ones left behind.

Grand prairies! Noble Illinois!—may we be worthy soldiers of our own, loved state! But I must enter into details.

At a late hour in the evening we crossed the state line, and about daybreak reached Logansport, Ind.,—thence we had a fine ride down the Wabash valley on the Jeffersonville, Indianapolis and Logansport railroad.[4]

From the great prairie sea we had been transferred to an immense forest— the real home of the genuine hoosier; and judging from the wild appearance of parts of the country—the log huts and little farms, we could hardly resist the impression that we were in the vicinity of "Posey county—Hooppole township."[5] Yet, we passed thro' some lovely towns between Logansport and Indianapolis, among which I may mention particularly, Delphi and Lafayette.

At Indianapolis we met a large number of the Mumfordsville prisoners, who were, as you know, released on parole by the rebel general.[6] They were a hardy looking set of men, and I do not believe they have been thus humiliated through any fault of theirs. Our boys faithfully promised them that they would "square accounts" with the rebels on that score.

A short distance south of Indianapolis, we met two trains carrying the remainder of the paroled men—in all, something over four thousand.—There were a great many troops drilling in the capital city, who greeted us with hearty cheers as we passed through. We saw there also, some of the "machinery of war"—rifled cannon, etc.

Our ride from Indianapolis to Jeffersonville (opposite Louisville,) was mainly after night, and I took but few notes. We reached Jeffersonville about two o'clock a. m., yesterday (Wednesday) morning. Various rumors of fighting across the river back of Louisville, reached us shortly after our arrival. Our guns were distributed and we slept on our arms last night.[7]

At one o'clock this morning the "long roll" was sounded, we received three days rations, and at daybreak moved out of camp and crossed the river on a pontoon bridge (made of flatboats,) passed through a portion of the city of Louisville, and are now encamped near Cave Hill cemetery.

Our boys walked with a proud step as they marched into the famous city, and felt they were entering the pretended dominions of secessia.—Our noble state received many fine compliments from the loyal citizens. A number of union flags were exhibited from the windows of dwellings and business houses. Three hearty cheers greeted the old flag whenever we passed it. Many of the citizens, however, looked "grum," and if I mistake not, *secessianity* is pretty deeply seated here.

The new levies are constantly pouring in from the north, and I think an overwhelming force will soon clear Kentucky of rebels. Our armies are in motion, and if the traitors do not "skedaddle" there will be warm work hereabouts ere this reaches you. Rumor says they are now on the retreat. Meantime I will keep you "posted" as we advance,—for the present, adieu.[8]

Ever yours,

S. F. F.

P. S. Shelbyville, Oct. 5.—We have made a forced march to this place, since I wrote the above—distance about 30 miles. I will give you details hereafter. The march was terribly exhausting.[9]

S. F. F.

(Rock Island *Argus,* October 15, 1862, p. 2)

1. The departure of the 102d was expedited by the worsening situation in Kentucky. Union commanders there were attempting to deal with two invading Confederate armies. One, under Gen. Braxton Bragg, was threatening Louisville, while the other, under Maj. Gen. E. Kirby Smith was in the vicinity of Frankfort. On September 16, Maj. Gen. Horatio G. Wright, commanding the Department of the Ohio at Cincinnati, wired the governors of Illinois, Indiana, Wisconsin, and Michigan: "Please send your troops till further notice to Louisville, Ky., and hurry them on as fast as they can be mustered and armed. The rebels are passing rapidly northward and must be met with larger forces than we yet have. Every day is of importance." *OR,* Vol. XVI, Pt. 2, p. 521.

2. In many of his letters Fleharty exhibits a fondness for literature and poetry. Here he quotes, if somewhat inaccurately, from Tennyson's, "The Charge of the Light Brigade" (1854). The correct rendering is: "Into the jaws of death,/Into the mouth of hell."

3. "Sucker" was a nickname for residents of Illinois. There were two explanations for its usage, neither of them definitive. The first stemmed from the practice of Illinoisans going up the Mississippi in the spring to search for lead in the region near Galena; a journey similar to that of the sucker fish, which also migrated upriver in the spring. The second explanation, perhaps nearer the truth, is that many of the early settlers of the state were the dupes of land speculators and promoters—"suckers."

4. By 1860, railroads crisscrossed the North with more than 22,000 miles of track connecting all major cities. This rail network allowed Union forces to move quickly to the seats of war.

5. One Posey County historian lamented: "Let a resident of Posey county go among strangers almost anywhere in the United States and tell anybody he came from Posey county, Indiana, he will be required to answer the question: 'Are you from Hoop-pole township?'" There is no such place. The name apparently derives from an incident that took place about 1833. A gang of drunken flatboatmen picked a fight with some citizens of Mt. Vernon, seat of Posey County. In the encounter, the locals were badly beaten. When some of their fellow townsmen heard of the defeat, they procured a number of hoop-poles from the cooper shop and soundly thrashed the rivermen. Word quickly spread among flatboatmen, and Mt. Vernon

became known as "Hoop-pole township." See John C. Leffel, ed., *History of Posey County, Indiana* (1913; rpr. Evansville, Ind., 1978), 85–86.

6. On September 14, 1862, Chalmers' Brigade of Bragg's army launched an attack on the Union garrison at Munfordville, Kentucky, an important post on the Louisville and Nashville Railroad between those two cities. The Confederates were repulsed with heavy losses. The victorious Federals under Col. J. T. Wilder held their ground only to be surrounded by Bragg and forced to surrender on September 17. The 4,133 Union soldiers were shortly paroled and sent north. See Long, *Civil War Almanac*, 267–68; and Boatner, *Civil War Dictionary*, 575.

7. On October 2, 1862, at Jeffersonville, Indiana, the 102d was initially armed with French and Belgian rifled muskets, and with 93 Colt and Remington revolvers. See Ken Baumann, *Arming the Suckers: A Compilation of Illinois Civil War Weapons* (Dayton, Ohio, 1989), 192.

8. The thirty-eight new regiments that were being forwarded to Louisville in response to General Wright's pleas for help were formed into two divisions in Maj. Gen. Don Carlos Buell's Army of the Ohio: the 10th under Brig. Gen. James S. Jackson, and the 12th under Brig. Gen. Ebenezer Dumont. The 102d was assigned to Ward's Brigade of the 9,000-man 12th Division (*OR*, Vol. XVI, Pt. 1, p. 665).

9. While Buell's main force operated against Bragg's Army of Tennessee, then at Bardstown, Brig. Gen. Joshua W. Sill's 2d Division (composed mostly of veteran regiments) moved against Kirby Smith's force at Frankfort. Sill's division was followed on the march by Dumont's 12th Division (composed of regiments newly arrived from the North, including the 102d Illinois).

◦— No. 4 —◦

Frankfort, Ky., Oct. 11.

I have detailed the prominent incidents of our "Kentucky campaign" up to the time of our arrival in Louisville, and in a postscript to letter No. 3, barely mentioned our arrival at Shelbyville. The events of that and subsequent marches will form the gist of letter No. 4.

Early in the morning of the day on which we left Louisville, we had marched about four miles. Late in the afternoon, we packed up knapsacks, three days' rations, arms, ammunition, &c., and marched out of town on the Shelbyville turnpike. The evening was very warm. For a time the boys kept their ranks well, but after two or three hours of brisk walking, they commenced dropping out one by one, then in squads, until towards the close of the journey there was not, on an average, ten men to a company on their legs[.] The boys will long remember how, as we kept slowly moving along at a late hour in the night, the remnants of different companies would endeavor to preserve some degree of order—scattered like a flock of quails, ever and anon would be heard the call, "company C," or whatever company the weary soldier belonged to.

Reinvigorated by short rests, a few thus continued for many tedious miles, and finally rolled themselves in their blankets by the road side, and slept the sweet sleep of the tired soldier. Those who continued thro' had marched about 15 miles—this too, in addition to a morning walk of 4 miles. At 11 o'clock next day, we started again, reaching the vicinity of Shelbyville that night at a late hour. Next day (Sunday) rested all day in the burning sun, on a sunburnt Kentucky hill. Monday evening (Oct. 6) removed to a camp two miles east of Shelbyville. Wednesday morning were on the march again—had traveled but a short distance, when we were ordered to give way to the right and left and permit a large body of cavalry that was coming rapidly up in the rear, to pass ahead.[1] Six regiments passed by—hardy fellows, toughened by over a year's service—mainly in Tennessee and Alabama. Continuing on until night, we entered a long, narrow defile, where the dust was deep and light as flour. Here rumors of fighting in advance reached us. The Chicago Board of Trade battery[2] came thundering up in our rear, and as gun after gun, and wagon after wagon of ammunition rolled by, filling the atmosphere from hill top to hill top, with clouds of dust that veiled the face of the rising moon, the terrible implements of war seemed about to be let loose. A few miles march brought us to Frankfort, and there we learned that our advance guard of cavalry had met the enemy's cavalry at the bridge across the Kentucky river, a few hours previously. All was quiet when we reached the place. One tier of the flooring had been torn from the bridge, but our cavalry arrived in time to stop the devilish work of the traitors. There were but few casualties in the scrimmage—the rebels, however, were routed, and skedaddled in fine style. The faithful cavalry boys were resting along the roadside rear [*sic*] the bridge—some sleeping on their horses, some on the ground. One of them told me that the rebels they had just routed were the same they had met before in Tennessee and Alabama.[3]

The moon was shining brightly, and the lovely city, hushed in deep repose, seemed not to indicate the presence of war. We filed through the city—up, up, up, a hill that seemed as if 'twould meet the sky. Reaching a level surface, we formed in line of battle and stacked our arms.

The enemy is near by and impudent, but I do not think he will venture to attack us. Troops are constantly arriving, and doubtless another forward movement will soon be made. Our regiment was detailed last night to support a masked battery,[4] and we slept on our arms. We still occupy the same position, and should the butternuts be foolhardy enough to attack us, methinks they will imagine that judgement-day is at hand, when they get within shooting distance.

I have, as yet, seen but little of the city of Frankfort.[5] It is situated among the hills, or rather is environed by hills, of almost mountainous proportions. The citizens are friendly, and some of them have indicated their friendship by substantial favors—giving the boys edibles, &c. The "contrabands" have indicated their regard for us and "de union" wherever we have been. All along the line of our march shining rows of ivory have welcomed our soldiers; Sambo's illuminated features often presenting a striking contrast to "massa's" gloomy countenance. During one of our marches we had a "culled gemman," with a team, carrying our knapsacks. "Uncle Billy," as he was called, would frequently meet his acquaintances, and various remarks were passed. One ugly, square-built, wretchedly dressed, but jovial daughter of Ham,[6] had a good word for every one. Meeting our driver she seemed almost frantic with delight. "Why, Uncle Billy! whar you be gwine?" Uncle Billy told her his business, then springing up and clapping her hands, she continued, "God bress de union! God bress de union!" The darkies furnish an inexhaustible fund of amusement. Friend G., who usually shares bed and board with the writer, called at one of their shanties today, to get some bread. Friend G. was in for a "hoe cake," I suppose, and asked Dinah for some corn bread. "No, sah! no sah! have no cawn bread, but a *pone* or two." Friend George got "a pone or two," and I can testify that Dinah understands making a "pone," if she does not know it is corn bread, when made.[7]

The sanitary condition of our regiment is good, and notwithstanding many privations, the boys are in good spirits. We are as yet without tents, but have good warm clothing and blankets—and good appetites.

Ever yours,

S. F. F.

(Rock Island *Argus*, October 18, 1862, p. 2)

1. The Battle of Perryville was fought on this day, Wednesday, October 8.

2. The battery was recruited in the summer of 1862 under the auspices of the Chicago Board of Trade. At the time of the Perryville campaign, it was attached to Dumont's division.

3. In his report, dated October 5, 1862, Sill noted that the rebel army had evacuated Frankfort at 3:00 P.M. on the previous day. In the process, the rebels burned the railroad bridge over the Kentucky River and tore up flooring and timbers on the turnpike bridge. It was all to no avail, for, as Sill reported, "the river can be forded." *OR*, Vol. XVI, Pt. 1, p. 1020.

Fleharty, however, seems to have been confused as to the timing of the various skirmishes. There had, indeed, been a fight between elements of Sill's leading brigade and Col. John S. Scott's Confederate cavalry at the Frankfort bridge, but it occurred on October 4, four days before the 102d arrived at Frankfort. By October 8, as Dumont's division was approaching Frankfort, Sill's division had advanced from Frankfort to Lawrenceburg in an effort to join Buell's main force. At Lawrenceburg, Sill was attacked by elements of Kirby Smith's army but drove them off with little trouble. This was undoubtedly the rumor of "fighting in advance" to which Fleharty refers. It is apparent that communication between Sill and Dumont was not what it should have been. In his report of the action at Lawrenceburg, Sill noted: "I know nothing of General Dumont's column, but I suppose he has moved on Frankfort." *OR*, Vol. XVI, Pt. 1, pp. 1020, 1028, 1134.

4. A masked battery was one "so concealed or disguised, as not to be seen and recognized by the enemy, until it opens its fire." See H. L. Scott, *Military Dictionary* . . . (New York, 1864), 408.

5. With the exception of a few weeks during Bragg's invasion of Kentucky in the late summer and early autumn of 1862, Frankfort remained in Union hands throughout the war.

6. Ham was the second of Noah's three sons (Gen. 5:32). Some traditions consider him the progenitor of the black and oriental races.

7. "Friend George" was possibly either Sgt. George Gregg of Berlin, Mercer County, or Sgt. George W. Allen of Coal Valley, Rock Island County. Both were members of Company C.

⌒ No. 5. ⌒

Camp Near Frankfort, Ky., Oct. 16.

I wish you could call into my *sanctum* this morning, Colonel, and make up your daily *melange* of items and editorials. A large white oak tree, forming a right-angle with the surface of mother earth, is the best substitute I could offer you for the chair editorial, for an office, a covering constructed mainly of cedar boughs. Rather rough quarters, most assuredly, but then, think of the romance of the situation! What pen would not fly more lightly over the paper, and receive fresh inspiration from the charms of camp life? Yet there are hours of trial, of gloom and depression, and an introduction to our camp this bright day, would furnish you with a more cheering picture than is usually pre-sented.—The weather is sufficiently cool to create a demand for all the blankets and overcoats that the law allows, yet the atmosphere is dry and we experience little inconvenience from sleeping so much in the open air. At night a lively picture is sometimes presented. The rude supper over, the boys occupy the intervening period before "taps," in telling stories around the camp fires, singing good old methodist hymns or sentimental songs, and often we hear borne on the night air, those sweet words—

Do they miss me at home—do they miss me?
'Twould be an assurance most dear,
To know that this moment some loved one
Were saying "I wish he were here."[1]

And again may be heard the more martial song of

Bingen on the Rhine.[2]

At such a time the thoughts of the soldier will wander from the rough scenes around him to the dearly loved ones left behind, and while, perchance, he leaves the gay crowd to get beyond the sound of the memory-awakening song, he turns his eye towards the north, and fixing it, perhaps, on the twinkling polar star, still *will* think of home, and wonder if there are those there who keep their night vigils in remembrance of him. Is it an exhibition of weakness? Methinks not; for rather at such a moment the true soldier resolves to discharge his duty faithfully, and return to his home *honorably, or not at all.* But enough in this vein—we are endeavoring to act our part in the dark drama of rebellion, and many at home are anxiously inquiring "What of the night?"

In response I will say I have made the best possible use of my limited means of observation, since our arrival in Kentucky, and am forced to the conclusion that the war is being carried on at a great disadvantage on our side. Regard for the union element has been one of the main causes of our weakness. Now if there is a true union element in any part of secessia, it should be willing to submit to the greatest sacrifices as cheerfully as we do in the north, in order to aid in restoring the authority of the federal government. But has this petted "armed neutrality" element shown such a disposition? Let us see—Kentuck, I think, is claimed to have a union majority at the ballot box. But what treatment have the forces of the respective combatants received at the hands of the Kentuckians in this vicinity? We are told that the rebels were feasted on the fat of the land, when here, a few weeks since. The rebel sympathisers [*sic*] would make it their business to cook for them, and of course, means of transportation and negro muscle were as freely placed at their disposal. On the contrary, I may safely say that we are received by a majority of the people with indifference, and our best friends seem to be the poor people and the negroes.

Although there is a large class that is professedly union in sentiment, and willing to submit quietly to a restoration of federal authority, *secessianity* is seated in their bones, and would become fully developed could they be assured of the final success of the rebellion.

Instead of being met with open arms and offers of kindness, we often found guards stationed at the gates of the wealthier class, and the weary, hungry and half-famished soldier had not the privilege of passing in to quench his thirst or obtain something to allay his hunger. It is true there were exceptions, and these shine out brightly, as stars through a clouded sky. One of these I will mention: During one of our most dusty marches, late in the night, a group stood at the gate of a dwelling by the roadside, handing out water to the thirsty soldiers. Half choked with dust as I was, I shall never forget the cooling draught received from the hands of these good Samaritans. But this does not change the general rule, and the position of thousands of non-combatants in this state may be summed up in the words of a contraband that came into our camp the other morning. He said, substantially, "Oh, massa, he good 'cesh' when de 'cesh' are about; and he good 'cesh' *when 'cesh' are away;* but when de union men come around, *he be good union man, den.*" A second cause of inefficiency, I think is a deficency [*sic*] of cavalry.[3] Let one half of our infantry force be placed on horseback, with liberty to subsist on the enemy, and trained to such work as has been accomplished by Stewart's[4] rebel cavalry, and they would, with the aid of light artillery, sweep over the state with the force of an avalanche. We must strike sudden and unexpected blows, and this is generally impracticable with infantry.—That the rebellion will yet be effectually crushed, I still earnestly hope—but it is evident that we have to rely on our great strength rather than our military skill. It may be presumptious [*sic*] to write thus, and doubtless is. Gen. Scott always entertained an opposite view in regard to the usefulness of cavalry, and possibly the present chief commander does, but they must permit an humble corporal to hold a different opinion.[5] No apparent mismanagement, however, shall alter my determination to exert all my feeble energies in sustaining our noble government, and its honored head, in suppressing the rebellion.

Our camp news is unimportant. The arrival of a contraband occasionally, and now and then a rebel prisoner, relieves the monotony of daily camp duties. Yesterday a scouting party brought in a real secesh flag—the stars and bars— made of coarse material, in size about 6 by 15 feet. It was taken from the

house of an old secessionist, where it had been laid away, the old cuss having concluded, no doubt, to "play union" awhile. He was brought into camp, and doubtless fully appreciated the dismal groans that greeted the triple-barred emblem of hell. But my letter is long enough. Good bye. S.F.F.
(Rock Island *Argus,* October 21, 1862, p. 2)

1. The words and music to "Do They Miss Me at Home?" were written by S. M. Grannis. The song was first published in 1852, but it did not achieve real popularity until the beginning of the war.

2. Caroline Norton wrote the words to "Bingen on the Rhine," and the music was composed by Judson Hutchinson. The song, originally published about 1850, tells of a young German soldier of the French Foreign Legion who is mortally wounded in the fighting near Algiers. As he lies dying, surrounded by his comrades, he fondly remembers the people and places he has known at his home in Bingen. Several later versions of the song also appeared, including one published in the South at the outset of the war, entitled "Richmond on the James."

3. Part of Rosecrans's reorganization of the Army of the Ohio (soon to be the Army of the Cumberland) was the revamping of its cavalry arm. An army historian noted that there was a "sad lack" of cavalry in the fall of 1862. "With his cavalry . . . immensely superior, the enemy constantly annoyed our outposts and forage-trains. The provision-trains between Nashville and Mitchellsville were constantly watched, and sometimes pounced upon." Feeling he lacked a "capable officer to instruct and lead them," Rosecrans secured the appointment of Brig. Gen. David S. Stanley as his chief of cavalry. In order to increase the effectiveness of his mounted arm, Rosecrans immediately requisitioned 5,000 revolving rifles and several pieces of light field artillery for its use. See John Fitch, *Annals of the Army of the Cumberland* (Philadelphia, 1863), 369–76.

4. Fleharty is no doubt referring to Confederate cavalry general J. E. B. Stuart (1833–64).

5. Winfield Scott (1786–1866) was general-in-chief of the United States Army from 1841 to 1861. The "present chief commander" was Maj. Gen. Henry W. Halleck (1815–72), who served from 1862 to 1864. It is possible that Fleharty is also referring to Maj. Gen. Don Carlos Buell (1818–98), who continued in command of the Army of the Ohio until October 24.

CHAPTER 2

"Further Out of the World"

⌒ No. 6 ⌒

Camp near Frankfort, Ky., Oct. 26.

Since writing my last letter we have been engaged in a general chase after John Morgan, the guerrilla chief. Rumors that Lexington had been retaken by the rebels reached our camp during last Saturday. While on dress parade in the evening the news was confirmed, with the additional statement that Morgan's cavalry was only twelve miles distant from our camp. Shortly afterwards a body of union cavalry, probably 800 strong, came dashing by at break-neck speed, from the direction of Frankfort; next came a battery, and then a large force of infantry in wagons—some drawn by four mules, some by six—all making the quickest possible *mule-time*.[1] "Fun ahead," thought we, and that night rolled ourselves into our blankets with the full expectation of hearing the long roll before morning. About midnight it sounded, and hastily equipping ourselves, we were soon on the march towards Frankfort, however, instead of Lexington. What did it mean? Where could we be going? We knew not, then, but have since learned the object of our Sunday morning walk. It appears that Morgan had heard of our cavalry, infantry and mule-wagon-movement against him, and was making good time from Lexington—southeast of this place—towards Lawrenceburg, a point nearly south of Frankfort, and distant thirteen miles— from our camp fifteen miles distant. Our business was to intercept him at Lawrenceburg. After passing through Frankfort we halted some time, proba- bly waiting dispatches. Starting again, we marched in quick time until day- light—then in the gray of the morning were ordered to halt, form in line of battle and load our guns. This done, we continued on to Lawrenceburg; but the game had escaped. Morgan had passed through the town an hour and a half before our arrival. Our cavalry, *wagon-mounted* infantry and a battery of light artillery continued the pursuit. I have not learned the result.[2] This much, however, is evident, the guerrilla chief would have been intercepted and probably the main body of his band captured, if the force that went out from this place had been mounted. Although the plan to catch the rebels was well designed, I think the result justifies the opinion that yesterday's severe marching was rather a painful verification of the remarks made in my last letter in regard to the ineffectiveness of infantry in a guerrilla war, and our great need of more cavalry.

The reader will pardon these criticisms—the opinions expressed are honestly entertained. Of course Uncle Sam will neither take my advice nor make me commander-in-chief, but as our armies are controlled almost as much by our editors as by our generals, I shall not have criticised in vain if the Argus and other influential journals, should be induced thereby to agitate the subject.

We learned at Lawrenceburg that our cavalry had taken 27 prisoners and one wagon loaded with stores. Morgan captured between 200 and 300 of our cavalry the day before at Lexington. The horses and everything valuable were taken from the men. The cavalry was commanded at the time by an Ohio captain.[3] All were paroled. During the time they were held as prisoners, the captain was introduced by Morgan to his mother, who resides in Lexington. His sabre and revolver were returned to him. In lieu of a good horse, however, he was compelled to come away on an old "crow-bait," which the rebels placed at his disposal. I am told that this mode of trading horses is quite common among the guerrilla bands—the rider of an inferior horse immediately making a forcible exchange whenever he finds one that is better.

We rested a few hours near Lawrenceburg—some sleeping, others munching hard crackers and eating smoked ham. The return march was made in slower time. Many of the boys, however, were completely worn out as they well might be, having marched fully thirty miles. We reached our old camp about 7 o'clock in the evening, and found a very good supper—hot coffee, fried crackers, &c., ready for us. The boys who had been left in camp, had heard of our coming, and immediately went to work to welcome us in a manner becoming soldiers. Their kindness as well as their coffee was fully appreciated.

With weary limbs we retired to rest, confidently believing that when the old-fashioned sail-vessels succeeds in making better time than the present fast-going steamer—when the stage-coach of fifty years ago travels faster than the modern locomotive, or when men can be found who are able to trot faster than "Patchen" or "Flora Temple,["]⁴ we will be able to capture John Morgan with infantry.

Yours truly,

S. F. F.

(Rock Island *Argus,* October 29, 1862, p. 2)

1. Fleharty was not the only person to recognize the potential of mobile infantry. German-born brigadier general August Willich, in March 1863, proposed that regiments of "wagon-mounted" infantry be formed. He suggested that "enough wagons should be constructed so that they [his men] could be hauled to their position during the approach march, positioning them sooner than the enemy would enable his men to be more rested and thus better able to fight." The idea was rejected. See James Barnett, "Willich's Thirty-Second Indiana Volunteers," *Cincinnati Historical Society Bulletin* XXXVII (1979), 63.

2. Morgan eluded his pursuers. See Fleharty, *Our Regiment,* 17.

3. Capt. George A. Gotwald, commanding four companies of the 4th Ohio Cavalry, surrendered to Morgan on October 18. See *OR,* Vol. XVI, Pt. 1, pp. 1147–48.

4. Both were noted racehorses of the day. On October 15, 1859, at Kalamazoo, Michigan, Flora Temple had trotted a mile in the record time of 2 minutes, 19.75 seconds. See Frazier Hunt and Robert Hunt, *Horses and Heroes: The Story of the Horse in America for 450 Years* (New York, 1949), 108–10.

✎— No. 7 —✎

Camp Near Bowling Green, Nov. 5.

At length I am able to resume my pen in the tented field, after an unpleasant absence of ten days from the regiment, which struck tents and started for this place on the 26th ult. Being quite unwell at the time, and therefore unfit to commence a long and severe march, I was permitted to accompany a number of others "likewise blessed," to Jeffersonville, Ind., where a hospital has been established for the especial benefit of the 102.¹ Those most seriously sick were placed under treatment in the hospital—the remainder, including the writer hereof, were placed in a building near by. After a few days of rest and recuperation we came on to this place over the Louisville and Nashville railroad, arriving in advance of the regiment. I will not detail our experience during those ten days of absence from the regiment, the changes that have taken place in the

102 requiring the principle part of my attention in this letter. I will, however, recur to the appearance of the country along the line of the L. & N. railroad. As the road passes within a few miles of the far famed Mammoth Cave, you will readily imagine that it is rocky and rough; but the wild grandeur of the scenery on some parts of the route, should be seen to be appreciated. While moving along in the most open and level parts of the country, we could see in the distance immense mounds, their peaks reaching far up towards the sky, and usually crowned with cedars. At times, however, we noticed a beautiful diversity of colors in foliage of trees and shrubs that covered the mounds— the orange, russet and golden hues that decorate a northern forest in autumn, being intermingled promiscuously with the deep rich green of the cedar. Leaving the open country, we would wind for a time among the hills—the road being located in many places about half way up the sides of precipitous, rocky bluffs. Moving rapidly along in one of these rugged places, we were suddenly plunged into utter darkness. I looked in vain to see the man who sat by my side. The train thundered along for more than a mile through the "blackness of darkness," and then emerged from the tunnel into a comparatively level country. But enough of landscape painting.

You have doubtless heard, are [*sic*] this, of the resignation of Col. McMurtry. It is possible that the colonel has been, to some extent, the victim of jealousy; but, independent of any such influence, both officers and privates had become convinced that the interests of the regiment required a change; and the resignation was tendered only after the will of the regiment had been publicly expressed. That the colonel is brave, no one can doubt, but there are other qualities essential to a good commander. He must be able to command himself. Alas! how many of our best officers have ruined their best prospects by being subject to a domineering vice! and how much our poor soldiers have suffered from that worst of all commanders, Mr. Double-barreled Canteen![2] Inexperience, too, should induce many officers yet in responsible places, to commit their trust to abler hands. For illustration, let us suppose there is a locomotive with a long train of cars, freighted with human life, ready to start from a depot,—a man who is totally ignorant of the structure and management of a steam engine, steps on board the panting monster, pulls the lever and moves off—intending to learn the art of engineering as he goes along! You would call it madness, but it is a degree of madness that is not without a parallel.

The colonel relinquished the command of the regiment before it left Frankfort, and for the present Lieut. Col. Smith fills his place. Various individuals are mentioned, in "official circles," in connection with the colonelcy, but it is not known who will be our future leader. Of course our first expectations have not been realized, but we are enabled to congratulate ourselves in view of the fact that a change so important has been effected without creating any serious dissatisfaction in the regiment. The future of the 102 seems propitious.

The march from Frankfort to this place was accomplished in ten days. The boys are generally foot-sore, but otherwise they appear remarkably well. They marched on an average fifteen miles per day. Our division will probably remain here until we are paid off and receive additional clothing, when it is thought we will move on Nashville. During the next tramp I will be with the boys, as I feel quite well again, and hope to be able to accompany the regiment hereafter in all its journeyings.

The grand army under Gen. Rosecrans has been passing here for several days. During the time we were awaiting the arrival of our regiment, at least twenty thousand troops passed our quarters. Almost every battle field of the war, west of the Cumberland mountains, is represented in the ranks of the great army. I conversed with veterans from Somerset, Pea Ridge, Donalson, Shiloh, Perryville and Rich Mountain.[3]

The soldiers seem to be generally well pleased with the removal of Gen. Buell and the appointment of Rosecrans as commander-in-chief of this department. I was told that the army was fast becoming demoralized under Buell's administration. Rosecrans seems to possess the confidence of the entire army. They say he has never lost a battle, and it is confidently expected that with the vast resources of men and means, at his command, he will strike a death blow at the heart of secession, and add new laurels to his already brilliant name.

I am told that the mail is about to leave, and must therefore, bid you adieu. More anon. S. F. F.

(Rock Island *Argus*, November 14, 1862, p. 2)

1. Jeffersonville, Indiana, situated across the Ohio River from Louisville, was located at "one of the principal gateways of the South." The men and supplies of the Union army operating in Kentucky and middle Tennessee funneled through the city and down the Louisville and Nashville Railroad. Consequently "vast storehouses, shops, factories, offices, hospitals and barracks were to be found scattered over all parts of Jeffersonville and its vicinity." Here, at Camp Joe Holt, a hospital was established and maintained until 1864. For more on Jeffersonville

during the war, see Lewis C. Baird, *Baird's History of Clark County, Indiana* (Indianapolis, 1909), 159–60.

2. Apparently, McMurtry's drinking problem was serious and of long standing. In an otherwise laudatory obituary, a local journal noted: "Governor McMurtry was a genial, large-hearted man; and, like too many men of generous impulses and public prominence was not free from the besetting social curse of intemperance." The notice went on to say that one of McMurtry's oldest friends had remarked after his death that "had it not been for this habit he might today have held a place in the hearts of the people of the entire nation." Galesburg *Republican-Register*, April 17, 1875, p. 1.

3. The battles to which Fleharty refers were, in chronological order: Rich Mountain, West Virginia, July 11, 1861; Logan Cross Roads (Somerset), Kentucky, January 19, 1862; Fort Donelson, Tennessee, February 12–16, 1862; Pea Ridge, Arkansas, March 7–8, 1862; Shiloh, Tennessee, April 6–7, 1862; and Perryville, Kentucky, October 8, 1862.

❧ No. 8 ☙

Camp "Lost River," near Bowling Green, November 10, 1862.

Have we not a pretty name for a camping ground? I will tell you whence it is derived: A short distance from camp a small stream rises apparently out of the ground, flows about two hundred yards, and then disappears into the mouth of a yawning cavern,—hence its name, "Lost River"[1]—which title has been well chosen to designate our excellent camp. The stream makes no approach in size to the dignity of a river. Local circumstances alone give it any importance.—Being determined, notwithstanding its retiring disposition, to seek a further acquaintance with the little river, I joined a party of explorers and penetrated the cave. Lighting our candles, we wandered over detached rocks far into the interior, beyond the sounds of the ever busy camp—far beyond the reach of daylight. The ceiling of the cave, in some places, reaches almost to the floor, in others rises in a dome-like form, so high that its outline could be but dimly discerned with our imperfect light. Our voices resounded with startling effect through the rugged aisles of the cavern. A pistol was fired by one of the party, and the sound roared through the distant recesses like the report of a cannon. The river murmurs along its dark passage, sometimes in view, and sometimes through deeper cavities. This is, of course, but an insignificant part, or section, of the great cavernous district in Kentucky; yet, unimportant tho' it may be, the rude apartments, and the solemn stillness of the place, broken only by the voice of man and the murmuring stream, render "Lost River Cave" well worthy a visit. I was told the cave has been explored a number of miles from its mouth. We spent an hour picking our way over and among the rocks, and were sufficiently tired at the end of that time to appreciate the advantages of a level surface and perpendicular position in pedestrian exercises. We entered another cave near here, which opens into quite an extensive room, about one hundred feet below the surface. A pure stream of excellent water flows through it. Enough, however, on this subject for the present—I may be enabled to make more extensive explorations hereafter, underground, in which case I will give you additional inside views of Kentucky.

We have remained quietly in camp here since the 4th inst., and the boys have had a good rest. The weather has been glorious. During leisure hours we have rambled thro' the woods, gathering hickory nut[s], walnuts and persimmons. Indeed we have experienced a pleasant relaxation of the arduous duties of a soldier's life, and pleasant memories will ever cluster about our recollections of Camp "Lost River."

Our division was reviewed last Friday by Major Gen. Rosecrans. All were anxious to see the general—the hero who has never lost a battle. At length he appeared, followed by a train of subordinate officers and his body guard. Riding to the head of the division, and then guiding his horse slowly along the line, he received the salutations of each regiment as he passed, and to each regiment addressed a few words. To the 105th Illinois he said, "Men of the 105th, when you come into battle, fire deliberately, and aim low.—Remember that if each one of you hits a man you will kill or cripple a great many. It is a short lesson, and I hope you will remember it." Then riding on, he said: "These are tall men—very tall; they must have been raised where they grow such tall corn." As he rode along the front of the "102" he asked how many men were in line. Major Harding stated the number, and the general responded: "The largest and finest looking set of men on the ground!" This *we* of the "102" construe into a handsome compliment, notwithstanding our native modesty!

Rosecrans *looks* the general, every inch; and although I have become somewhat cautious in estimating the qualities of military men, I must say that his manly bearing suggested the idea that he would not rank unworthily by the side of Napoleon's famed marshals. He has a pleasant countenance, and the soldiers are of the opinion that in becoming a general, he has not forgotten that he is a man. The review was an imposing spectacle, and one that will be long remembered by those who witnessed it.[2] The rays of the setting sun gleamed from many thousand polished bayonets, and that long line of loyal hearts was animated by a common feeling—confidence in their united strength, the justness of their cause, and the ability of their new general.

Since I commenced this letter, I have learned that we are to start for a new camping ground to-morrow—at or near Scottsville, about 25 miles east of Bowling Green. A scarcity of forage in this vicinity is said to be the cause of our removal. Some, however, entertain a different opinion, and pretend to have discovered in the movements of our armies, and in certain mysterious rumors from diplomatic circles indications of an important change in our domestic complications. What are the signs of the times? Some say peace, others say war—doubly fierce, doubly bitter, against an allied foe.

The result of the recent elections in the north seems to have impressed many with the belief that the war will soon end. Whether this opinion is well founded, I am, of course, unable to say. Of this much, however, we are convinced—the discarding of radicalism, and the introduction of a conservative element (call it by what other name you will—republican, democratic or union) into the councils of the nation, will be for the good of the whole country. All we ask is loyalty to the constitution and the union—away with your Lovejoys on the one hand and your Vallandighams on the other. If the result should be an honorable peace, none will hail the moment of its inauguration with greater joy than the war-worn volunteers; but peace on any other terms would involve the anathemas of all loyal soldiers.[3]

I am told that Lieut. Col. Smith will permanently fill the position vacated by the resignation of Col. McMurtry. Major Mannon, of Mercer county (one of the very best men in the regiment) becomes lieutenant colonel, and Capt. Harding of Co. A (a man of fine military talents) is our major.[4] Company C, [my company] has been recently under the exclusive control of your old friend, Lieutenant Almond Shaw, who is very popular with the boys. Our worthy captain, Frank Shedd you have probably learned, ere this, is at home on a short furlough in consequence of sickness. Our second lieutenant, Watson C. Trego, has tendered his resignation on account of continued ill-health. We regret the necessity for this step, but the nature of the disease with which the lieutenant is affected renders it inexpedient for him to continue longer in the service.

The boys are suffering considerably from colds and coughs. Since we arrived in Kentucky three of the regiment have died. I have not learned their names in full; will report them hereafter. To-day a member of the 108th Ohio, in camp here, was accidentally shot through the head and instantly killed. A comrade sportively cocked his gun, aimed it at him—supposing it unloaded—pulled the trigger, and the poor fellow fell dead at his feet. It was a sad accident, and the wretched survivor has learned a lesson in blood which should have been the legacy of common sense.

But I must close, as my letter is long, and the night air is growing cold. I must rest to-night, for to-morrow we march.

Adieu,

S. F. F.

(Rock Island *Argus*, November 20, 1862, p. 2)

1. Lost River, known locally as the shortest river in the world, is near Bowling Green. The stream emerges from underground in a valley on the south edge of town, proceeds about three hundred yards and enters Lost River Cave, where it again goes underground, eventually emptying into Jennings Creek west of Bowling Green.

2. When Rosecrans took command of the Army of the Ohio, he found a mixture of veteran regiments, thinned by disease and battle, and new units filled with raw recruits. "The former were poorly clad and equipped, and the latter inexperienced in drill or discipline, with officers often ignorant and sometimes incompetent." The commanding general thus began reviews of the divisions, examining the men and their equipment "with earnest scrutiny," while simultaneously "the new troops were drilled incessantly." Fitch, *Army of the Cumberland*, 369, 371.

3. Lincoln's issuance of the preliminary emancipation proclamation in September, together with his suspension of the writ of habeas corpus shortly thereafter, created a storm of Democratic protest throughout the North which was noticed by the voters. In the mid-term elections that fall, Democrats carried Ohio, Illinois, and Indiana; elected governors in New York and New Jersey; and gained thirty-five seats in Congress that had been held by Republicans. This apparently met with Fleharty's approval. See Phillip Shaw Paludan, *The Presidency of Abraham Lincoln* (Lawrence, Kans., 1994), 157.

Owen Lovejoy (1811–64), Republican congressman from Illinois from 1857 to 1864, was the brother of Rev. Elijah P. Lovejoy, the "abolitionist martyr," who had been killed by a pro-slavery mob in Alton, Illinois, in 1837. The only full-scale biography of Lovejoy is Edward Magdol's *Owen Lovejoy, Abolitionist in Congress* (New Brunswick, N.J., 1967).

Clement L. Vallandigham (1820–71) was a peace-at-any-price Democratic congressman from Ohio from 1858 to 1863. His antiwar speeches were considered treasonous by the administration, and he was eventually arrested and banished to the Confederacy. See Frank L. Klement, *The Limits of Dissent: Clement L. Vallandigham and The Civil War* (Lexington, Ky., 1970).

In calling his readers' attention to Fleharty's commentary on the election, editor Danforth noted that Fleharty "is one of the strongest republicans in this region of [the] country, or was when he enlisted." Rock Island *Argus*, November 20, 1862, p. 1.

4. Capt. Roderick R. Harding of Galesburg, Illinois, served only as acting major. He had originally been a company officer in the 17th Illinois Infantry from April 1861 to May 1862. In September 1862 he was mustered in as captain of Co. A of the 102d. *Adj. Gen. Rep.*, V, 594.

❦ No. 9 ❧

Camp Near Scottsville, Ky.,
Nov. 15, 1862.

We were on the eve of marching to this place when I closed my last letter. At the appointed time the division was put in motion: We followed an apparently unfrequented road, winding over hills and through valleys,—the hills in some places so steep that the wagon trains moved with great difficulty. We marched at a very moderate pace, and reached Scottsville on the evening of the second day.

Nothing of particular interest occurred during the march, yet the wild appearance of the country, and the apparently anti progressive character of the people, could not fail to attract the attention of those who have been accustomed to the wide awake spirit that pervades western society. I do not wish to draw unjust comparisons, but I must say it would be a source of positive pleasure, to view, once more, a neatly built, white-painted Illinois farm house. The majority of the dwelling houses in this country are log-cabins. There is one redeeming feature, however, about these rough buildings: they all have the old-fashioned fire place, which always suggests a picture of happiness that is never realized in connection with the modern arrangement of house-warming. Looking at these well worn hearthstones, the mind of the native western boy reverts to the time—long ago—when, as one of a happy family circles [*sic*] he was accustomed to sit beneath the paternal roof, before a brightly blazing fire made of hickory logs. Oh! there is not in the wide world another such place to dream "day dreams" and build air castles!—and those who have not enjoyed the luxury of listening to the snow storm raging without, while gazing into a bed of glowing hickory coals, have been deprived of one of life's sweetest pleasures. There is an inexhaustible supply of wood for these cheerful fires, and Kentucky must present many happy winter-evening fireside scenes.

We noticed one school house on the road, the best we have seen in the state. The children were out, en masse, looking at the soldiers; and here let me say that, notwithstanding the apparently sterile nature of the soil may indicate an unproductive country, the troops of children gathered about the cabin doors, furnished tangible evidence that the injunction to "multiply and replenish the earth" (an order, by the way, which appears to have been entirely superfluous) is not disobeyed in this part of Kentucky. One would think, indeed, that there is a degree of rivalry between the white and black races in this respect, so equally were the two classes represented.

In more than one respect there are marked peculiarities in the character and manners of the people. The majority of them use the vulgar negro brogue, and if they should endeavor to say, "since the war broke out, we poor folks have seen hard times," the words would be enunciated as if written thus: "Since the *wah* brooke out we *po'* folks have seen *hawd* times." Butternut colored clothes are almost universally worn. I do not mention these characteristics in any inimical sense. As good men as ever wore broadcloth may and do wear this homespun material. That there should be so much difference in dress, habits and manners, between the people of a common country, and so closely allied as Kentuckians and Illinoisans, seems, however, remarkably strange, and before we had made any personal observations, in Kentucky, we were impressed with the belief that similar comparisons had been made between the respective sections in a prejudicial spirit.

No one who has cultivated a western farm would be contented to live in any part of the state we have seen. The soil generally looks as if it had been blasted by a thousand years of furnace heat; and the hazy atmosphere of an Indian summer day—reflecting the red rays of sun, in connection with the yellow robes of the forest trees, and the red and yellow soil beneath our feet, would seem to be sufficient to give any one the yellow jaundice—a disease that is not uncommon among our troops.

In the life of Daniel Boone, it is said that the old hunter was fairly enraptured when he first viewed the wilds of Kentucky; and this was a very natural feeling, for Boone looked at Kentucky with a hunter's eye. His romantic and adventurous nature rendered him at home only in the great forests, and in the vicinity of the nimble deer, the wildcat, the panther and the red-skin. But to the eye of the western farmer, this portion of the state, at least, presents few attractions. Of course there are staple articles that may be produced with great facility, and very profitably, when the land is thus cleared, and chief among these is tobacco—large quantities of which we noticed drying in the tobacco houses by the roadside. The boys call it "Kentucky scrip," and indeed it may be said to be the only kind of currency here on which there is no discount.

The people in this vicinity appear to be as loyal as those who reside nearer the Ohio river, and I have fully as much confidence in the patriotism of Scottsville as I have in the patriotism of Louisville.

Our camp is located near the town, on the sunny side of a long hill. There are twenty or thirty acres of cleared land here, suitable for camping purposes. A heavy forest covers the sides and summits of the surrounding hills. A stream of excellent water runs near camp. It is thought by some that we will remain here some time, and if the necessities of the service do not demand our removal elsewhere, we are perfectly willing to serve our country for a time in this secluded place. We seem to be further out of the world than we ever were before; and have even heard the north spoken of by the soldiers as *"the other world."*

We left Camp Lost River last Tuesday morning, and up to this time, Saturday noon, have not heard a word of news from the north or east. What have you been doing during these five long days? Perhaps we will be wakened some fine morning from our Rip Van Winkle repose, to hear something important. Of the war movements that may be in progress, we know nothing. Indeed, we do not know precisely why we are here, and cannot tell whether the nearest rebel force is within ten or one hundred miles of camp.

Scottsville is the county seat of Allen county, and probably at one time contained three hundred inhabitants. About half of the houses are constructed of logs, and the rude appearance of the village would readily suggest the idea that we are not many miles distant from the region of illiterate judges and backwoods sermon-singing parsons. Indeed, we confidently expect that we will yet find the preacher that preached, and the identical pulpit from which was delivered the celebrated sermon beginning with the text:

An' he played on a harp of thousan' strings, sperits of jus' men made perfec.'

We are said to be only about ten miles from the Tennessee line, in which state that modern, but somewhat mythical apostle of darkness is said to have flourished. In our peregrinations we will keep a sharp look-out also for that other Tennessee evangelist—the author of the "Curse of Congress!"[1]

But I must not tire you longer with these idle speculations. We have one more item of camp news that may interest you: A squad of refugees—seventeen in number—came into our division last Thursday night. They were greatly rejoiced at their deliverance, and have all enlisted in the union army. We trust it may be our lot to accompany the grand army of the union into Eastern Tennessee, and witness the deliverance of the oppressed patriots of that section from the thraldom of Confederate tyranny.[2]

Our time is occupied here in drilling, and performing various camp duties. The weather is very pleasant, our rations amply sufficient, and we are having rather a good time generally.

Permit me, in conclusion, colonel, to thank you for the regular receipt of the Weekly Argus, which is ever a welcome camp visitor.

Ever yours, S. F. F.

(Rock Island *Argus*, December 1, 1862, p. 2)

1. Fleharty probably refers to William G. "Parson" Brownlow.

2. The geography of eastern Tennessee had never supported a slave culture. A region of hills and mountains, that part of the state had seen the development of an agriculture based on small independent farms. In 1860 only 9 percent of eastern Tennessee's population were slaves. On February 9, 1861, when the call for a secession convention was voted on, 81 percent of east Tennessee voters opposed it. When the state finally left the Union on June 8, 69 percent of the region's voters still cast their ballots against secession. Even after Tennessee had cast its lot with the Confederacy, the people of east Tennessee remained loyal to the Union. In the 1861 state elections, for instance, Federal congressmen were elected in each of the districts in the region. As resistance to the Confederate government continued, east Tennessee was subjected to increasingly harsh counter-measures, including occupation by a Confederate army. For a succinct, but excellent, discussion of the plight of the people of east Tennessee, see Stephen V. Ash, "Tennessee," in *Encyclopedia of the Confederacy* (New York, 1993), IV, 1574–80.

∽ No. 10 ∾

Camp Near Scottsville, Ky
November 20, 1862.

Rain, rain, rain, has been the order of the day, so far, during this week; and we imagine that the constant "pattering on the roof" (?) to which we are accustomed to listen, is not heard away up north, where the short November days freeze such vapor-laden clouds as the one that is passing over us, into gently falling flakes of snow. Perhaps even now, the boys "we left behind us" are luxuriating in an abundance of Buffalo robes, among the fair northern belles, guiding the elegant cutter over the glistening snow, while the air is filled with the tinkling of merry bells. We don't anticipate any such enjoyment here, even if the snow should come, for soldiers can only *seem* to realize such bliss during the fleeting moments of delusive dreams. Our camp is so situated that we experience very little inconvenience from so much rainy weather; but any forward movement now, would be next to impossible, as the adhesive nature of Kentucky soil when mixed with water, renders the roads almost impassable.

I have but few items of news to communicate, and in the absence of more entertaining matter, will occupy a leisure hour in detailing the routine of camp duties, and some incidents of our experience as soldiers. Inquiring friends desire to know how often we drill, how we cook, eat, sleep, &c. I will furnish the desired information.

At 5 o'clock in the morning—perhaps in the midst of sweet dreams, wherein the forms of absent friends appear, and the voices of loved ones are heard—bang! goes a gun from the battery near us, the sound rolling off among the hills, and reverberating with the voice of seven thunders. The roll of the drum is then heard, and the camp is soon astir with life. The companies form in line, the roll is called, and then the boys disperse, following the inclinations of the moment.—Some build fires, some post off to the spring with camp kettles for water; others, desirous of a little more "folding of the hands" in slumber, retire to their tents, and remain till the cook calls for breakfast, which is usually served between six and seven. The victuals are cooked in camp kettles, over fires made of logs and rails. If the weather is inclement, we take our meals within our tents, forming a circle around the centre pole, and sitting in Turkish style; at other times we eat at random, around the camp fire. Our company is divided into five messes, or rather was so divided, but owing to a slight disagreement in one of the messes, a number of its members seceded and set up an independent "confederacy." How it will end, we can no more predict than we can foretell the termination of a certain other quarrel which has assumed formidable proportions from a very small beginning!

Those detailed for guard duty are called together a little before eight o'clock, and the ceremony of guard mounting takes place. The number detailed for camp guard from each company, per day, varies from four to six. The number of pickets placed out, varies according to the nature of the country and the probabilities of an attack. The inner line of pickets is stationed a half or three-quarters of a mile from camp; the outside line of infantry pickets is placed out two or three mile[s]; beyond these are the cavalry pickets. The camp guards are on duty two hours, and off four, alternately, during the twenty-four hours; the pickets are governed by the same rule, but are usually compelled to remain in the open air during the whole time. One can hardly conceive of a position more lonely than that of the faithful pickets, when in the darkness of the dead hours of night, and perhaps in a driving rain, they stand on the alert for any approaching foe.

Company drill occupies the time intervening between ten and half past eleven o'clock a. m., and dinner is dispatched at half-past twelve. Battalion or regimental drill begins at half past one, p. m., and ends at four. Dress parade takes place at four. We have supper between the hours of five and six, in the same style that we take breakfast and dinner, with a very slight variation of dishes. "Tattoo" (roll call) is sounded at half-past eight; "taps" at nine, when all lights must be extinguished, and all noise must cease, and this ends the daily round of our duties while in camp.

Our fare has of late been unexceptionable. During one week of the time we have been encamped here, our company drew rations as follows: Pork, 320 lbs; beef, 138 lbs; sugar, 80 lbs; crackers, 560 lbs; coffee, 43 lbs; soap, 11 lbs; beans, 19 qts; and 31 candles. This was not more than an ordinary draw. We have opportunities every day to purchase edibles from citizens, who bring in and retail pies, apples, corn bread, corn meal, dried apples and dried peaches. The only draw back to a lively traffic in these articles is a remarkable scarcity of currency among Uncle Sam's boys. This deficiency some of them have partially remedied by playing off their inevitable "Yankee tricks," and in some cases imposing, I must say, most shamefully upon the credulity of an ignorant people. You would not have supposed that there could be found within the limits of the United States a community so completely wrapped in the night of ignorance. I will relate one or two incidents, that will verify all I have said on this subject. One of our soldiers, in order to make a raise, has repeatedly shelled a little corn, placed it in a small sack, and traded it off as coffee for pies and other luxuries. One of our pickets recently tried to make a small purchase of a citizen, offering to give him some postage stamps in exchange for the article desired. The stamps were refused, the citizen stating that he had some of them already in his possession, and had found them to be worthless. The picket asked him to show his stamps, whereupon he drew forth a number of *sutler's tickets*,[1] that had been issued by the sutler of an Ohio regiment which removed from this place sometime since. Apropos to the subject under consideration, I will here relate the personal experience of my friend A. H. Trego, our orderly sergeant, who, besides being an excellent orderly, has acquired something of a classical reputation as a scholar from a long intercourse with the *savans* gathered about Galesburg institutions of learning, and better than all is a first rate judge of feminine beauty. Friend T. was purchasing some pies of an interesting young lady, and wishing, no doubt, to prolong the interesting interview, he entered into conversation with her, in the course of which he asked her how far it is to the Tennessee line; and noticing that she looked at him inquiringly, without immediately replying, the question was repeated. "What? Tennessee Line?" said she "No such folks lives around here. I've lived here all *my* time, and there's nobody of that name about here, *I'm shore!*" Here the conversation ended, Orderly T struck a bee-line for his quarters, musing as he went on the words of the poet—

Where ignorance is bliss, 'twere folly to be wise.[2]

The exposures and privations to which the regiment has been subjected has greatly reduced the list of effective men on its muster rolls, and some of the companies report only about two thirds of their original number as fit for duty. The following are the names of those who have died since we left Knoxville: Chas. H. Rodgers, of Co. A, from Abingdon, Ill.; Wm. Drury, of Co. F, from Galesburg; Robert Watson, Co. D, from Knoxville; David Hocke, Co. B, from Utah, Warren county; and Orlando Kinney, of Co. A, from Pope Creek, Mercer county.[3]

Friday Nov. 21.—The rain clouds have dispersed, and the weather is much cooler.

I have one more item of news to add, which must close my "jottings" for this week. In consequence of the resignation of Lieut. W. C. Trego, the non-commissioned officers of our company have been promoted—each being advanced one grade. Orderly Trego becomes, accordingly, our second lieutenant.

Very truly yours, S. F. F.

(Rock Island *Argus*, December 2, 1862, p. 2)

1. Francis A. Lord notes in *Civil War Sutlers and Their Wares* (New York, 1969), 36: "In lieu of change and to prevent soldiers from buying elsewhere, individual sutlers issued their

own 'money.' This was either metal 'tokens,' usually about the size of a penny, or small 'card-board chits.' In both cases the sutler's name, unit, and denominational value were stamped or printed."

2. This is Fleharty's slightly incorrect rendering of a line from Thomas Gray's poem, "On a Distant Prospect of Eton College" (1742).

3. Pvt. Charles H. Rogers (Co. A) died October 21, 1862; Pvt. William Drury (Co. F) died October 23; and Pvt. Robert Watson (Co. I) died November 1, all in Frankfort, Kentucky. Sgt. David Hocker (Co. B) died November 4 in Jeffersonville, Indiana; and Pvt. Orlando Kenny (Co. A) died November 20 in Scottsville, Kentucky. *Adj. Gen. Rep.*, V, 595–96, 605, 610. In all cases the spelling here is that given in the *Adj. Gen. Rep.*

◦— No. 11 —◦

Gallatin, Tenn., Dec. 3, 1862

Our friends at home can hardly realize the difficulties under which soldiers labor in preparing for their perusal and gratification those messages of friend-ship and love which are intended to cheer their hours of loneliness, and enliven, perchance a broken family circle—the soldier's letter—crumpled and blotted though it may be, is consecrated to true friendship by the circumstances under which it is written. Our wandering life renders it difficult to preserve materials for writing, and at the close of a march we sometimes find our inkstands empty or lost, our stock of writing paper reduced to a few crumpled half sheets—no envelopes, no stamps, and perhaps empty pocket-books! In addition to this, the chill December winds benumb our fingers, and sometimes a drizzling rain renders everything uncomfortable. My mind has been directed into this channel by the circumstances under which I now write. Having decided that the day and the hour had arrived in which I should have my accustomed chat with the readers of the *Argus,* I endeavored to secure a comfortable place, where intruders would not interrupt, and where my fingers would not become numb with cold. Noticing that there was a fire in one of the tents, I entered it; the atmosphere was blue with smoke, and half suffocating I quickly retreated. The next effort was more successful. Entering my own quarters I made the following disposition to meet the exigencies of the case: drew on my overcoat, pulled off my boots, rolled the lower extremities in three or four blankets—thrust my right hand into my only remaining mitten which has independent receptacles for the thumb and forefinger, the remaining part being undivided; armed myself with a pen that appears to have borne the brunt of many wordy battles, and then with my portfolio on my knees, and a plate of hard crackers by my side (which I "nibble" when ideas come slowly) felt that I was armed and equipped.

And now I will take up the thread of our regimental history, which has been roughly traced, up to the time we were encamped at Scottsville. On the morning of the 25th ult., we left our pleasant camp at that place and started on a two day's march to this point. During the few remaining miles over which we marched in Kentucky, we saw nothing in the appearance of the country to redeem it from the reputation for roughness and sterility already established, and the last prominent landscape picture that came under our observation may not inaptly represent the rough appearance and impoverished condition of the state. The picture was this: a little farm on the side of a precipitous hill,—here and there among the rocks were scattered hills of stunted corn; in the centre of the field were two forlorn little donkeys, struggling to maintain a perpendicular position, and seeking to gain a scanty subsistence from the products of the barren soil. As we looked upon the lonely picture we could not help thinking of the miserable destiny that evidently waited those feeble and diminutive donkeys—may their probable fate never be realized by the desolated state which they seemed to represent.

After marching a few hours, and while passing a long deep valley, loud cheers were borne to our ears from the head of the column. We were crossing the state line, and cheer after cheer echoed through the valley as the different regiments shook the dust of Kentucky from their feet.

We marched until after dark, and at a time when we were expecting every moment to be halted for the night, commenced descending a narrow valley,—down, down, down, deeper and darker the valley grew. Between the precipitous hills there was but little more room than was taken up by the road. Where could we camp? This question was soon answered; the long train stopped. The men stacked arms near the roadside—the wagons halted in the road—and then there was a scene of apparent confusion that is indescribable; some were getting water, others securing blankets, &c., that were in the wagons; the majority proceeded to lay in a stock of rails with which to build fires. In the midst of the melee, while seeking a sleeping place, I climbed a fence that stood near, and at the time felt it reeling and swaying beneath me;—returning about two minutes after, there was no fence to climb—hardly a vestige of it remained; but many bright fires began to cast their fitful gleams of light through the surrounding darkness—the rails had all been confiscated and were being rapidly consumed. Owing to the lateness of the hour and the inequality of the ground, we were unable to pitch our tents, and slept that night beside the camp fires and near the roadside. On the following morning we took up the line of march at an early hour, and passed through what appeared to be the nucleus of a town, which could never realize the "manifest destiny" which its ambitious projectors contemplated, in consequence of the unpropitious nature of the country—the surrounding hills having evidently forced the citizens to enlarge their city in only two directions—up and down the valley. The village or neighborhood is called Rock House Valley. We noticed at this place a most excellent commentary upon the conduct of Bragg and Buell—represented on the door of a blacksmith shop. Some rustic genius had painted two caricatures in black, about half life size, respectively representing the union and the rebel general. They were nice, gentlemanly looking fellows, and appeared to be chatting in a foppish, hail-fellow-well-met style—one of them smoking a pipe, the other a cigar. Doubtless both the union and rebel soldiers appreciate that picture.

From Rock House Valley to this place the country gradually improved in appearance, and we were once more cheered with a view of neat farms and tasteful residences. We reached Gallatin in the evening and encamped near the city—if it may be proper to honor a town of about two thousand inhabitants with that appellation. The town contains a number of neat residences and public buildings, and the citizens seem to have imbibed something of a western spirit, in the enterprise and taste they have shown in decorating their grounds and ornamenting their buildings.—We noticed some very pretty groves of evergreens in connection with which the neat white residences, imperfectly visible, present a quiet summer picture that is hardly in harmony with these cool December days.

Extensive fortifications were being erected here, and the troops encamped in this vicinity will probably remain until they are in an advanced state of completion. The different regiments take their turns in working upon the fortifications, which, when completed, can be held by an inferior force against a greatly superior foe.

Having sketched the principal events of our march to this place, I will attend now to a subject that will be as deeply interesting to you as it is to us. I refer to the mission of our mutual friend and fellow citizen, Capt. John A.

Jordan, the object of which mission is to furnish the soldiers of the 102d and 112th regiments Illinois volunteers with many good things contributed by their kind friends at home.[1] The captain reached the regiment while it was yet at Scottsville. The boys had been anxiously awaiting his arrival, and it was amusing to listen to their speculations on the subject. All felt that there was a rich treat in store for them, and some would repeat long catalogues of luxuries that Ma or Pa, sister or brother would be sure to send; and the desire to receive the goods was only equalled by the desire to grasp the generous hand of Capt. Jordan, who is esteemed wherever known, as the soldier's friend. At length the word came that he had arrived, and the news spread like wildfire through our camp. All demonstrations of joy were immediately repressed, however, as we learned that he came into camp very sick. After a little rest and repose Capt. J., though feeble and pale, appeared among the boys, and was joyfully received. The captain expressed himself highly pleased with our condition, location, etc., remarking that if we should ever be attacked by the enemy, he hoped it would be in that place, as the grounds furnished great natural advantages for defensive operations. He had experienced great difficulty and delay in fulfilling his mission up to that time. The goods had been shipped to Louisville, but failed to arrive when expected. After waiting in that city some days, and paying daily visits to the Jeffersonville and New Albany railroad depots in Indiana, in search of the delayed supplies, he came on to the regiment, and only learned of their arrival in Louisville when we were on the eve of marching to this place. Again he went to Louisville, marked all the boxes for transportation to this city, and again reached our camp on the evening of the 24th ult. Still the supplies do not come, and we are informed that Gen . Rosecrans has issued an order prohibiting the transportation of all goods at this time over the Louisville and Nashville railroad, excepting government stores—the scarcity of supplies in this department absolutely requiring the enforcement of the order. Of course we can receive no luxuries under this order.[2]

Independent of all assistance from our state government and from other sources, Capt. Jordan has expended liberally of his private means, in order to further the object in view—the delay attending the forwarding of supplies compelling a considerable and very unexpected outlay for telegraphing, railroad and hotel fare.

Notwithstanding the many disappointments and vexations that have attended his humane efforts, the captain has been permitted to pass a very pleasant season with us, and both officers and men deeply regret the circumstances that will probably compel him to return to his home ere he has delivered and, we have received from his own hands the evidences of his self-sacrificing efforts, and the precious tributes of affection from loved ones at home.

Perhaps I am encroaching on your space, Mr. Editor, and prudence may dictate a truce to further gossiping to-day, therefore I bid you farewell. Ever yours, S. F. F.

(Rock Island *Argus*, December 9, 1862, p. 2)

1. John A. Jordan, a respected Mercer and Rock Island County farmer, raised a company of volunteers known as the "Ellsworth Guards" at the outbreak of hostilities. In August 1861, part of this company and part of the "Rock Island Rifles" consolidated to become Company A of the 37th Illinois Infantry, of which Jordan was elected captain. Because of a slight stroke, however, Jordan resigned his commission December 31, 1861.

Jordan's twenty-year-old son, Byron, enlisted in Company C of the 102d on August 5, 1862. Initially a sergeant, on May 6, 1863, he was commissioned 2d lieutenant, serving in that capacity for the rest of the war.

In October 1862, Captain Jordan was appointed by Governor Yates to receive articles from area soldiers' aid societies for the 102d, which he pledged to personally deliver to the regiment in Kentucky. Rock Island *Argus*, October 21, 1862, p. 2.

The 112th Illinois Infantry was organized in the summer of 1862 and was composed largely of men from Henry and Stark Counties.

2. When Rosecrans took command of the army, he prepared for "an active and vigorous campaign" against Bragg. After breaking the Confederate siege of Nashville, he began to concentrate the army there. To supply this force he repaired the damage done by the Confederates to the Louisville and Nashville Railroad. By November 6, 1862, the railroad had been reopened to Mitchellsville, and by the twenty-sixth trains were again operating from that point to Nashville. "Up to this time it had been barely possible to subsist the army by running wagon-trains." Gallatin, where the 102d was camped, is about halfway between Mitchellsville and Nashville on the L & N. (Fitch, *Army of the Cumberland*, 370–71, 376).

CHAPTER 3

"Near the Scene of Stirring Events"

⌒ No. 12 ⌐

Gallatin, Tenn., Dec. 10, 1862.

We are near the scene of stirring events, but the daily telegraphic dispatches have ere this furnished you with the war news that is current in this vicinity, therefore I will not anticipate the painfully interesting occurrences that have recently transpired in close proximity to us, but will proceed in the order of time, and link this with the chain of preceding letters.

Our regiment enjoyed the privilege of listening to a speech from our former fellow-citizen, Gen. E. A. Paine, at the close of battalion drill, last Thursday evening. The general has earned an envied reputation among our military commanders, and the boys naturally felt some degree of pride in being permitted to listen to the eloquent words of the gallant Illinoisan. Gen. Paine referred, in the course of his remarks, to the anomalous position of the amateur soldier; the strict discipline necessary to the proper discharge of his duties, being diametrically opposite to all the feelings and inclinations of the free American citizen. The necessity of proper discipline, however, should be apparent to all, and it should be the pride of the soldier, to bear with patience the unavoidable hardships of his position. He himself had stood guard when the thermometer indicated ten degrees below zero, and he thought he would be frozen through and through. He stated also that in earlier years our commander-in-chief, Gen. Rosecrans, performed guard duty at his bidding. He had placed him on guard when he himself was sergeant, and had commanded him to "present arms" whenever the officer of the guard or any field officer should make his appearance. Thus, he said, the lowest officer in the ranks, or any private, with energy and laudable ambition, may advance to a high position in the service of his country.[1] He referred to the fact that we represented a common section of country, alluded with some feeling to the many familiar faces around him, and enjoined upon us the high duty of preserving untarnished the brilliant name Illinois has already won in the present war. At the close of the speech we gave him three hearty cheers.

Gen. Ward of our brigade, then addressed the soldiers, briefly alluding to the peculiar circumstances in which, as soldiers, we are placed, and paying a high tribute to the gallant sons of Illinois. The general is a very fluent and eloquent speaker. In appearance there is a very striking contrast between the two commanders. Gen. Paine preserves the precise demeanor of the strict disciplinarian. Gen. Ward, in his unique uniform, plain rough and ready hat, heavy boots, with pants inside the tops, or boots and pants meeting in square conjunction, appears to represent the opposite character, yet he rigidly enforces strict obedience to orders, and is evidently an officer who believes in earnest work. Gen. Ward's speech was well received.[2]

The different companies of our regiment have been sent out on picket duty, each in its turn, since our arrival at this place. Company C was sent out last Saturday, and we had a fine time gathering nuts and cracking them by the side of our excellent camp fires. The day would have passed for a bright October day at home—just cool enough to render our spirits vivacious, but the following morning revealed a different scene. A cloud had overcast the sky, the air had grown much cooler, and as we crawled out from our bunk in the fence corner to cook our breakfast of pork, crackers and coffee, the snow was coming down thick and fast. It continued to fall for some hours, melting, however, as it fell, and disappearing entirely in the course of two or three days. The weather is again as pleasant as could be desired.

During the time we were on picket we availed ourselves of every favorable opportunity to converse with citizens, in order to learn views in regard to the difficulties that distract the country. A large majority of the people sympathise [sic] with the rebellion, and we were informed by a citizen who claimed to be loyal, that there were but two or three union men among a large circle of acquaintances in his neighborhood. He himself had been compelled, at a former era of the rebellion, to flee to the woods and remain for weeks, receiving sustenance from home by stealth, and thus avoiding the universal persecution visited upon loyal men. This man was riding by the side of a sheepish-looking secessionist, who reluctantly acknowledged his secession proclivities, when pressed by his neighbor to avow his sentiments. It was a source of gratification to witness the excruciating torture that afflicted the poor devil, as, with the air of a convicted villain, he uneasily awaited the movements of his fellow-traveler, who seemed to be in no hurry to relieve him of his misery. Generally there is very little intercourse between the rebel and loyal citizens. An intelligent slave with whom we conversed, appeared to possess a very general knowledge of the country and the character of the people in this part of the state. He was very communicative, and expressed his opinions with all the pomposity and volubility of the semi-educated negro. Being questioned as to the whereabouts of Morgan's men, he answered: "You see men riding around here every day, in citizen[']s clothes, don't you? Well, when you see one of dese, you may say dar goes one of Morgan's men." He said the rebels declare it is the intention of the Yankees to take their slaves, ship them to Cuba, and sell them to pay the expenses of the war! In answer to the question whether he would prefer a state of freedom to that of bondage, he gave the following sensible reply: "If I could live in a country like this and work when I please, eat and sleep when I please, and go to bed when [I] feel like it, I wouldn't care to be free; but if I should be sent to some wild country among the varmints, I wouldn't like it so well."

A Happy Sunday.

Near the close of last week, Capt. Jordon [*sic*] learned that the sanitary supplies designed for our regiment, had been forwarded from Louisville direct to Nashville, and immediately upon being apprised of the fact, he took the train for the last named city. There he found the missing goods, and kept track of them thereafter, until they were safely deposited in our camp. According to military orders, no one is permitted to ride on a freight train on this road except those having the train in their charge. The captain succeeded, however, in getting a permit from the proper authorities to accompany the train, which reached the depot at this place last Sunday morning, and the goods were distributed, under his supervision, during the day. The goods came through in as good condition as could be expected, considering the time they were subject to the tender care of railroad employees. The universal satisfaction that beamed from every countenance, when they arrived, testified how deeply the generous gifts of our friends at home are appreciated by their friends in the army. The business of distributing the supplies produced an active scene during the usually quiet hours of the Sabbath. The happy recipients of the luxuries distributed, with smiling faces, the good things sent them; here a crowd could be seen testing the quality of a nice roll of butter, or a can of preserves; there another gathered about a promiscuous pile of cakes, green apples, dried apples and cheese; while others were in ecstacies over warm mittens, gloves, socks, and an endless variety of minor articles that are a desideratum in camp, such as pens, ink, paper, thread, needles, pins, &c., *ad infinitum.* Every one felt happy, from corporal to colonel—all the way down! Our adjutant was jubilant over a variety of cakes, sweetmeats and Illinois butter; and the rubicund face of our popular sergeant major was luminous over the many rich things that he—didn't get.[3] Of course, however, among so many friends, he could do no better than test the extreme capacity of his gastronomic organization, and feel as happy as the happiest among us. The boys have liberally shared their luxuries with each other, and we are yet enjoying the privilege of sitting down to our meals with the consciousness that there is a heavy discount on fat pork and hard crackers. After our meals are dispatched, we gather about the camp fires, and lighting our fragrant cigars, while away the evening hours with all the gravity becoming gentlemen of ease!

The satisfaction with which the supplies were received, was equalled only by the pleasure which Capt. Jordon realized in delivering them. He bade us adieu on the following morning, and set out for home, carrying with him the good will of the boys, and the assurance that his work has been well done.

Blue Monday.

You have doubtless, ere this, received details of our disaster at Hartsville. The first report of the affair reached us on Sunday evening, during the heighth of our enjoyment in disposing of the first instal[l]ment of home luxuries placed before us. Morning confirmed the painful intelligence, and with depressed spirits we awaited the details of the engagement. After much inquiry I am enabled to give what appears to be an authentic account of the battle.

The enemy, about 6,000 strong, crossed the Cumberland at or near Harts-ville, about 15 miles from this place, on Sunday morning last, and succeeded in surprising the brigade encamped near that village, under command of acting Brig. Gen Moore. The brigade was composed of the 106th and 108th Ohio; the 104th Ill. regiment; Nicklin's Indiana battery, and about 300 Indiana cavalry. The fight commenced a short time before daybreak. One of the Ohio regiments surrendered without firing a gun; the other did but little better, yet made some show of resistance; the 104th Ill., it is said, fought like tigers, and maintained the unequal contest almost unaided, for an hour and twenty minutes. Pressed, at length, on every hand by superior numbers, they were compelled to yield. The greater part of our cavalry was captured; also one section of Nicklin's battery. The wagon train stores belonging to the brigade were taken. Acting Brig. Gen. Moore was wounded.[4]

Learning that reinforcements were coming up under Gen. Miller, the rebels hastily retreated with their prisoners and booty to the opposite side of the river.[5]

A Scandinavian friend of ours, by the name of Charley Peterson, who formerly resided near Berlin, Mercer county, was in the engagement, and received a ball in his right arm.[6] After the surrender, on pretence of going to get his wound dressed, he succeeded in making his escape. He came into our camp to-day. His story confirms the above in all essential particulars. He says about 50 were killed on our side—probably the federal loss in killed and wounded reaches 175. The rebels left 30 dead on the field, and carried a number away with them. These are the main facts that have transpired, and they indicate a degree of cowardice and imbecility on the part of both officers and men that is deeply humiliating.[7]

On the morning following the day of the battle, we were ordered up at an early hour, and told to be ready to march at a moment's notice, but the expected order did not come. During the latter part of the following night, we were ordered to hold ourselves in readiness to meet the advancing enemy, but no enemy came. Again last night the long roll beat, and the boys tumbled out of their beds, and were rapidly forming in line, when we learned that we were again the victims of a false alarm.—It is said that Rosecrans has sent a strong force to the rear of the enemy, which may drive them in this direction. Our generals have evidently been expecting an attack—let the traitors come on; they will find more Illinoisans here than they encountered at Hartsville. Ever yours, S. F. F.

P.S.—We have just received orders to march to-morrow at eleven o'clock. It is thought we will move to some point on the railroad, near here, and go into winter quarters. I have also learned, since closing my letter, that Gen. Dumont has been deprived of the command of our division, and Gen. Paine

will hereafter have control of all the troops in this vicinity, including this division. We do not regret the change. S. F. F.[8]
(Rock Island *Argus*, December 18, 1862, p. 2)

1. Brig. Gen. Eleazer A. Paine (1815–82), an Ohio native, was graduated from the U.S. Military Academy in 1839. He stood twenty-fourth of thirty-one in a class that included future Union generals Isaac I. Stevens (first), Henry W. Halleck (third), Edward O. C. Ord (seventeenth), Henry J. Hunt (nineteenth), and Edward R. S. Canby (thirtieth). He resigned his commission in 1840, practiced law in his native state, and served as deputy U.S. marshal and brigadier general of state militia. He moved to Monmouth, Illinois (just a few miles south of Fleharty's home in Mercer County), in 1848, where he practiced law until the outbreak of the war. He was colonel of the 9th Illinois before being promoted to brigadier general and commanded troops at New Madrid, Island No. 10, Fort Pillow, and Memphis. See Ezra J. Warner, *Generals in Blue: Lives of the Union Commanders* (Baton Rouge, 1964), 355–56.

The incident described by Paine would have had to occur during the winter of 1838–39. At that time Paine was a senior and Rosecrans a plebe at the U.S. Military Academy. They did not serve together again prior to the Civil War.

2. Brig. Gen. William T. Ward (1808–78), a Kentucky lawyer, Mexican War veteran, and former congressman, commanded a brigade of Dumont's 12th Division from September to November 1862. During the latter month, Ward's Brigade (consisting of the 102d and 105th Illinois, 70th Indiana, 79th Ohio, and 13th Indiana Battery) became part of the garrison of Gallatin, Tennessee, commanded by Brig. Gen. Eleazer A. Paine. The 102d would serve under Ward, as brigade and division commander, through the rest of the war.

3. The sergeant major at this time was Jacob H. Snyder of Galesburg, Illinois.

4. Fleharty's description of the engagement at Hartsville, Tennessee, a railroad town garrisoned by a brigade of Union troops, is fairly accurate. At daylight on December 7, 1862, John Hunt Morgan with about 2,100 men surprised and captured the Union garrison (composed of the 104th Illinois, 106th and 108th Ohio, parts of two cavalry regiments, and an Indiana battery), commanded by Col. Absalom B. Moore of the 104th Illinois. The only unit to offer any significant resistance was the 104th Illinois. Victor Hicken, *Illinois in the Civil War* (Urbana, Ill., 1966), 122–23; James A. Ramage, *Rebel Raider: The Life of General John Hunt Morgan* (Lexington, Ky., 1986), 129–31; and Long, *Civil War Dictionary,* 293–94. A detailed history of this action may be found in Edwin C. Bearss, "The Battle of Hartsville and Morgan's Second Kentucky Raid," *Register of the Kentucky Historical Society* LXV (January 1967), 1–19; (April 1967), 120–23; (July 1967), 239–52; and (October 1967), 304–23.

5. Col. Abram O. Miller of the 72d Indiana Infantry, commanding the 40th Brigade of Dumont's 12th Division at Castalian Springs, near Hartsville.

6. Pvt. Charles F. Peterson of Peru, Illinois, served in Co. K of the 104th Illinois Infantry. He mustered in August 12, 1862, and mustered out June 6, 1865. *Adj. Gen. Rep.,* V, 660.

7. Fleharty's numbers are not far off the mark. The official casualty figures for the Federal force at Hartsville were 58 killed and 204 wounded, a total of 262. The Confederate loss was 21 killed and 104 wounded, totaling 125. *OR,* Vol. XX, Pt. 1, pp. 45, 65.

8. Brig. Gen. Ebenezer Dumont (1814–71), an Indiana lawyer, had originally been colonel of the 7th Indiana Infantry. He was promoted to brigadier general of volunteers on September 3, 1861, and had seen action against Robert E. Lee in West Virginia. After the reorganization of the army under Rosecrans, Dumont became commander of the 5th Division of the Army of the Cumberland. He went on sick leave in December 1862 and resigned his commission on February 28, 1863. Warner, *Generals in Blue*, 132.

No. 13

Gallatin, Tenn., Dec. 24.

The march we were about to make when I closed my last letter proved to be a very short one. Gen. Ward's brigade, to which our regiment belongs, has been assigned to the duty of guarding the railroad bridges between Mitchellsville and Nashville, and also furnishes a provost guard for this city and a garrison for the fort that is being constructed here. The 102 moved to the vicinity of the fort, about three fourths of a mile from our previous camp. Several companies of the regiment have been detached as provost guard, and have very comfortable quarters in the city. Those remaining in camp have been busily engaged preparing for inclement weather. A brick kiln near by furnished material for chimneys, and almost every tent is supplied with its underground fireplace.—Some of the wall tents have regularly built fireplaces which indicate much artistic skill in their construction. The chimnies [*sic*] are of all sizes and patterns; some of them erect and neatly finished; others leaning and irregularly put up. These rude subterranean fireplaces render the tents quite comfortable in cold weather. Company C was detailed about a week ago to guard a railroad bridge three miles out towards Nashville. We set out for our destination in a drizzling rain, which was reinforced and came down in torrents when we reached the bridge. A dilapidated house three or four hundred yards distant promised a temporary shelter. In double quick time we passed over the intervening space and took possession of the rude building. It was a two story log house, and had, in better days, no doubt been a pleasant abode for some hospitable family—this inference was drawn from the fact that a comfortable fireplace, both above and below, had served to warm the building. The windows and doors were all gone, and a number of logs had fallen from the second story on one side. We immediately went to work and closed up the apertures on the windward side, built a huge fire in the fire place, cooked our supper, and those who were not on guard retired to rest. The rain continued to fall with unabated fury until late at night, but the following morning was bright, clear and cool. As we threw off our blankets and surveyed the group of soldiers sleeping, dressing, cooking and eating, the scene that was presented would have been a fit subject for the pencil of the painter. Near the entrance, a number of the boys were busily at work cutting and carving what, they called a *possum*. It was apparent, however, that the animal belonged to the species that "divideth the hoof," and we were permitted to realize, at breakfast, the superiority of fresh pork over ancient bacon. Of course we asked not whence it came, and if we had been so impertinent, the boys would undoubtedly have made the usual reply—"We sold eggs and *buyed* it."

A stockade has been erected near the bridge—and near this our company is quartered. A number of the men sleep in their tents, others in the stockade, and others, with characteristic western enterprise, have erected comfortable wooden quarters. One quiet day shortly after our arrival, we were suddenly startled by a rumbling, crashing sound, and upon looking towards the place where the ancient log house had been standing, nothing but the loan [*sic*] chimney appeared above the ruins. A number of the men had upset the building in order to secure the roof, which, being cut into two parts and placed upon the ground in its original shape, and boarded up at the ends, adds two very comfortable houses to our encampment.

The change from our regimental camp to this place has a very exhilerating [*sic*] effect upon the boys. They have few duties to perform, and seem to have regained their native liberty, the loss of which, though a necessity, is one of the severest privations of the American soldier. A clear little creek runs over a rocky bottom near the camp. The weather has recently been pleasant, and we have had pleasant rambles along the creek bank and in the woods. In view of all the advantages of the situation, we might appropriately give our encampment the name of "Happy Hollow."

I am enabled to furnish you with a few additional particulars in regard to the recent defeat at Hartsville. A gentleman who was within the rebel lines a few days since, under a flag of truce, informed me that he conversed with Col. Bennett of Morgan's cavalry.[1]—The rebel colonel complimented the Illinois soldiers very highly. He said, "The Illinois regiment fought like h——l, and the Ohio regiments ran like the devil!" After the Ohio regiments ran, the Illinois regiment was subject to a cross fire that was terribly destructive. He stated also that they found two of our pickets asleep, and said that when they came within view of our camp our boys were preparing breakfast, and he "really felt sorry for them, as he knew the fate that awaited them." Nearly two thirds of the killed were of the Illinois regiment. Our informant observed, as a remarkable fact, that nearly all those killed outright were shot though the head. Many of the wounded will yet die.—Poor fellows! it is hard indeed, after leaving the comforts of home to serve their country to become victims of incompetent officers and cowardly comrades, yet we have the proud satisfaction that the sons of Illinois acquitted themselves nobly.

The camps in and about town were aroused last night and warned to be in readiness once more for Morgan. A dispatch was received early in the night by Gen. Paine from Gen. Hall, stating that he was menaced by a force of rebels from 7,000 to 10,000 strong and asking for support if he should be attacked.[2] Other messages were received in quick succession, confirm[ing] the first. The brigade of Gen. Steadman was ordered in from Pilot Knob, and was held in readiness to support Gen. Hall, who is encamped about six miles out on the Hartsville road.[3] The rebels did not attack. It is believed, however, that they were in considerable force in that vicinity, and it is thought that Morgan is making a raid on some railroad point between this place and Bowling Green.

There was a lively scene at Gen. Paine's headquarters during the time we were awaiting the expected attack. Brig. Gens. Ward and Reynolds, and a number of inferior officers were there awaiting the issue of events.[4] Our ears were constantly filled with clanking and jingling of sabres against the pavement, as the couriers moved to and from. The generals were seated around a writing desk. But few words were spoken. The disposition to meet the attack had been made. General Paine sat motionless as if wrapped in deep thought. Gen. Ward, with the air of a rough and ready warrior, seemed to be praying for a brush with the traitors. Gen. Reynolds, a smooth-faced, business-like man, received and answered dispatches. Thus during the greater part of the night the "council of war" continued in session, and to an amateur in military matters it appeared that the union cause has able and vigilant defenders here.

Under an order lately issued by the war department, a medical board of examination recently commenced the work of examining sick and convalescent soldiers at this post with a view to discharging all who will not soon be fit for duty. There are about 1,500 convalescents in this place, and up to this time a majority of those examined have been discharged. The order is a humane one, and should have been issued long ago. Many happy homes have been rendered desolate by the heartless policy heretofore pursued by the government in this matter. Men who were evidently useless to the army, and who were gradually approaching the end of a miserable existence, have been compelled to remain in barracks and camps, apparently almost forsaken by God and man.

Through the changes of army life, I am again disconnected from the 102d, having been detailed as clerk at Gen. Paine's headquarters. The regiment is in very good condition at present. There is general harmony between men and officers. Our colonel, F. C. Smith, takes a deep interest in the welfare of his men, and is an excellent commanding officer. The *morale* of the regiment has greatly improved since he was placed in command.

It is painful to leave kind comrades and good officers, though it be only for a short season. I promise the friends at home, however, that they shall hear from the 102d thro' your columns, by your permission, as long as I am enabled to communicate personally with the regiment. Respectfully yours,

S. F. F.

(Rock Island *Argus,* January 9, 1863, p. 2)

1. Col. James D. Bennett of the 9th Tennessee Cavalry.

2. Col. Albert S. Hall of the 105th Ohio Infantry commanded the 1st Brigade of the 5th (late 12th) Division, Army of the Cumberland.

3. Brig. Gen. James B. Steedman commanded the 3d Brigade of the 3d Division (late 1st Division, 3d Corps, Army of the Ohio).

4. Brig. Gen. Joseph J. Reynolds succeeded General Dumont as commander of the 5th Division, Army of the Cumberland.

ᴏ⁓ No. 14 ⁓ᴏ

Gallatin, Tenn., Dec. 31, 1862.

Owing to the uncourteous conduct of John Morgan in cutting off communications with the north, my last letter is probably still on this side of the Ohio river. I write again, however, with the hope that my communication will escape the hands of the guerrilla traitors, and speed quickly on its way to your pleasant sanctum.[1]

It is thought the railroad will soon be in running order again, and then we will all be gladdened by the receipt of letters from home.

You are no doubt surprised at the facility with which the rebels are enabled to "play around us," but the difficulties of the situation in which the union forces are placed are not fully appreciated by those at a distance from the scene of operations. Aside from the source of weakness heretofore mentioned—a lack of cavalry—we labor under all the disadvantages of carrying on the war in the heart of a country that is bitterly, and almost universally hostile. You hear men talk of armies fostering a union sentiment—there is very little of that sentiment here, and the little that there is will never be increased by the conciliatory (?) conduct of an invading army. There are some lawless men among all troops, and the utmost vigilance of our officers will not suffice to shield the innocent at all times from the depredations of unprincipled soldiers. A bitter feeling of hostility is naturally engendered, and we find the citizens ever willing to aid the armed rebels in all their designs against us. We have a long and precarious line of communication with the north to keep open, and it would require an immense army to guard every bridge and protect every mile of railroad at all times from destruction. These raids will continue until a mortal blow is struck at the rebellion, and then the power of the guerrilla chief will be broken.

The rebels have recently been prowling around in close proximity to this place. A few nights since Gen. Paine received information that a heavy force was about to cross the Cumberland at a ford about three miles from town. Every preparation was at once made to give the traitors a warm reception,— troops were held in readiness for action—a portion of the 102d was ordered into the fort, the streets were barricaded with wagons, close up together, so close that they would effectually check a charge of cavalry. Gen. Paine and staff rode out on the pike leading to the ford. A short time after daylight we heard cannonading, and it really appeared that the ball had opened. The sum of the whole matter was, that our pickets were fired upon by a small body of rebels in the vicinity of a dwelling house on the opposite side of the river; the fire was returned; two field pieces were ordered into position; the house was vigorously shelled; the rebels hastily retreated, and thus the fight ended—no one being hurt on either side. A party of our men who visited the house after the shelling ceased, reported that the breakfast table had been prepared for forty men that morning; they were of the opinion, however, that no more rebels would enjoy rebel hospitality in that house, as they saw it disappear in smoke and flames.

Much excitement was created here a few days since, by the cold-blooded murder of an inoffensive citizen. The horrible deed was evidently committed about daylight, as he was seen at six o'clock by a neighbor. He was robbed of a gold watch and a small sum of money. I looked upon the murdered man, as he lay with his clothes disarranged, and his face all bruised and gory,—the body lying in the corner of a blacksmith shop, apparently as if it had been dragged there by the fiend or fiends who committed the deed, in order that they might search the person of the murdered man with less fear of molestation. As I turned, heart-sick from the scene, the tho't was suggested to my mind, that for all the honor and all the wealth of earth, I would not carry with me for one day, the recollection of having committed a deed so horrid—annihilation would be a delightful destiny for a conscience thus ever haunted—how terrible the *thought*, even, of an eternal existence with the remembrance of such a crime ever recurring to the mind! Soldiers who had walked, almost thoughtlessly among the dead and dying of the battle-field, turned away with horror from the ghastly spectacle.—There is no clue to the perpetrator of the deed.

The work of examining and discharging the convalescents at this post is rapidly progressing. The mortality among these poor fellows has been very great. One hundred and ten have died within two weeks. These men—many of them—could have been at home but for the insane policy which has held them nominally in the service.

There has been much disorder in the management of the convalescent barracks; and much suffering has resulted from the uncleanliness of the buildings and of the men themselves. Under the rule of Gen. Paine, a different policy is being inaugurated, and the many abuses that have shocked humanity here will be abolished. There would be ample work in this place for the philanthropic ladies of the north, were they able to endure the privations of the situation. Many of our brother soldiers are perishing, who would live long and happy lives, could they but have, at the critical moment, a mother or a sister's tender care.

The only class of people that seem to be really happy, in the midst of so much misery, is the negro population. They enjoy their usual holiday festivities, and those who have attended their "cotillion parties" state that they are generally well dressed. No doubt the enjoyment of these festive occasions is hightened [*sic*] by the near approach of "emancipation day." A friend tells me that he heard them conversing very jovially in regard to the pleasant prospect that they seem to think awaits them in the near future. One of them said: "We gwine to be Massa Linkum's children new year's mornin'!" Another thought the blue coats would be willing to give them "Christmas three or four times a year," whereas the grey coats (butternuts) only give them one. Intelligence of "Massa" Linkum's emancipation proclamation has doubtless reached every negro household from Mason and Dixon's line to the Gulf of Mexico. They express grave doubts as to the success of the president's policy, but seem to be very generally in favor of setting up for themselves. A short period of time will indicate whether their dream of liberty is to be realized.

I am writing late at night. The last hours of 1862 are passing into eternity. I have written in a somewhat melancholy vein, for the surrounding associations are solemn. Fly quickly by! oh, evil-freighted year! Let another black chapter of national misery pass from our sight! Let us hope, however, that the thick gloom of the present will soon be displaced by a glorious future of peace and prosperity.

It is now midnight! the old year dies! the new year dawns! Adieu. S. F. F. (Rock Island *Argus*, January 31, 1863, p. 2)

1. This letter was published January 31, 1863, more than two weeks after Number 15 had appeared. According to editor Danforth: "The one published to-day has been delayed a long time somewhere, on the road, but we publish it in order to make his series complete." He also noted Fleharty's employment of a new title for the column. It had formerly been called "Jottings from the 102d," but from now on would be, "Jottings from Dixie." Rock Island *Argus*, January 31, 1863, p. 3.

The raid by John Morgan's cavalry that resulted in the disruption of the mail has become famous as the "Christmas Raid." Morgan's command moved into Kentucky on December 22, 1862, with the objective of destroying the Louisville and Nashville Railroad trestles at Elizabethtown and cutting Rosecrans' communications with the North. In their wake the raiders left sixty miles of damaged track, halting traffic between Louisville and Nashville for several weeks.

⌁ No. 15 ⌁

Gallatin, Tenn., Jan. 7.

Philosophers have furnished us with lengthy dissertations on the properties of the elementary mechanical powers. There is another power, however, which might be classified with these, that I am not aware has ever received the attention of philosophical writers. I refer to the *power of the shoulder strap.*—There is this remarkable peculiarity about the power of the shoulder strap—it operates diametrically opposite to all known mechanical principles, and in this respect may be said to supercede [*sic*] or overcome the powers hereto fore [*sic*] known in the laws of mechanism:

It supercedes the power of the lever,—the subject of its influence receiving an upward impetus the moment the straps are placed upon it.

It supercedes the power of the screw and the wheel and axle—its elevating power being far greater.

It supercedes the power of the wedge and the inclined plane,—having derived its properties chiefly from the wedge that divided the union, and overcoming the power of gravitation, because it ever tends to lift the subject of its influence towards the stars—a general's insignia. The shoulder-strap is of no importance, however, when considered apart from its influence on the human species; and the law that governs the operation of its power, like many other laws, has it exceptions. A certain class of individuals are entirely exempt from its influence. They are the solid men of the army—the golden treasures of their mind, common sense, outweighing the power of the magical strap. I have treated thus at length, upon this novel subject because it is a new candidate for philosophical consideration, and also from the fact that I have been for some months in a situation that is every way favorable to the acquirement of a perfect knowledge of the principles that govern the operations of this remarkable mechanical power. It is a pleasant reflection, however, that those with whom I have been most intimately associated, and who were placed in a position where they were liable to experience its effects, have not yielded to the upward pressure.

As a natural result of the principles above enumerated, I have witnessed the following phenomena:

I have seen individuals whom nature had sorely neglected, when completing the final story, pomposly [*sic*] giving orders to those whose natural endowments were far superior, and have seen the superior execute the commands of the inferior with the mute obedience of the dumb ox.

I have seen individuals who appeared utterly destitute of all sympathy for the men they brought into the service—the men being looked upon as so many pawns to be used in securing their personal elevation.

I have seen the bearers of these magic straps admitted to the most elevated social circles, winning, through their influence, the sweetest smiles of fair ladies, and the most choice dinners.

I have observed that many of these affected by its power, conduct themselves as if an impassable gulf separated them from the common soldier—which may be the case hereafter, where all distinctions of title cease—the relative positions of the parties being reversed, as on a former occasion.

A few days since, while passing through the streets of this city, the personal inconvenience of traveling without the straps was well illustrated. While walking briskly along an unfrequented street, a guard with fixed bayonet commanded "halt!" adding that he was ordered to "let no one pass through that street"—the commissioned officers, of course, excepted. I asked him why such an inexplicable order had been given him. He was profoundly ignorant in that respect. At the moment I was turning to retrace my steps, two tidily dressed officers passed the guard, whereas the writer was compelled to walk some distance on the back track and across lots before reaching the centre of town. Now do not infer that I write in a cynical spirit—such circumstances are more amusing than irritating. Only let me say, however, Mr. Editor, that if you ever conclude to become a soldier, by all means supply yourself with the magical straps.

A Negro Wedding.

We learned a few evenings since that a negro wedding was about to take place in the outskirts of town. Our curiosity was naturall[y] excited, and we soon struck up a bargain with a sable son of Africa to procure admittance for three of us into the festive hall.—The bridegroom received us with all the urbanity of an educated gentleman of color.—We were ushered into a dark and dingy room but were told that the ceremony which joined "two willing hearts in one," had already been performed, and that in consequence of a want of room, the customary "hoe-down" would be omitted. Notwithstanding these disappointments, we were well recompensed for our little tramp, as we were politely invited to partake of an excellent supper, comprising roast turkey, roast pig, pie, cakes, & c. Our northern scruples, as to the color of the cook's hands were quickly overcome, and we did ample justice to the viands set before us.

I have seldom seen a northern lady dressed more elegantly than were some of the negro women. One, in particular, seemed loaded with silks and superfluities. All evinced the Etheopian [sic] partiality for showy apparel. The bride appeared to be a mere girl, and we were not a little surprised to learn that she had already served an *irregular* apprenticeship in the *nursery business.* Perhaps this qualification added an important item to the bridegroom's prospective happiness. The night was dark and gloomy, the room dimly lighted, and the guests were mainly of the ebony hue. In the midst of this dusky scene the Caucasian features, represented in the person of a moderately fair northern lady, appeared strikingly fascinating—or, to say the least, would have appeared charming to one of an impressible nature. We noticed that the gentlemen with the magical straps, were very well represented on the occasion.

A Tennessee Heroine—Suffering of the Border State Patriots.

The union cause is not destitute of heroines in the south. One morning, recently, two young ladies (apparently) rode up to General Paine's headquarters, and the elder of the two stated that they came from the vicinity of Scottsville, that her companion was a brother whom she had dressed in woman's clothing and brought into the union lines. She stated that an older brother had been captured, and was then in prison at Scottsville.—They set out for this place at midnight—both mounted on one horse, and the young lady, having placed her younger brother in safe hands, immediately started on her return home, intending if possible, to effect the release of her elder brother from the clutches of the rebels. The distance from this place to Scottsville is about thirty miles, and the entire journey would be considered something more than a pleasure ride by the best lady equestriennes, besides being an undertaking that required no little nerve.

This, however, is but one of many similar occurrences, the adventurers not always succeeding so well in carrying out their plans. I conversed with an old man, recently, whose locks had been whitened by the frosts of seventy winters; who had been virtually an exile in his own country, having passed thro' all the terrors of the rebellion, and witnessed the estrangement of friends and neighbors through the influence of the secession mania. Respect for the old flag was intertwined with all his feelings, and the fire which yet burned in his eye indicated well where his strength would be thrown, were he yet young. In answer to the question whether he had any union neighbors, he replied that he had, but they lacked the nerve to declare their sentiments.

The full history of this war will never be written. All the researches of the best historians will fail to bring to light the numberless incidents of suffering and daring, that have marked the progress of the war in the border states.

The Battle of Murfreesboro.

How goes the great battle? This was the oft-repeated inquiry that fell from anxious lips during the great struggle at Murfreesboro. Day after day we were held in suspense. At times rumors of disaster reached us, again we were told that Rosecrans was crowding them steadily backward, gaining every inch of ground, however, at a fearful sacrafice [sic] of life. Then came the news of the loss of Houghtelling's battery, the death of the brave Col. Roberts, and the loss of Col. Garesche, chief of Rosecrans' staff.[1] These calamities enabled us to judge of the terrible nature of the conflict. "Rosecrans himself, leads the gallant army of the union into the battlefield." The intelligence thrills every breast, and the prayer of every one is, "God save Rosecrans, and the victory is ours."—Day after day goes by; prisoners, paroled on the battlefield by the rebels, begin to arrive, clad in butternut clothes, the rebels having made a forcible exchange. At length, on the morning of the 5th, we received reliable news that the enemy were in full retreat.—Our gallant soldiers had met the enemy on his chosen ground and defeated him. The smoke now begins to clear away from the terrible battlefield. How many noble men have perished? How many homes have been made desolate by those five days of sanguinary carnage! The field of Murfreesboro will rank in the world's history with those of Leipsic [sic], Eylau and Waterloo.[2]

At this distance from the battle field I am unable to obtain a connected account of the struggle. We have learned enough, however, to convince us that our troops fought with the most determined obstinacy. Three companies of the 21st Illinois regiment lost all their commissioned officers, and all their sergeants, and yet their thinned ranks were bravely led forward by the remaining corporals!

The news of defeat is a sad disappointment to the secesh in this vicinity. They have thought the position of the rebels impregnable. I have heard the opinion expressed by one of our leading military men that the rebel army of the west is a wreck. "Old Rosy," as the boys call our great commander, had given the rebellion a blow that will probably free Tennessee and Kentucky of armed rebels. The Tennessee rebel troops fought with great determination. They wished to fight the decisive battle in their own state—they staked all and have lost.[3] These troops will be of little use to the Confederacy hereafter.

You have doubtless received details of the five days' struggle, and as accurate estimates of the loss on each side as I can give, from the meagre accounts received here, therefore, I will close this lengthy letter, promising to give your readers hereafter whatever items of interest I may glean, from the accounts of those who participated in the battle.

As ever yours,

S. F. F.

P. S.—I have just returned from the solomn [*sic*] ceremonies attending the burial of another member of our company, Geo. Hoffman. Also learned of the decease of T. B. South, another comrade. I have inadvertently failed heretofore to record the death of Charles Anderson, which occurred some weeks since. His mother, a widow lady, lives near Berlin, Mercer county. Thus the hand of the destroyer is busy at work in our midst.[4]

"Rest, soldiers, rest; your warfare's o'er."

S. F. F.

(Rock Island *Argus,* January 16, 1863, p. 2)

1. The Battle of Stones River was fought from December 31, 1862, to January 2, 1863. On the first day of the battle, the brigade commanded by Col. George W. Roberts (42d Illinois Infantry) was shattered by the Confederate attack, and Roberts was killed. Battery C of the 1st Illinois Artillery, commanded by Capt. Charles Houghtaling and attached to Roberts's brigade, lost all of its six guns to the enemy, and Capt. Houghtaling was wounded. The same day, Col. Julius P. Garesche, chief of staff to General Rosecrans, was decapitated by a shell as he rode by his commander's side.

2. The Napoleonic battles to which Fleharty refers were: Leipzig (October 16–19, 1813), Eylau (February 7–8, 1807), and Waterloo (June 18, 1815). Eylau was an indecisive encounter between Napoleon's forces and the allied armies of the Russians and Prussians. Leipzig and Waterloo were decisive defeats for the French emperor.

3. Tennessee produced some of the South's best and hardest-hitting units. For a history of one, see Christopher Losson, *Tennessee's Forgotten Warriors: Frank Cheatham and His Confederate Division* (Knoxville, 1989).

4. Pvt. Thomas B. South died January 4, 1863, and Pvt. George Huffman died January 6, both at Gallatin. Pvt. Charles Anderson died December 15, 1862, but his place of death is not given. All were members of Company C. *Adj. Gen. Rep.,* V, 598–99.

ᲙᲐ No. 16 ᲙᲐ

Two Pictures—Look on That and Then on This.

Gallatin, Tennessee, January 23, 1863.

Scene 1st.—A home circle. Evening—A bright fire burning in the grate—Husband enters the elegantly furnished room, and seats himself in his comfortable arm chair, having closed a profitable day's business, when the following conversation ensues:

Husband.—Well, my dear, what do you find in the evening paper—you appear to be intensely interested?

Wife.—Nothing. Really nothing worth repeating. The papers are remarkably dull now-a-days. There are no accounts of battles in the east or in the west. I wonder what our armies can be doing that they do not move forward. This state of inactivity is becoming very uninteresting.

Husband.—It is indeed; and I have just been thinking how insipid the papers will be when the war is over. How will we be able to endure such monotony? There are thrilling pages of history being originated now, and one is loth to read the closing chapter. There are daring deeds performed and bloody scenes enacted, that will render this an heroic age. Is it not a high privilege to live in such an era?

Wife.—Yes; and how much material there will be for "thrilling novels," and then there will be endless tales of the great ["]rebellion," which will in some measure relieve the monotony of newspaper reading.

Scene 2d.—A hospital in Tennessee. A pale sufferer, wasting with fever, lies helpless on his cot—his eye falls on the ubiquitous daily paper:

Sufferer.—What is there in the paper to-day? (he asks a comrade.) Read to me. Are there no indications of peace? Are the rebels not willing yet to lay down their arms? It matters but little to me, however, only I wish to see my country at peace with itself, and the thousands of languishing, feeble and broken down soldiers released from military bondage before I die. It is noble to give one's life for the good of a noble government. If I perish not in vain, it is well to become a sacrifice for such a government as ours. But I would have the war end—honorably end. I have a father, a mother, and sisters, hundreds of miles away. Among them I was idolized, but who besides our kind physician and yourself cares for me here? Pardon me, good comrade; I am talking wildly to-night—my brain is frenzied with fever. Will you read to me?

His comrade reads; but the sick soldier, after endeavoring for a moment to fix his attention upon the subject, becomes insensible to external impressions. His mind wanders, and in broken utterances the words "sister," "mother," "home," fall from his lips.

Another day dawns—the face of the fever-stricken soldier is fixed and lifeless, and ere the newsboy comes around again, with his bundle of papers, a soldier's funeral is witnessed. Slowly, solemnly, with measured tread the procession moves; plaintively the music plays; solemnly the sound of the muffled drum falls upon the ear. Another patriot is gone. And thus it is day after day. Noble young men, and honored men of age, are falling on every hand—in hospitals, in barracks and on the battle field. These are the rough scenes of war, that are not realized by those that are charmed by its romance.

In looking upon such scenes we are impressed with the weighty responsibility that rests upon all who hinder the speedy suppression of the rebellion, which is carrying desolation to so many hearthstones.*

The Emancipation Proclamation—Gen. Paine's Policy with Rebels, Etc.

Probably no subject that I could suggest would interest you more than a statement of the manner in which the emancipation proclamation is received here. It is admitted that many of the Kentucky union troops have deserted and gone home, and the conviction is gaining ground that hereafter Tennessee and Kentucky troops will play a very insignificant part in suppressing the rebellion. As these states are exempt from the operation of the proclamation, it would seem that we are reaping its evil effects without receiving whatever benefits may result from it in other states.[1]

There has been considerable sensation among the colored population since their minds have become impressed with the idea that they will be free. If they could be positively assured that they would remain unmolested in their liberty a great many would come within the union lines. As it is, numbers are coming in and applying for protection. The post quartermaster here supplies them with rations and work, at $10 per month.—Whether the proclamation is yielding good fruits in the cotton states, I am unable to say.

The grand question presented to our minds at this crisis is, whether the embittered feelings engendered is [*sic*] recompensed by a weakening of rebel strength, in depriving them of their negroes. As Uncle Abe has said, the whole subject is "piled high with difficulties," and it may be well for us to suspend judgement upon a question that cannot be decided by any opinion of ours.[2] Time must work out the solution of the great problem that convulses our people—*What shall be the status of the negro in the future organization of our government?* If the slavery question was a vexed question years ago, it seems to be inexplicable now.

Notwithstanding the general opposition to the government there seems to be but little disposition among those who have heretofore been non-combattants [*sic*], to take up arms against us. They are heartily sick of the war.

The policy of Gen. Paine in all his intercourse with the rebels is very commendable. Their property is taken whenever it is needed for our men. Our commanders are authorized to forage from union men also; but the secesh must suffer first. In all cases receipts are given, which will entitle union men to a final adjustment of their demands. Traitors will get nothing.

Although the general deals sternly with rebels he is not void of humane feelings, as is too often the case with those who occupy positions that give them authority over their fellow men. On the contrary, he hears the complaints of his men patiently, and in every case where he can consistently aid the needy, his assistance is freely given. Recently a northern lady applied to him for transportation for the body of her husband, to Louisville. This, of course, could not be given at the expense of the government. The general said— "Madam, I don't know what in the world to do," and then, after a moment's pause, he turned to a clerk and said, "Give this lady an order on the post quartermaster for transportation, *and tell him to charge it to me.*"

Citizens are brought before him daily, arrested under various charges, and the cross-questioning process which they undergo generally elicits their true character. A captain under his command brought in a prisoner who had avowed that he would not take the oath of allegiance. The captain wished to know whether the general approved of the arrest. "I do," he replied, "we must make these rebels feel that the government is not dead yet," and the rebel went to the guardhouse. A secesh lady living near town refused to sell some potatoes for the use of the hospital. The general sent a squad of men to take the amount of potatoes wanted, and give the customary receipt for them. Since then, other property has been taken, and on the face of the voucher given by the quartermaster, the significant word "disloyal" was written, which settles that account.

More Contrabands.

Yesterday morning, bright and early, a squad of negroes, eleven in number, rode up to headquarters in charge of two soldiers, who brought them in from the picket line. They took the horses from the stables of their masters. Darkies and horses are all now in the employ of the government. In "good times" here, I suppose that the property that came in on this occasion would represent the snug little sum of $12,000.

Regimental News.

The "102" is in *statu quo,* so far as position is concerned. Regimental changes have occurred, however, and in place of Act'g Major Harding, and Adjt. Pitman, resigned, we have Capt. Wilsie, of Galesburg, as acting major, and Sergeant Major J. M. Snyder is acting adjutant. The office could not be filled by a better man.[3]

An amusing episode that occurred in conjunction with one of our periodical Morgan alarms has been the theme of conversation in camp for several days past. The story, which is perfectly reliable, runs thus:

The impression generally prevailed that Morgan was near by in force, and would attack us at daylight, without fail. Two prominent officers, or ex-officers, of a certain regiment stationed here, naturally became very solicitous for the safety of their war horses, which animals, it appears, possessed qualifications that would be of eminent service on a retreat. Keenly alive to the importance of saving their noble chargers from the clutches of Morgan, and with a surprising degree of indifference to personal danger, they made the following dispositions to meet the exigencies of the case. An immediate advance on Bowling Green was decided upon. They determined to go unattended, even leaving a faithful hired boy who had attended one of them through his five months' campaign, and would doubtless have been a faithful body-guard during the expedition about to be undertaken. And here let me say that the "military necessity" which compelled them to leave this faithful attendant in a penniless condition, must have been very imperative. Indeed, this apparent inhumanity is regarded by military men as the only objectionable point in their strategy.

In order to cover up their real designs more effectually, a candle was left burning in their tents, and then—

"To horse! to horse!" the valiant Major cries;
"To horse! to horse!" the Adjutant replies.

"There was mounting in hot haste,"[4] and through the thick gloom of terror inspiring night, the heroes urged their coursers on.—Perchance the baying of startled canines, and the unearthly hooting of the night owl added to the terrors of the adventure. But the extraordinary enterprise was successfully accomplished. The valuable horses were placed beyond the reach of danger, Bowling Green was re-inforced, Gallatin was not taken, and while we mourn an adjutant and major lost, we are consoled by the reflection that—

Since they have "went and rund away,"
Ther'll be more "grub" for those who stay.

In the style of a somewhat famous modern writer, we say; "Unekalled patriats, adoo."[5]

And now to you, Mr. Editor, lest many words tire your patrons, I tender a temporary and respectful good-by.

S. F. F.

---

*And our correspondent might have added: upon all who, by their agitation of sectional questions, which did not concern them, added to bringing on the war. There is where the responsibility for all the loss of life and treasure, and the destruction of the best government on earth, must rest at last. [ED. ARGUS.] (Rock Island *Argus*, February 3, 1863, p. 2)

1. The proclamation was effective only in those states or parts of states then in rebellion against the United States. The slave states of Missouri, Delaware, Kentucky, Maryland, and West Virginia were unaffected, as was Confederate territory then occupied by Union forces. The latter included parts of Louisiana and Virginia and the entire state of Tennessee.

2. The quotation is from Lincoln's second annual message to Congress (December 1, 1862), a speech containing some of the president's most memorable prose. He said, in part: "The dogmas of the quiet past, are inadequate to the stormy present. The occasion is piled high with difficulty, and we must rise with the occasion. As our case is new, so we must think anew, and act anew. We must disenthrall our selves, and then we shall save our country." See Basler, *Collected Works of Lincoln*, V, 537.

3. Capt. Roderick R. Harding of Company A and Adj. John W. Pittman resigned January 7, 1863. The resignation of Adjutant Pittman led to the promotion of Sgt. Maj. Jacob H. Snyder to fill the vacancy. Fleharty, in turn, replaced Snyder as sergeant major. Capt. Horace H. Willsie (Company D) of Galesburg, who succeeded Harding as acting major, resigned as well, on April 9, because of ill health.

4. This line is from Byron's "Childe Harold's Pilgrimage," Canto 3, Stanza 25.

5. The two officers Fleharty so whimsically refers to were, of course, Captain Harding and Adjutant Pittman.

CHAPTER 4

"The Dead Sea of Inactivity"

∘— No. 17 —∘

Gallatin, Tenn., March 3, 1863.

Almost as a stranger I resume my pen to claim my accustomed place in your columns. Rapidly the weeks have flown by since my last talk with your readers, and often during the interval a remembrance of promises made long ago, has recalled my attention to the obligations assumed. And yet there is but little transpiring in our immediate vicinity, worth recording. We seem to be placed in the dead sea of inactivity, while we hear from every other source the rush and roar of contending waves. From this comparatively placid region, we listen to the increasing storm, and sometimes in imagination hear the creaking of the timbers that still hold together the old ship of state. How fearfully she labors now! Beset on every hand by deadly foes! The fact that she still survives the storm—that the old banner still waves amid the gloom of political night— indicates how well those timbers were framed—how nobly the artists who constructed the vessel accomplished their work.

What will the end be? Every mail brings intelligence of a gathering storm in the north. As a nation have we not already sinned beyond the hope of pardon? Why would our people, therefore, endeavor to consummate this last fiendish act in the great tragedy of national suicide? Can any plea be offered in justification of such madness? Let us suppose ourselves on board a vessel which has sprung a leak—all hands are called to work at the pumps; a portion of the crew believe that there is a misapplication of power in working them, and refuse to assist. Not satisfied, however, with a condition of neutrality, they insanely endeavor to "shiver the timbers" of the vessel in some other vulnerable quarter. Thus all are in imminent danger of being wrecked, whereas, should wiser counsels prevail, the ship would ride into a haven of safety.

These manifestations of armed opposition in the north are infusing new life into the rebellion. The secesh in this vicinity are decidedly hopeful, and predict brilliant results from the co-operation of traitors in the northwest.

On the contrary our friends write gloomily from home. One writes of "secret meetings" of hostile parties, securing arms, and so bitter, so deadly the feud appears to have become, that it seems as if the "next gale that sweeps from the north may bring to our ears the clash of resounding arms."

Another who has almost grown up with the government, declares that "if the old ship that has borne us so proudly and so long, must at length be wrecked, it shall go down in a sea of blood." With such intimations of impending danger, constantly coming to our ears, we cannot but be apprehensive of the result.

At this perilous moment American statesmen and people should be calm, and yet firm as adamant in their endeavors to preserve the legacy of liberty inherited from our forefathers. Suppose the means adopted do not meet with our approval, is there not strength sufficient in the north, if united, to *crush treason?* and admitting that we have the power to accomplish this great purpose, who will deny that the American people have the will and the ability to *kill fanaticism at the ballot box?*

This division of sentiment should be counted upon as one of the incidental accompaniments of the war, experienced by the rebels as well as by patriots, and cannot patriots sacrifice personal and party preferences with as much unanimity as traitors do?

The only atidote [*sic*] for armed rebellion is *coercion:* the true corrective for abuses of constitutional power is the *ballot box.*

Two long years of darkness have passed since we witnessed the setting of the sun of peace, and as we look back through the shadows of night, and view the glories of those halcyon days, their splendor becomes ever more apparent to our vision, and yet if we are faithful, united and determined, we may see those days of glory rivalled in the dawning of a permanent peace—when the American eagle shall place at the feet of the Goddess of Liberty the lifeless form of the trio serpents which threaten our country's destruction, viz: the rattlesnake, the blacksnake and the copperhead.

It is not in our line to grind out political speeches, but we wish once for all to protest against the suicidal policy of clambering for peace on the best attainable terms that may be made with the traitors at this time.

The 102d.

We are enabled to furnish the friends of the 102d with regimental statistics, showing the total loss of the regiment on account of deaths, discharges and desertions. The record is as follows:

Deceased,	41
Discharged,	74
Deserted,	10
Total,	125

In addition to these, 12 commissioned officers have resigned, which makes a grand total loss of 137 men. The regiment originally numbered 912. These figures indicate a heavy ratio of loss during six months service, in which we have not experienced any casualties on the battle-field. To our Richland Grove friends we will state that Co. C has lost 6 men—2 have been discharged, 3 died, and 1 deserted.

The prospect at this time of a brush with the enemy seems more distant than ever, and the nearest approach to a battle that I am able to record is a recent skirmish between our worthy major and a noisy animal of the genus bovine. Regularly as roll call would be heard the boo-oo-oo of the major's enemy was near his tent. The major is remarkably good natured, but coming to the conclusion one day that forbearance had ceased to be a virtue, he loaded a shot gun and opened the attack on his bellicose foe. Round after round was fired,—the natural defenses of the foe proved impregnable, and the major was reluctantly compelled to quit the field, leaving the enemy in undisputed possession; and to this day his periodical visitations have been continued.— The ground upon which the battle was fought may hereafter be designated "Major Wilsie's defeat." We have every reason to believe, however, that the major will come out *first best* in the first encounter with the common enemy.

We have already been luxuriating amid the beauties of opening spring. The green fields, bursting buds, and singing birds remind us of the first days of May at home.—The boys have had fine sport playing ball and other games. Away with your interminable Illinois winters! Why will you endure them?

The friends of the 102 will be pleased to learn that our popular young friend J. Hamlin Snyder has received the appointment of adjutant. Truly yours, S. F. F.

NOTE:—Our correspondent deals some pretty hard blows on the abolition midnight meetings—"secret meetings of hostile parties securing arms." We know of no "traitors in the north" unless they are found in these secret oath-bound abolition societies.—The rebels may well be "hopeful and predict brilliant results" from the tendency of such organizations to provoke hostilities among ourselves. But there *is* "strength sufficient in the north" to crush these dangerous organizations and "kill fanaticism at the ballot box"—to destroy the "trio of serpents." We know of no men who "clamor for peace on the best attainable terms," except abolitionists, and no newspapers which advocate it except Greeley's *Tribune* and its echoes. The democrats will never be for peace on any terms except a restoration of the whole union.—EDITOR ARGUS. (Rock Island *Argus*, March 10, 1863, p. 2)

⌒ No. 18 ⌒

Gallatin, Tenn., March 16, 1863.

Six months experience, as soldiers, has effected no inconsiderable change in the habits and manners of the men who left their quiet homes in Mercer, Knox and adjoining counties, and united their destinies with the 102. Men who were only accustomed to the arts of peace, and who never dreamed, in early days, of adopting a military life, have learned to perform their daily duties as soldiers with a degree of promptness that has become "second nature." As I write the energetic notes of command reach my ear: "Right, face!" "Right shoulder, shift—arms!" &c., all of which Farmer Frugal and Carpenter Chisel obey with heads erect and soldierly bearing. My mind reverts here, however, to one individual, who seems almost proof against the effects of military regulations. Although a faithful soldier, he retains much of the individuality of the farmer. Always having esteemed it an inalienable right to "express his opinion" in the most independent style, he finds the restraints of military discipline very inconvenient, and at times asserts his independence and his contempt for 'strap officers,' in a manner that would be dangerous to his remaining personal freedom, where his eccentricities are not well understood. No, "Uncle George," they will never make a military man of you, notwithstanding your soldierly qualities. The rugged original will predominate over the slight military education, and we can only see Farmer E. after all, shambling in his gait, and handling his gun as if he wished it were a pitchfork.[1]

We have all become thoroughly disciplined in the use of rude tinware and rough cooking utensils, in all our culinary operations. It may not be uninteresting to give here a description of our table ware—the mess being composed of a physician, a gentleman bearing the rank of first lieutenant, and the undersigned. There are tin plates, ordinary knives and forks, tin spoons, and what may be called medicine bowls, from which we sip our coffee. They originally contained some kind of medicine, but owing to the skill of Bob, the colored cook, they now present an appearance of whiteness and purity that would do honor to any lady commander of the kitchen department. For a sugar bowl we have a huge tin can, which in size is very much out of proportion to the amout [sic] of sugar it usually contains—on the outside it is labelled "Epsom Salts—10 lbs." Our pepper bottle is labelled "Sulphate de Quinine," and on the outside of our salt cellar we read "Cantharides Cerate." Thus from diverse sources our table has been supplied with a very respectable array of dishes and miscellaneous commodities.

As appendages of the mess, I may also mention Bob, aforesaid, and Peter, a playful little Tennessee canine. Bob is, in some respects, entitled to distinction in colored society. In the days of chivalry, when Gallatin was the centre of fashion for this section, and was celebrated for its fast horses and fine exhibitions, Bob was employed at training likely stock for the turf. He states that when he became too large and consequently too heavy to train the horses, his master put him through a process of "sweating," in order to bring him down to the required standard of weight. Bob represents this operation as having been anything but agreeable. It appears that he learned many of the bad habits of the fast gentlemen at that time, and we were not a little astonished the other morning, when he exhibited a roll of bills—greenbacks, &c.—which he won at card playing.— When asked if he did think that "his Satanic Majesty" would have a dark account to settle with him hereafter, he thought "there would be lots of folks in the same fix, for dat game dun been carried on 'bout here mighty free—dat I knows mysef," and during the delivery of the speech, Bob's enormous lips would oscillate with a motion not unlike that of a Mississippi sawyer, in a strong current. With a provoking stoppage in his delivery, he at times presents a most ludicrous spectacle in endeavors to make himself understood.

The distinguishing characteristic of our family pet—the little canine—is the representation of a pair of shoulder straps, which the doctor has sheared upon him, and then stained with an indellible [*sic*] red color. He ranks as captain, but does not seem at all proud of his newly acquired honors—this may be attributed to his secession origin.

But enough about lieutenants, doctors, negroes and dogs.

A Ride to the Cumberland.

In company with a friend I had a glorious ride to the Cumberland yesterday. The day was very pleasant, everything indicating the presence of spring. The farms have a quiet and peaceful appearance that can hardly be reconciled with the strife that is raging between man and man. Some of the residences are surrounded with a dense growth of evergreens, the general appearance of grounds and dwellings indicating the presence of wealth and taste. A brisk ride of about three miles brought us to the bank of the river—the historic Cumberland—ever to be famous in connection with the existing war. We spent a pleasant hour wandering along its banks. A huge rock juts out into the stream at one point, and affords an excellent view both up and down the river. The rock is shaded by a group of cedars, whose immense roots derive sustenance from its crevasses, and present very distorted shapes in conforming themselves to surrounding circumstances.—The river is quite full, and the current setting in shoreward at this point, flows violently against the jutting rock, and the reaction produces a natural series of eddies. From this and other attractive features of the place, we named the place "Eddy-stone View." The scene from this point is exquisitely beautiful. Far down the river a group of trees on a diminutive island, dot the mirror-like stream. In the opposite direction, miles above, the rocky bank, at one spot, presents the appearance of some ancient ruin—the broken and disfigured columns only remaining. In commemoration of our visit to "Eddy-stone View" we plucked a number of twigs from the rude old cedars, taking them from boughs that overhung the eddying flood which rolls at the base of the rock. One of these I dedicate to the editor of the *Argus,* one to friends at home, and the other to—well, no matter whom. Our ride to the river was highly exhilerating [*sic*], and we heartily wished a score of our friends at home were with us to enjoy it.

Traitors in Blue.

Not those guerrillas who prowl about the country in federal uniform—such characters are already placed without the pale of civilized warfare, and according to a late order of Gen. Rosecrans, are to be shot whenever captured. According to recent developments we have, if possible, a more dangerous element in our midst. The circumstances are these: A rebel captain by the name of Kirkpatrick effected his escape from confinement in the court house a short time since, and suspicion was at once aroused that some one or more of our own soldiers were implicated. The escape was made at night, yet so well was the building guarded, it would seem that no one could escape without the connivance of the guard. I am sorry to state that two men of the 102 have been arrested on suspicion of having aided the absconding rebel. For the present I withhold names, and earnestly hope the accused may establish their innocence.

Regimental News.

By a recent order from the commander of the post, the 102 has been relieved from provost duty, and, with the exception of company C, which still remains at the railroad bridge, is again united. The command of Fort Thomas has been assigned to Col. Sweet of Wisconsin, and the 102 has been placed at his disposal for its defense.[2]

Death has again entered our ranks, and company C has lost one of its best non-commissioned officers, Sergeant J. [sic] N. Roberts.[3] Sergeant Roberts was a faithful soldier, ever ready to perform his duty, and capable of filling a much higher position in the service. He could not have had an enemy in the company, and will always be remembered by his comrades as a generous and true friend. His friends and relatives at home will rest assured that in this sad bereavement they have the heartfelt sympathy of the company.

Sergeant Roberts resided, before his enlistment, in the northwestern part of Mercer county. His disease was typhoid fever.

The general health of the regiment is better than it has been at any period since our arrival at Gallatin.

Respectfully yours,

S. F. F.

(Rock Island *Argus*, March 21, 1863, p. 2)

1. Fleharty is probably referring to Pvt. George Eckley of Company C. Eckley was a farmer from Richland Grove Township, Mercer County. He was mustered in with the 102d on

September 2, 1862, and mustered out on June 6, 1865. See "Descriptive List of Co. C," Record Group 301, Illinois State Archives.

2. Fort Thomas was located on the southwest side of Gallatin, across from the Louisville and Nashville Railroad depot. Some of the companies of the 102d had gone into winter quarters at Fort Thomas the previous December 12 (see Letter 13). Col. Benjamin J. Sweet (1832–74) commanded the 21st Wisconsin Infantry.

3. Cpl. Isaiah N. Roberts (Co. C), of Berlin, Mercer County, died March 4, 1863, in Gallatin.

◦— No. 19 —◦

Gallatin, Tenn., May 3, 1863.

Lovely May is here! The dense foliage that robes the trees, the advanced state of vegetation, and the warm summer-like days remind us that the "heated term" is close at hand. But methinks I hear you say, What have you been doing up to the first of May, that you have not dropped us an occasional line? Really, now, editor and friends, I shall make no apology [f]or my remissness. We soldiers in blue are becoming the most independent fellows in the world! Dictate to us, would you?—No, sir; Uncle Sam's boys have been paid up to the first of March, get excellent "grub," feel contented—what more could they wish? Shall we pass our precious time preparing palatable food for the pampered appetites of epicurean readers? Well, yes, we will—*if we feel like it!* Now, if I have succeeded in making both editor and readers quite angry with me, I will proceed with No. 19.

Since writing my last a few incidents have occurred in this vicinity that may be worth recording. First, then,

The Fight at "Negro Head Cut."

That is the outlandish name of a place about 30 miles from Gallatin, on the Louisville road. On the morning of April 27th, an order was received for 200 of the regiment to prepare two day's rations and form immediately in line for a march. The line was quickly formed, under the immediate command of our colonel, F. C. Smith, Col. Sweet, the commander of Fort Thomas, having the general direction of affairs. In quick time we marched—to the depot. Having arrived at the depot, it was found that the train would not accommodate all, and fifty men were sent back to camp.

The day was lovely. The trees all coming out in heavy robes of green—many varieties being in full bloom and scenting the air with sweet fragrance. One could not think of war amid such loveliness. We had proceeded about 25 miles in the direction of Louisville, had passed the pretty little village of Franklin [where 50 more of our men were left, under Lieut. Conger,] and the train was thundering along through a wild uncivilized region, when as we approached a dense wood it suddenly stopped, and bang! bang! bang! went firearms in the woods near by. Quick as thought a roar of musketry from the cars answered the rebels, who immediately skedaddled in fine style. We formed in line outside the cars, a party of skirmishers were sent out, and Col. Smith, with Capt. Wilson, of Co. K, and 50 men went out to support them. The remainder awaited the issue of events in line of battle at the train. Our men returned, however, without having found the rascals.

In making their arrangement to capture the train, the guerrillas displaced a rail, and secreted themselves a few miles distant from the track, awaiting their booty. The engineer discovered the break in time to stop the train. There was an immense sum of money on board, in charge of one of the U. S. paymasters. In addition to this, large sums were being sent home by the soldiers. The rebels had evidently learned by some means that the money was on the train. They were a sadly disappointed set of fellows. Gen. Paine had been apprised of their intentions, and sent the detachment from the 102d, to aid the usual train guard, in anticipation of an attack. It appears that there were about 35 rebels. They had dismounted and hitched their horses at some distance in the woods. They were commanded by a Capt. Gordon, and were well armed with short English muskets and revolvers. We were informed that they were Texas Rangers. The result of the affair is accurately given in the following complimentary order issued by Col. Sweet, which I have abridged:

Headquarters 102d Illinois
Volunteers,}
April 28, 1863.}
General Order No. 5.}

The colonel commanding on the railroad train yesterday, compliments Col. Smith, 102d Ill. Vol., and the men of his command, for their promptitude, bravery and soldierly bearing in repelling the attack made upon the train by the rebels under Capt. Gordon at "Negro Head Cut," between Franklin and Woodburn, on the Louisville and Nashville railroad.

The promptness and effectiveness with which the fire of the enemy from behind trees, and at a distance of not more than five rods was returned from the car windows, shows that behind our guns were brave hearts and steady nerves, while the quickness with which the commands fell out of the cars, formed line of battle and gave pursuit to the flying enemy, who escaped on horses, evinces that officers and men are alike brave and trustworthy in battle. *****

Three killed, and three wounded of the enemy, taken prisoners, and six horses captured, is the result of the enemy in his attempt to throw the train from the track and rob its passengers. Four of our own brave boys were wounded, two mortally (since dead). For the dead we sorrow; to the wounded we give our warmest sympathy and admiration. *****

B. J. SWEET,

Colonel commanding Fort Thomas,

A. H. Trego, Lieut. and Act'g Adjt.[1]

A little drummer boy of another regiment, who was going home on a furlough, was severely wounded in the leg. A considerable sum of money was immediately raised among the soldiers and passengers, and presented to the poor little fellow.

The railroad having been repaired, we got under way again, and continued on towards Louisville, until we met the express train from that city, a few miles this side of Bowling Green. We were transferred to this train and returned to Gallatin that evening. As we left the train that had been saved from capture, the passengers gave cheer after cheer for Illinois.

On repassing the scene of the raid, we noticed one of the rebels, with his heels turned towards us, still lying on the ground. He had paid a terrible penalty for his crime. The secesh of that vicinity probably buried him that night, and wept bitter tears over his richly merited fate. Oh! ye boasted southern chivalry! are ye not rather a band of highway robbers and murderers, than honorable warriors?

One of the wounded rebels remarked that he thought it "too bad that we should serve them in that way, for they were *forced* to make the attack!" The poor wretch received very little sympathy from the union boys.

These are the men who are constantly receiving the aid and encouragement of citizens at home. As a perfect cure for southern brigands, our prayer is that every sympathizer may be subject to the tender mercies of these guerrillas.

Enough, however, on this subject. The raid was only a small affair, but it may serve to show you the state of things in this vicinity.

The regimental news is unimportant. Under the judicious act passed towards the close of the last session of congress, a few of the boys are going home on a short furlough.—This is as it should be. Men will endure the privations of soldiering with much more fortitude and will be far more effective, when permitted, occasionally, though at long intervals, to visit their homes and those they love best of all on earth.

The business of war will yet become a systematic arrangement with us. Our beloved commander-in-chief, appears to exercise both a general and particular supervision of matters in his department. Even the manner of preparing grub receives attention at departmental headquarters, as we have before us a department order regulating the manner of cooking certain articles in the soldier's bill of fare. Under such a general who would not willingly fight? I have yet to hear the first word of dissatisfaction expressed in the army with reference to the character and achievements of Gen. Rosecrans. In our humble opinion he is the rising star of the republic. "Little Mack" has great abilities, and we hope the future historian will award him that degree of merit which contemporaneous writers deny him. Misfortune and jealousy effected his overthrow. "Old Rosy," on the contrary, seems to be little embarrassed by either, and we all predict for him a glorious career.

S. F. F.

We are very glad to hear from our genial friend "S. F. F." again—he has been silent for a long time. We hope his letters, in future will be more frequent. But we would suggest that he, and all other soldiers make a great mistake in adopting the spirit of abolition slang about northern sympathisers [sic] with treason. We know of no man in the north who sympathizes with brigands, and thieves, and robbers, and traitors. There may be such people, but we do not know who they are—and we think that abolitionists should, instead of applying opprobrious names to all men who do not agree with them in every thing, be compelled to designate, by name, the men they mean when they talk about "copperheads," "sympathizers," &c, &c.

(Rock Island *Argus*, May 9, 1863, p. 2)

1. See Col. Sweet's report in *OR,* Vol. XXIII, pp. 323–24, for an account of the action.

Letter of Withdrawal

Our Regular Correspondent.—We publish a letter to-day from S. F. F., who will continue to be a regular correspondent of The Union from Tennessee. His letters are graphic and readable, and our readers will be highly entertained and instructed in their perusal. The following note sent to the *Argus* having failed to appear in their paper we publish it in these columns to inform the reader the cause of the change of direction of our correspondent[']s future communications. We are pleased to know that we shall have the privilege hereafter of laying before the reader the "Jottings from Dixie." Here is the note to which reference is made above:

Stewart's Creek, Tenn.,
June 9th, 1863.

Col. J. B. Danforth—*Dear Sir:* Hereafter the "Jottings from Dixie" will appear in the columns of The Rock Island Union.

In justice to yourself and the readers of the Argus, I deem it my duty to state frankly my reasons for choosing another medium of communication with friends at home.

It is the habitual practice of many Northern papers to criticise the war measures of the Administration with much apparent vindictiveness—awakening distrust in the minds of the people, and thus embarrassing the Government in all its efforts to suppress the rebellion.

In my opinion, the influence of the Argus has long been and still is of this character.

It is the evident duty of loyal men to discountenance all efforts tending to thwart the Government in the prosecution of the war for the restoration of the Union.

It is equally evident that bullets and bayonets must decide whether the Union or the Constitution is a failure, and until the storm of bullets is over individuals should sacrifice personal opinions and prejudices for the good of our common country. To do otherwise is to connive at treason.

Certainly I will not question the sincerity of those convictions of duty by which you are governed, nor would I have you for a moment imagine that I assume to dictate your newspaper policy. If my conclusions are erroneous or unjust, I have only to say that they are my honest convictions—reluctantly given.

The want of some other satisfactory medium of communication with those who have urged me to continue my correspondence, has induced me to postpone the meditated change until the present time.

In conclusion permit me, Colonel, to acknowledge the uniform kindness and courtesy shown me in the columns of the Argus, and in other ways.

Respectfully yours,

S. F. F.

(Rock Island *Weekly Union,* June 24, 1863, p. 1)

CHAPTER 5

"The Most Glorious Times Imaginable"

⌒ No. 20 ⌒

Stewart's Creek, Tenn.,
June 9th, 1863.[1]

The reader naturally inquires, where is Stewart's Creek? This is the name of a small stream that runs between Lavergne and Murfreesboro, about five miles south of the former place.

How and when our regiment reached this place, I will state, giving other news after a general sketch of a recent visit home. On the 17th of May, thanking Providence and General Paine, I started on the Louisville and Nashville Railroad for the Prairie State, having received a furlough of twenty days. I will not attempt to give the details of the journey, lest I infringe upon your space and my own limited time. Some general impressions are received during a trip of this kind that it may be profitable to reproduce.

On the cars from Gallatin to Nashville, the passengers were principally soldiers. There were a few citizens and very few ladies. The soldiers were going home—some discharged, others on furlough. The effects of campaign life are thoroughly represented on such a train. Those who appear to be well have the rugged and bronzed appearance always acquired by Northerners during a sojourn in the South. Here is one who has been through the trying scenes of real war, and the stump of a leg, supported on a cushion, explains the remarkably pale and tender appearance of his countenance. Others are mere walking skeletons, and have become thus emaciated through want of attention as much as from disease.

I will relate an incident connected with the return of these invalid soldiers, for the truth of which a gentleman of veracity stands ready to vouch. The omnibus had reached the wharf near the Ferry landing at Louisville; the passengers had taken their baggage and were going on board the boat to cross over to Jeffersonville, when my friend who tells the story, whom I will call Mr. B., heard some one ask for assistance in getting his baggage on board. Turning he observed a mere skeleton of a man feebly moving towards the boat with his knapsack. Taking the knapsack he assisted the invalid on board the boat. On arriving at Jeffersonville, the sick soldier was unable even to walk up the steep bank alone. The great mass of passengers immediately left, without devoting a moment's thought to such cases of distress. Instructing the soldier to remain quietly at the landing, Mr. B. went up into the city, and procuring a hack after much delay and difficulty, the sick man was taken to the Depot—about three-fourths of a mile distant. The hack driver was a negro who strongly objected to making the trip, as he said his time was limited. A white man who was with him, but whose heart was in the right place although he was somewhat intoxicated, swore that the black fellow should take the soldier to the depot. He would not see a man perish from neglect in that way—not he.

"What is your charge?" asked Mr. B. of the black hackman on arriving at the depot.

"One dollar, sir."

The dollar was promptly paid, and the invalid feeling weak and faint, Mr. B. procured a bottle of wine or brandy and some cakes which somewhat refreshed him. He was well supplied with Greenbacks and promptly paid Mr. B. for any expense incurred in his behalf. There was a tremendous pressure at the ticket office, and it would have been utterly impossible for him to procure a ticket in his condition. Tendering his portmonia[2] to Mr. B., who offered to procure his ticket for him, he remarked:

"Take this; I am not afraid to trust a man that has cared for me—an entire stranger—as you have."

The ticket was obtained, and after much difficulty the invalid was placed on board the train. On the following morning the train reached Indianapolis. The cars were soon vacated with the exception of the one containing Mr. B., the sick soldier, and another invalid soldier even more feeble than the first, who seemed also to have been deserted by his friends if there had been any with him. Calling an omnibus driver, Mr. B. asked him to assist the man into his omnibus and drive to a hotel.

"I am not allowed in the depot, sir," was the reply; "there is a man" (pointing to an artillery man) "who will assist you."

"Certainly, sir," said the honest hearted son of thunder, "I will do anything in God's world for a sick soldier."

The train backed out of the depot and switched off on a side track two or three hundred yards distant. Here the sick men remained a half hour while a vehicle was being procured to convey them to the Soldier's Home, where Mr. B. was advised to take them. A hack having been obtained they were placed in it, and the driver was directed to drive to the Soldier's Home. On arriving at the "Home," Mr. B. was told that there was no room for the invalids, and he was directed to the Hospital about one mile distant. The most feeble of the two men could hardly give his name and place of residence (Peru, Ill.,) when asked by one of the officers of the "Home." At the Hospital the sick men were received by the steward and carried by attendants into the building, and there they have probably received the kindest attention.[3]

I have taken up more space with this sketch than I designed, but the facts, being unquestionable, are of interest, as they indicate a criminal neglect of the suffering soldiers on the part of many who have the power to relieve them. Are our Sanitary Commissions entirely blameless in the premises? Would it not be well to have a number of Sanitary Agents at such important points as Louisville to aid returning invalid soldiers?[4]

After leaving Indianapolis we fully realize we are in a peaceful land. But few soldiers are seen upon the train. Ladies and babies become more numerous; the familiar face of the driving man of business, and the pleasant countenance of the "affluent old gent with spectacles," reading the news, are again before you. As you pass through the woods and dense underbrush, you have no suspicions that guerillas may be ready and waiting near at hand to send their messengers of death into the flying train.

Homeward bound! How exhilarating the thought! And how inexpressibly charming to an Illinoisan is the first view of the prairies after a long absence. Even the low, swampy land of northern Indiana looked delightful. On reaching the rolling prairies of his own State and viewing the broad expanse, clothed here and there with island groves, his happiness is complete.

A "Twenty Days' Furlough"—its pleasant and its painful incidents may be sketched in a few concise words. Riding and rumbling for days and nights over all kinds of railroads and in all kinds of cars; jolting hurriedly from depot to depot in "busses"; meeting all sorts of people; and finally astonishing everybody at home by dropping down suddenly in their midst when all supposed you were in Dixie; the old folks cry with joy and a tender-hearted soldier feels like crying also; the girls are overjoyed, and completely subservient to the magnetic influence of the blue uniform; the days pass quickly away, the sun rising and setting with amazing rapidity. A few pleasant rides[,] hurried meetings, sudden partings! A few hours of quiet conversation with special friends, and the hour of separation again has come. Much that you would wish to say must be left unsaid. Yet one feels when moving away from the circle and scenes of home, that he has become better fitted for the duties of the soldier from the brief intercourse with sympathetic and ever generous friends.

Happy, prosperous North! Though mourning the loss of so many brave sons, still happy when compared with the scourged and desolate South. The great Northern marts of commerce echoing to the hum of business pursuits, while through the streets of Southern commercial cities the roar of hostile cannon reverberates. Really it appears that the North may carry on the war and grow in wealth and strength at the same time.

Before commencing the return trip to the regiment, I learned that it had moved to the front. Leaving Galesburg on the 2d of June, I reached Gallatin on the evening of the 5th, and finding only the ruins of our camp where we had passed so many pleasant months. The Brigade had been taken to Lavergne via Nashville on special trains.[5]

After passing one night at Gallatin and another at Nashville, I was enabled to rejoin the regiment on the 7th inst., and felt that I was *at home again*—in my adopted home with the boys of the 102d.

My letter is already too long, and I must defer some observations concerning the trip from Gallatin to Lavergne, and a description of ou[r] present situation until a more convenient time.

S. F. F.

(Rock Island *Weekly Union*, June 24, 1863, p. 1)

1. This is Fleharty's first contribution to the Rock Island *Weekly Union*.

2. *Portmanteau* is evidently the word Fleharty is attempting to spell.

3. The Indianapolis Soldiers' Home and Rest was built in June and July 1862. The 150′ by 24′ building, paid for by the state of Indiana, was built in a grove near the White River, north of the railroad. A 100-foot section of the structure was fitted with bunks and bedding supplied by the Indiana Sanitary Commission, while the remaining 50-foot section was set up

for dining. The Soldiers' Home opened August 1, 1862, with the expense of its operation (except the purchase of food) borne by the Sanitary Commission. Local citizens contributed such things as butter, fruit, eggs, books, and paper. The Indianapolis postmaster donated stamps for the soldiers' use. The original building was soon outgrown. Late in 1862 a larger structure (250' by 24') was added and used exclusively as a dining hall. Three tables, extending nearly the length of the building, accommodated from 900 to 1,000 diners. The dining facility in the original home was then converted to dormitory use. By 1863 a third building (150' by 24') was added for use as a hospital. During that year the home served 817,656 meals. By the end of the war the total had risen to more than 3,700,000. See W. H. H. Terrell, *Indiana in the War of the Rebellion* (Indianapolis, 1869), 363–64, 366.

4. The Indiana Sanitary Commission was an independent organization, not affiliated with the United States Sanitary Commission. Terrell, *Indiana in the War of the Rebellion*, 339.

5. From November 26, 1862, until the end of May 1863, the 102d was stationed at Gallatin, Tennessee, guarding a portion of the Louisville and Nashville Railroad. As Rosecrans prepared for the Tullahoma campaign, the rear-echelon troops were organized into the Reserve Corps under Maj. Gen. Gordon Granger. The 102d was part of the 2d Brigade, 3d Division of this corps. On June 1, 1863, the brigade was ordered to Lavergne, Tennessee, to guard the railroad between Nashville and Murfreesboro. The section of the Nashville and Chattanooga Railroad assigned to the 102d was near Stewart's Creek, six miles south of Lavergne. See *Adj. Gen. Rep.*, V, 614–15; Frederick H. Dyer, *A Compendium of the War of the Rebellion* (Des Moines, 1908), 1,090.

◦— No. 21 —◦

Stewart's Creek, Tenn.,
June 19, 1863.

The country in which we are now encamped has experienced the effects of war in all its stern features. The little village of Lavergne—*that was*—is represented now by ashes and charred remnants of dwelling and business houses. It was evidently at one time a pleasant little town. The destruction of the place occurred during and after the battle of Stone River. Skirmishing between the two armies was carried on very briskly in this vicinity. Notwithstanding the general destruction of fences, and the loss of property occasioned by the fierce conflict that raged so near, there are some evidences of returning prosperity even in this neighborhood. An old gentleman who lives about two miles this side of the battlefield, states that at one time the Union forces were compelled to fall back and encamp upon and in the vicinity of his farm. His fields were one grand encampment and his fences disappeared in many brilliant camp-fires, yet he is raising a fine crop of grain. Everything has been put in repair since the battle.

Our Situation

If I mistake not I promised a description of the locality where we are encamped. The right wing of the regiment is garrisoning an earthwork which we call Fort Smith, in honor of our Colonel. We are about a half mile from the railroad. Three companies of the left wing are encamped near the railroad bridge at Stewart's Creek (in the direction of Lavergne). An earthwork has been thrown up at that place also, and the boys call it Fort Mannon, in honor of our Lieut. Colonel, who commands the garrison. Co. B, is about one mile beyond Stewart's Creek, at Smyrna. Co. H is stationed at a railroad bridge four miles in the direction of Murfreesboro. Thus you will observe the 102d is quite extensively distributed along the railroad. The position is considered very much exposed to a cavalry raid, and every precaution is taken to prevent surprise. Guerillas are prowling through the country and have fired upon soldiers passing between this place and Lavergne, since we arrived here.[1]

The boys have been busy at work felling trees that might protect an attacking party, and also repairing and improving the forts. A beautiful garrison flag was raised yesterday, its ample folds fluttering in the breeze as proudly as in the proudest period of our national glory, and must awaken a sense of remorse in the hearts of traitorous citizens who look upon it—and then view the desolation they have brought upon this once peaceful country.

A Ride to Murfreesboro

Obtaining two days' leave of absence from camp I left last Tuesday morning for Murfreesboro. Col. Walworth of the 42d Ill. vols., and Major Leighton of the same regiment, were returning to Murfreesboro from a visit with friends here, and it was my good fortune to join them on the Pike, before reaching the battlefield.[2] The effects of the desperate struggle are yet marked and distinct. Approaching the ruins of a building on the right of the Pike the colonel remarked: "There Rosecrans had his headquarters during a part of the ever-memorable 31st of Dec." Off in the woods to the right the most desperate fighting occurred on that day—the enemy having massed his forces there to turn our right flank. A short distance farther the graves of the slain become quite numerous. Some appear to have been buried promiscuously in trenches, others were buried singly. The carcasses of horses that were killed in the battle are yet laying [sic], shriveled like mummies, upon the field. Passing through an opening where there were numerous graves, the colonel remarked: "Here within forty rods of you, lay at one time, two thousand dead rebels."

Trees by the roadside are well marked with musket balls and lacerated with shot and shell, but it is said that these evidences of the fierce nature of the conflict are more apparent at some distance from the pike in the thick woods.

I intend soon to visit the battlefield, and view at leisure the different localities of interest, when I will write down any impressions that may appear to be worthy of record.

The distance to Murfreesboro—nine miles—seemed very short. The immense encampments of the grand army of the Cumberland burst upon our view before we reach[ed] the town; intermingled with these, appear the extensive series of fortifications—known under the general title of Fort Rosecrans. The panorama of camps and fortifications is very imposing. It would require some time and study to comprehend the arrangement of the works. They certainly appear very formidable, and apparently command every possible point of attack. The fortifications are principally in a northwesterly direction from the town—within easy range; and it is said that the town will be destroyed if the enemy should approach from that direction.[3]

On reaching Murfreesboro I learned that the brigade I wished to visit was out on picket duty. A ride of three and a half miles in a south-westerly direction from town on the Salem pike, brought me to the camp of the 27th, 42d, 51st and 22d Ill. vols., of which the 3d brigade of the 3d division in the 20th army corps is composed. Here were friends whom I had not met since the summer of '61, and our meeting in a Tennessee forest, so far away from the scenes of former acquaintances, was pleasant indeed.

This brigade has been through many severe engagements, and has earned unfading laurels on every field.[4] One cannot but admire the bronzed but honest determined features of these veterans. Time seems to have added intensity to their patriotism. One of them, with whom I have been long acquainted—who means all that he says—remarked that if his time of service should expire before the close of the war, he would "go in again, and see it through."

While with my old friends in the 27th, I walked out to the line of pickets about three-fourths of a mile distant.[5] The picket force is very heavy. The outposts, about fifty yards in advance of the reserve force, are from eighty to one hundred yards apart. A well-beaten path from post to post marks the line of infantry pickets around the grand army—beyond there are the cavalry pickets, or videttes.

A religious revival is in progress in this brigade. Numbers have been baptized and the work is still going on. Services are held at night in the woods. The novelty of the scene, I admit, more than any devout feelings, led me to the place of meeting. Four stakes driven into the ground supporting rough boards formed a kind of table or pulpit. Rude logs were arranged parallel with each other in front of the pulpit. On these and on the ground were seated a quiet and attentive audience. The preacher was of the Baptist pursuasion [*sic*], was evidently thoroughly in earnest, and it was quite as evident that he was preaching to earnest men. It was an impressive occasion. Amidst the shadowy gloom of the forest, near the picket line of the army of the Cumberland!—an audience of soldiers who had faced death on many bloody fields! How strongly and with what evident effect those earnest words appealed to the emotions of the listeners! The speaker dwelt upon the uncertainty of the soldier's life, and depicted all the imaginable horrors of punishment beyond the grave.

One could but admire his deep devotion, and his earnest labors in behalf of the soldiers, however widely differing from him on theological questions. During the prayers that followed the sermon, a petition was offered up in behalf of the pickets on the lonely outposts, and a simultaneous responsive prayer was echoed from the lips of the kneeling audience.

Returning to Murfreesboro on the following day in company with friends I visited other camps. It is stated that some lady visitors recently announced, after calling on Hooker and taking a very superficial survey of affairs, that in their opinion "JOE COULD NOT BE WHIPPED."[6] A declaration of this kind in reference to Rosecrans, may appear to be the result of superficial observations; yet I do but speak the minds of his veteran soldiers, when I state that in my own opinion he will never be driven by the rebels, but will in due season advance to certain victory.

Murfreesboro appears to have been a very pleasant village of about 2,500 inhabitants. The streets present a lively appearance now—but the life that pulsates through them is that which springs from the stern exigencies of the war.

The return ride to camp was marked by no incident of peculiar interest.

Respectfully,

S. F. F.

(Rock Island *Weekly Union*, July 15, 1863, p. 1)

1. The "right wing" consisted of Companies A, C, D, F, I, and the regimental headquarters. The companies of the "left wing," under Lieutenant Colonel Mannon, were E, G, and K. Fleharty, *Our Regiment*, 34.

2. Col. Nathan H. Walworth and Maj. James Leighton of the 42d Illinois were both residents of Oneida in Knox County. Major Leighton was killed at Chickamauga on September 20, 1863.

3. Immediately after the battle of Stones River, the Army of the Cumberland occupied Murfreesboro. While re-equipping and reorganizing his men, Rosecrans saw to the construction of an impressive series of fortifications around the city. An early historian of the army described the defenses of Murfreesboro: "Earthworks of the strongest type were thrown up on the high ground between the town and Stone river, on each side of the railroad and Nashville turnpike, and on the elevated ground north of the river. These heavy works were commanded in turn by a succession of forts which offered vulnerable sides to the great central fortress. And besides the heavy forts and intrenchments, there was a circumvallation in front of the extended camps of the army. These defenses subsequently furnished refuge for troops stationed for the protection of communications and the depot of supplies at Murfreesboro, but no great army ever had an opportunity of repelling a greater army through their friendly help." Thomas B. Van Horne, *History of the Army of the Cumberland, Its Organization, Campaigns, and Battles.* (Cincinnati, 1875), I, 288.

4. The brigade would experience another "severe engagement" in September at Chickamauga. Commanded by Col. Luther P. Bradley of the 51st Illinois, the 3d Brigade suffered 517 casualties in the engagement, including 58 killed. *OR*, Vol. XXX, Pt. 1, p. 75.

5. Most of the men of Company G were from Mercer County.

6. Maj. Gen. Joseph Hooker (1814–79), commanding the Army of the Potomac, could be, and indeed had been "whipped." Hooker had been badly beaten May 2–4, 1863, at Chancellorsville. On June 28, just nine days after Fleharty wrote this letter, Hooker would be relieved of his command, only three days before the pivotal encounter at Gettysburg.

꙰— No. 22 —꙰

Stewart's Creek[,] Tenn.,
July 1st, 1863.

In company with Lieut. T. H. Andrews, I rode to the Stone River battle-field yesterday morning.[1] The morning was auspicious. The earth had been deluged with heavy rains, and the comparatively clear sky and cool atmosphere indicated a pleasant day. A short ride brought us to Overall's Creek, which may be considered as representing the north western boundary line of the battle-field. About three-fourths of a mile beyond this we reach Cedar Hill—a point on the pike to which the right wing of the Federal army was driven during the terrible hours of December 31st, 1862. The Federal line of battle was originally formed at right angles with the pike and directly across it, extending on the left to Stone river and on the right through the woods to Wilkinson pike.

This wing, borne down by superior forces, routed and disorganized, fell back until the extreme right rested as I stated above, at Cedar Hill—the line of battle of the right wing, forming a slight crescent from that point to the point where the original line of battle was formed across the pike.[2]

Intending to visit all the prominent parts of the field, we proposed procuring a guide, and preliminary to a move in this direction, rode to a point where an acute angle is formed by the conjunction of the railroad and pike. Here a vidette, forming one of the outer line of pickets around Murfreesboro, halted us. We were without passes—no pickets having previously been posted through the battle-field, there was apparently no necessity for passes. We were desirous of visiting the clump of woods within the picket line, between the railroad and the pike, as some of the most desperate fighting had taken place in the angle above mentioned. The vidette told us we could ride in the reserve, a hundred yards distant, and the Lieutenant in command would probably give us a pass. We rode in. The Lieutenant was not present, and the Sergeant advised us to remain a few moments as the Lieutenant would be there in a short time. We waited—in the meantime riding into the "neck of woods" making observations. The trees here are terribly scarred. To acquire an idea of the intense fire that blazed among them imagine that a party of marksmen have placed a target on one side of a tree about one foot from the ground and fired until the ball holes become so numerous that they move the target round to avoid confusion and thus finally girdle the tree—imagine it girdled thus from within a foot of the ground to a height of fifteen feet above. I noticed one ball at least twenty feet from the ground, and there were doubtless many such wild shots fired. All the trees in this vicinity are thus marked. The fighting here appears to have been mainly with small arms, as there are but few marks of cannon shot or shell.

Near by we observed a small enclosure wherein were buried a number of the heroes that fell in the bloody contest. On a rough board were the following expressive words:

"The Slain of Hazen's Brigade."

A monument is being erected to their memory. Those who have read a detailed account of the battle, know how nobly Hazen with his brigade fought, and how poorly the noblest monument can represent the worth of the fallen patriots.[3]

We picked up a number of misshapen musket balls and returned to the pike. The Sergeant of the pickets met us, and as the Lieutenant had not made his appearance, he thought we had better go in to Gen. Van Cleve's [*sic*] headquarters and get passes, at the same time intimating his unwillingness to permit us to return through the outpost line without them.[4] Possibly our movements in the clump of wood—crossing and recrossing the railroad—had awakened his suspicions. We could not blame the faithful boys for being on the alert, and cheerfully went with one of them to the line of infantry pickets, thence to headquarters of the Lieutenant on duty as officer of the guard. The Lieutenant directed us to Gen. Van Cleve's headquarters, and thus we were compelled to visit Murfreesboro during the time we proposed to spend on the battle-field. To add to the romance of the occasion, a heavy shower came up, and the rain fell in torrents. Laughing at the awkwardness of our predicament, we hurried on. An immense wagon train—the beginning and the end of which could not be seen—was crossing the narrow bridge over Stone River, going to the front. Whipping, cursing, and at times sticking in the mud, the teamsters made slow progress with their incorrigible [*sic*] slow mules. At length we succeeded in running the gauntlet at the risk of breaking our necks over an embankment as we crowded past the teams. But our adventure was not yet ended. The Lieutenant applied for a pass. The General sent him to the Provost Marshal, where something like the following conversation ensued:

Provost—"What credentials have you?"

Lieut.—"I have no official documents with me, sir, that would establish my character and position." [And then the Lieutenant related how innocently we came within the picket lines, our business, etc.]

Provost—"Have you no letters?"

Lieut.—"Only this one" (drawing forth a neat billet-doux that bore an excellent specimen of lady penmanship,) "read it."

The Provost glanced at the post-mark, address and signature and returned it.

Provost—"This is hardly satisfactory. We are compelled to be very careful since the army has advanced, and left us with but two brigades with which to hold the town."

Lieut.—"Well, really, Captain, I imagine your proper course with me now would be to put me at once in close confinement, since you have been so kind as to give me your fighting strength."

Provost,—(slightly disconcerted)—"Oh, d——n it, you're all right! Clerk, give them passes!"

After crossing Stone River a novel spectacle attracted our attention. A crowd of men dressed in homespun, whitish-grey clothes, and enclosed by a circle of blue coats! Secesh prisoners! Now we are paid for visiting Murfreesboro. They numbered 480, and belonged to Wheeler's cavalry, and were captured a day or two previously near Shelbyville. They are a rough, hardy looking set of fellows, and are evidently fighting men[.] They did not seem despondent; thought they could fight a number of years yet; and those who had conversed with them stated that they were quite independent and insolent. Their clothing is comfortable and they have apparently been well fed. We desired very much to have a friendly chat with the rascals but they were surrounded with guards and crowds of spectators, which rendered profitable conversation impracticable.

Leaving the secesh we repaired to the sutler's tent, disposed of a wholesome dinner, tested the quality of the "Sparkling Catawba" that my friend, the Lieutenant, had provided for the occasion, and were soon on the pike leading to our camp at Stewart's Creek.[5] Arriving again on the battle field, we had barely commenced making observations, when the heavy clouds rolling up from the north west, and the continued roar of Heaven's artillery warned us that if we tarried a drenching rain would soon be upon us.

"We must reach the next courier post, two miles ahead," remarked the Lieutenant, and we galloped away from the field, having failed to accomplish our original purpose, yet feeling well satisfied with our adventure.

We reined up at the courier post just as the storm burst upon us, and found shelter with a squad of genuine East Tennessee soldiers. These soldiers are terribly in earnest. They long to visit their homes, bearing the "old flag" that they have been taught from infancy to love. Frank, intelligent and sociable, they do honor to the home of Brownlow and the cause in which they are engaged.[6]

One of them inquired particularly in regard to the strength and designs of the Copperheads, and in the presence of these exiled patriots, I felt loth to admit how deeply our own State is disgraced by the presence of these traitors within its borders.[7]

Speaking of guarding rebel property, one of them remarked that it would not be well to leave that business to them, for they had not yet forgotten how their property had been destroyed, and they themselves hunted from their homes. East Tennessee is yet loyal! No one will doubt this assertion after conversing with these brave young men.

The rain over we rode into camp, and of course related how we captured the Federal pickets and escorted them into Murfreesboro.

S. F. F.

(Rock Island *Weekly Union,* July 15, 1863, p. 1)

1. First Lt. Theodore H. Andrews of Galesburg enlisted July 25, 1862, in Company A of the 102d, and was named one of four sergeants. He was promoted first lieutenant of the company in January 1863, and on July 12 was promoted captain. *Adj. Gen. Rep.,* V, 594.

2. See Peter Cozzens, *No Better Place to Die: The Battle of Stones River* (Urbana, Ill., 1990) for an excellent account of the battle.

3. This brigade (2d Brigade, 2d Division, Left Wing, Army of the Cumberland), commanded by Brig. Gen. William B. Hazen, consisted of the 110th Illinois, 9th Indiana, 6th Kentucky, 41st Ohio, and Battery F of the 1st Ohio Artillery. During the first day's fight (December 31, 1862) the brigade lost forty-three men killed. The monument commemorating these men was constructed just days later and can still be seen just east of the Stones River National Cemetery. See Hazen's report of the action in *OR,* Vol. XX, Pt. 1, pp. 542–48.

4. Brig. Gen. Horatio P. Van Cleve (1809–91) commanded the post of Murfreesboro from November 1863 to the end of the war.

5. "Sparkling Catawba" is a light, sparkling wine made from the Catawba grape (Vitis labrusca). It was first produced about 1830.

6. William G. "Parson" Brownlow (1805–77), a Methodist clergyman, had been the editor of a number of Whig publications in Tennessee before the war. His strong pro-Union stand as editor of the Knoxville *Whig* led to the paper's suppression and his imprisonment by Confederate authorities. Released early in 1862, he resided in Ohio until Union forces regained control of eastern Tennessee in 1863. He was active in state government and served as governor from 1865 to 1869, then as U.S. senator from 1869 to 1875. See E. Merton Coulter, *William G. Brownlow, Fighting Parson of the Southern Highlands* (Chapel Hill, 1937).

7. "Copperheads" (a term usually denoting anti-war Democrats) were particularly active in Illinois and several other midwestern states. Copperhead activities in Illinois included attempts to discourage the enlistment of Union recruits through the use of antiwar propaganda, obstruction of conscription officers in the performance of their duties, and inciting the desertion of Union troops. Copperhead resistance to the war measures of the Lincoln administration took several ugly turns in Illinois, particularly during the war's latter years. Organized bands of guerrillas and deserters terrorized loyal citizens, using threats of violence and intimidation, and in some cases deadly force, especially in the counties of central and southern Illinois. In March 1864 there was even a pitched battle between copperheads and Union soldiers in the streets of Charleston in Coles County. For a detailed account of these and other copperhead activities in the state, see Arthur C. Cole, *The Era of the Civil War, 1848–1870,* Vol. III of The Centennial History of Illinois; Springfield, 1919), 305–11.

⌒ No. 23 ⌒

Stewart's Creek, Tenn.,
July 21st, 1863.

"A ten acre blackberry patch," remarked someone in our hearing the other day.

"Where?" was the eager inquiry.

"About a mile and a half from camp, in the direction of Smyrna."

Ten acres of blackberries were not to be seen every day, and we took the first opportunity to visit the locality named.

The blackberry season was fairly opening, and the tall bushes were literally burdened with the tempting fruit. The "ten acre" lot was no exaggeration, and the thickets of briars were so dense as to be in some places nearly impenetrable. We "laid siege" to them, and by regular approaches, succeeded in reaching regions hitherto unmolested. Crushing the immense briars around us, a perfect wall of berries seemed to impede our further progress. Great, luscious, juicy berries they were, too, and melted rapidly away in our appreciative mouths.

The whole country is full of berries. We have had them for some weeks and the supply seems inexhaustible. Morning, noon and evening they are placed on our table, and we have had stewed blackberries, blackberry pie, blackberry dumplings, blackberries and cream—or, rather milk, for the former luxury can seldom be obtained. The berries are an excellent sanitary addition to Uncle Sam's bill of fare.

Peaches are beginning to ripen, and there will be an immense crop of them.

Since our regiment came into Dixie I have sketched some of the rough scenes of army life, and others of an opposite character. We spent two pleasant weeks at Scottsville, Ky., and many pleasant days at Gallatin, but we are having the *most glorious times imaginable here.* Although ever willing and eager to share in the dangers, sufferings and honors of the advance troops, our regiment has, up to this time, been used to strengthen important points in the rear of the main army; and now, while we will cheerfully respond to any "forward" order, we are all praying that *the peaches may ripen before we move.*

It would be pleasant to have friends from home visit us here. We would go with them blackberrying; would invite them to witness the intricate evolutions of the regiment on battallion [*sic*] drill; and then when the shadows of evening close around camp, they could stroll to the Adjutant's quarters and hear our musical Adjutant, with his excellent guitar, sing a variety of sweet songs. Mingling with the rich notes of the guitar, might be heard the beautiful words:

> Weeping, sad and lonely,
> Hopes and fears how vain,
> Yet praying—
> When this cruel war is over
> —Praying that we meet again.[1]

and then again:

"Oh! wrap the flag around me boys," &c. or that other incomparable piece of music, commencing:

"We shall meet, but we shall miss him," &c.[2]

Perhaps nothing contributes to the enjoyments of life in our present situation, more than these little musical entertainments. His Adjutancy, quite unconscious of the fine compliments I am bestowing upon him, is just now very innocently and energetically repairing an old rusty pistol, as if thoughts of war really do occasionally cross his mind.[3] And undoubtedly they do, for we imagine his music has conquered more than one susceptible young lady, whose heart had been "fired" with the spirit of the "master race." It is amusing to observe how quickly his impromptu concerts will collect an audience in front of his quarters—the boys all listening with quiet but intense interest. Friends at home, will not these pleasant pictures induce you to visit us?

Captain "Bob."

In a previous letter I mentioned the peculiarities of "Bob"—at that time acting in the humble capacity of cook for our mess. Insignificant, stammering, black Bob, the cook, has taken a slight step upward in the world. Bob has caught the prevailing military mania. I cannot say that, through the thick gloom of semi-barbarism which has ever enveloped the race, any incendiary ideas of liberty are struggling, but it is evident that Bob, notwithstanding his impediment of speech, and the dilatory oscillations of his immense under lip, is determined to carve for himself a niche in the temple of military fame. After the work of the day is done Bob collects all the black boys of the regiment together for drill. He has learned the different commands very well, and handles his squad with no little ability. If his boys are inattentive he very authoritatively commands attention—"Get in the [*sic*] dar," and "Walk up *even* dar," "Stop dat 'ere talkin' in the ranks!" Bob is a rising star!

Recent Victories, Etc.

We have all been, and are yet, jubilant over the recent Federal victories. When the news that Vicksburg had fallen reached us, the companies were marched out in front of the Colonel's tent, the news was read to them and then followed a wild and deafening outburst of cheers.[4]

An incident occurred here consequent upon the advance of Rosecrans, that is worth recording.[5] Three old gentlemen and a young lady, from the vicinity of Chattanooga, were going North, and halted a few moments near our camp. They had been liberated from rebel rule by the general advance. While conversing with our boys a passing breeze caused our beautiful flag to unfurl its folds and float gracefully before them. At the sight of it the horses of the travelers became much frightened; a dog that was with them caught the panic and barked lustily at it.

"It is not surprising," remarked one of the old men, "that they should be frightened by that flag, for it has not been seen among us for nearly two years."

Guerillas

The guerillas are still prowling in this vicinity. Three couriers at a Courier's Post one and a half miles from our camp, in the direction of Murfreesboro, were captured a few nights since. Yesterday afternoon a squad of cavalry and a detachment from our regiment were fired upon while returning to camp from Triune. The rebels were pursued, and "in the hurry of the moment," one of them lost a pair of old-fashioned saddle-bags containing a number of articles useful to the soldier, and, strange as it may appear, among them was found a well-worn pocket bible! How inconsistent is man! This deluded individual undoubtedly thinks he is doing God-service in following his dishonorable mode of warfare. S. F. F.

(Rock Island *Weekly Union*, August 5, 1863, p. 1)

1. This was one of the most popular songs of the Civil War in both the North and the South. The words to "Weeping Sad and Lonely (When This Cruel War Is Over)" were written by Charles C. Sawyer and the music by Henry Tucker. See Irwin Silber, *Songs of the Civil War* (New York, 1960), 117.

2. "Wrap the Flag Around Me, Boys" (words and music by R. Stewart Taylor) refers to the occasional practice of using the national colors as a winding sheet in the burial of Union dead:

O, wrap the flag around me, boys,
To die were far more sweet,
With freedom's starry emblem, boys,
To be my winding sheet.
In life I lov'd to see it wave,
And follow where it led,
And now my eyes grow dim, my hands
Would clasp its last bright shred.

"We shall meet but we shall miss him," was the first line of "The Vacant Chair." The song, Henry J. Washburn's poem set to music by George F. Root, was popular in the North and the South. Silber, *Songs of the Civil War*, 119.

3. Adjutant Jacob H. Snyder.

4. The first week of July 1863 had been a disastrous one for Confederate arms. First, on July 1–3, the Army of the Potomac had stymied Robert E. Lee's invasion of the North at Gettysburg; then, on July 4, Vicksburg, the Confederacy's last stronghold on the Mississippi, surrendered to Grant.

5. In May 1863 the Lincoln administration, fearing that Braxton Bragg (whose army was drawn up in a defensive position north of the Duck River, between Columbia and McMinnville) would detach units to reinforce the rebel forces at Vicksburg, urged Rosecrans to move out of his defenses at Murfreesboro and attack the Army of Tennessee. When Rosecrans finally moved, during the last week of June, he directed a textbook campaign of maneuver that forced Bragg to retreat from his position by the end of the month. For a more detailed sketch of the campaign, see Boatner, *Civil War Dictionary*, 850–51.

◦— No. 24 —◦

Stewart's Creek, Tenn.,
Aug. 6th, 1863.

Our regiment has been quite active since arriving here in ferreting out the secret resorts of the rebels in this vicinity. Scouting parties are out almost daily, and frequently remain out all night. It is true these expeditions have not been as s——l as could be desired, yet they have inspired the guerillas with a wholesome dread of the Union scouts. I propose giving the readers of THE UNION a sketch of a ride last night of this character.

About sundown word ran through camp that a scouting party was going out, and eveery [*sic*] available horse was immediately saddled by soldiers eager for a little extra fun. Yet all who wished to go could not get horses, and among the disappointed the writer seemed doomed to figure. But there was another resource, and it was developed in this wise: "Mike," a dashing young Lieutenant, wished to go also, and was equally at a loss where to get a horse.[1]

"Mules! let us get mules!" said one.

"Agreed; I will if you will," was the reply, and off we posted to the Teamster's Department.

"Doc, have you a mule that's fit to ride?"

"Yes," [*sic*] I have a *little* one," answered our Richland Grove friend, whom the boys have dubbed "Doc."

"A little one," I mused with ominous forebodings of evil; but that was no time for indecision.

"She is very small," continued Doc, "but she will 'knock the socks' off anything in the camp for a riding animal. We call her 'Sis' and she is the universal pet of the teamsters."

"Sis" was soon bridled and saddled, and I observed at once that she was, as editors say, "all that could be desired," except, of course, in bulk. Let me give you an idea of her diminutiveness. I must premise, however, by saying that for some wise purpose, the exact nature of which cannot be clearly understood, the writer is endowed with "walking qualifications" of the highest order, insomuch that he finds no little difficulty at times in obtaining "unmentionables" of sufficient length to hide the fancy leather of his boot-tops. When in the saddle I could, without the least difficulty, strike my boot-heels together beneath the saddle-girth around the little animal.

"I say, young man, you should exchange places with your mule after riding awhile, or dismount and stow it away in your coat pocket, and 'tote' it around in that way until it gets rested!" "Have you got the soles of your boots iron-plated? They should be by all means! The rocks will wear the soles and the hide all off your feet before you get back!" Thus some of my jovial friends of the squad were disposed to make merry at our expense, all of which was endured with philosophic and mulish indifference by myself and little "Sis."

The party was composed of fifteen or twenty men of the 10th O. V. C.[2] and a number of volunteers from our regiment. A ride of three miles brought us to the place where we were to obtain a guide—a repentant rebel who had been into camp that day and informed the Colonel that a number of "Rebs" would assemble at a certain point beyond Stone river that night, with the intention of departing on the following morning for some more congenial part of Dixie.

The guide could not be found—his lady stating, however, that he had gone to the house of a neighbor. To the house of the neighbor aforesaid we galloped—"not there; had been there that afternoon." The old gentleman and lady at this house were much irritated by the cross-examination to which they were subjected.

"Can't *catch us* in a lie," said the old woman vehemently; "that's been tried before."

The evasive manner and irratability [*sic*] of the old couple had awakened suspicions that they knew more than they were willing to divulge. The house was searched through and through for the migratory gentleman whom we expected to obtain as guide—now considered a spy. The search was unavailing, and the old lady no doubt realized immense satisfaction from the fact that she had not been caught "in a lie."

Thence we hurried away to Stone River, forming a long line in single file as we passed the historic little stream. Passing on to a farm house, a colored guide was procured to pilot us to a house about two miles distant where it was thought the man we were seeking could be found. "Cuffey" led off quite briskly, and for a mile we clattered over rocks, and through thick brush at break-neck speed. At length the senseless haste of "Cuffey" was checked, and we found that the main body of cavalrymen were far in the rear. Continuing on, we arrived—six of the 102d—in the vicinity of the place to which we had been directed. Rapidly galloping to the house and surrounding it we found no one there but a pleasant featured lady with her little children. Happily she was not afraid of the "Yankees" and seemed quite composed, notwithstanding the sudden charge upon her premises, for which we of course, gave ample explanation. Nothing could be learned here of any advantage to us. The remainder of the party were now so far in the rear that we knew they could not find us, and we were confident that if they continued on in any direction, it would be quite as difficult for us to find them.

"Take us to Jefferson," said "Mike"—the mule-mounted Lieutenant previously mentioned,—and for Jefferson, a little village about two miles up the river, we started.—Mike was full of mischief and yelled out to the negro guide to hurry forward—*"faster!"* and away we went through the brush, over logs and into dense bodies of cedars. *Faster* yells the Lieutenant, and over the rocks, leaping, slipping and stumbling—the horses' shoes striking fire,—on we rode. At length the mad-cap Lieutenant was induced to rein-up. "Sis" had not made a single miss-step, which could not be said of some of the lubberly horses in the squad. Lieut. C. who laughed heartily at the unique appearance of "Sis" and her ———— at the beginning of the ride, had the satisfaction of gathering himself up from the ground once during the expedition. Luckily he was not seriously hurt, although his horse fell partially upon him.

Fording Stone River again we found ourselves in Jefferson—once the Capital of Tennessee—a quiet antiquated little village in a picturesque locality, that to all appearances might have been the identical dwelling place of Rip Van Winkle, during his years of seclusion.[3] The moon had fairly risen, and shedding its silvery rays over the quiet scene, rendered the picture really romantic. All the inhabitants were wrapt in slumber—neither friend nor foe were to be seen, and, dispensing with our guide, who did not seem to appreciate the necessity or romance of our night ride, we turned our mules and horses in the direction of camp. Another idiosyncrasy seized upon Mike however. Mike must have a swim in Stone River! The majority wished to continue on to camp. Both parties were obstinate. Lieut. W. (sometimes called "Parson W.") joined Mike, and away they went to have a swim.[4] The remainder of the party leisurely rode into camp—a distance of five miles—which was reached at two o'clock in the morning. The swimmers came in shortly afterwards, and the entire detachment an hour or two later. The expedition failed of its purpose through want of a guide, yet it was sufficiently interesting to repay us for the fatigue and drowsiness that oppress us to-day.

Respectfully,

S. F. F.

(Rock Island *Weekly Union*, August 19, 1863, p. 1)

1. Second Lt. Michael L. Courtney, a native of Ireland, was living in Knox County, Illinois, at the time of his enlistment in July 1862. Originally a sergeant in Company I, Courtney was promoted 2d lieutenant of Company A in April 1863, and 1st lieutenant four months later. On December 21, 1863, he was commissioned lieutenant colonel of the 16th U.S. Colored Infantry, in which capacity he served until mustered out in April 1866. Courtney then obtained a commission as second lieutenant in the 39th U.S. (Colored) Infantry. He served with that regiment for three years until it was consolidated with other units to form the 25th U.S. (Colored) Infantry. He remained in the army until his death, as a captain, on July 16, 1886.

See Francis B. Heitman, *Historical Register and Dictionary of the United States Army* (1903; rpr. Urbana, Ill., 1965), I, 330.

2. 10th Ohio Volunteer Cavalry.

3. Jefferson, Tennessee, was on the Middle Fork of Stones River, about ten miles northwest of Murfreesboro. (It now lies covered by the waters of the J. Percy Priest Reservoir.) Fleharty was understandably mistaken about Jefferson's having been the capital of Tennessee. For the first forty-seven years of Tennessee's history as a state, political leaders were themselves confused about just where to locate their capital. Before being permanently located in Nashville in 1843, it was at Knoxville (1796–1807), Kingston (1807), Knoxville (1807–12), Nashville (1812–15), Knoxville (1815–17), Murfreesboro (1817–26), and temporarily at Nashville (1826–43), until the legislature at last made up its mind. For an interesting discussion of the dispute over the location of Tennessee's capital, see Robert H. White, "Tennessee's Four Capitals" in *Tennessee Old and New, Sesquicentennial Edition, 1796–1946* (Kingsport, 1946), I, 319–32.

4. The identity of Lieutenant W. remains a mystery. He was most likely either 2d Lt. George W. Wooley (Company F) of Henderson, Knox County, or 2d Lt. Samuel E. Willits (Company K) of Aledo, Mercer County.

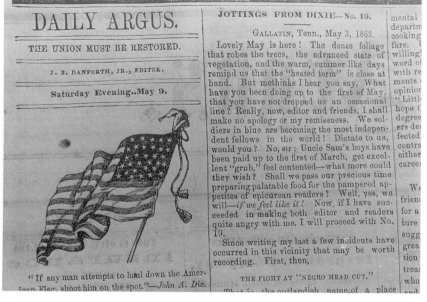

DAILY ARGUS.

THE UNION MUST BE RESTORED.

J. B. DANFORTH, JR., EDITOR.

Saturday Evening..May 9.

"If any man attempts to haul down the American Flag, shoot him on the spot."—*John A. Dix.*

JOTTINGS FROM DIXIE—No. 19.

GALLATIN, Tenn., May 3, 1863.

Lovely May is here! The dense foliage that robes the trees, the advanced state of vegetation, and the warm, summer-like days remind us that the "heated term" is close at hand. But methinks I hear you say, What have you been doing up to the first of May, that you have not dropped us an occasional line? Really, now, editor and friends, I shall make no apology or my remissness. We soldiers in blue are becoming the most independent fellows in the world! Dictate to us, would you? No, sir; Uncle Sam's boys have been paid up to the first of March, get excellent "grub," feel contented—what more could they wish? Shall we pass our precious time preparing palatable food for the pampered appetites of epicurean readers? Well, yes, we will—*if we feel like it!* Now, if I have succeeded in making both editor and readers quite angry with me, I will proceed with No. 19.

Since writing my last a few incidents have occurred in this vicinity that may be worth recording. First, then,

THE FIGHT AT "NEGRO HEAD CUT."

The opening of installment No. 19 of "Jottings from Dixie." This letter was the last in the series to appear in the Rock Island *Argus*. Because of the ongoing criticism of abolition, the government's handling of the war, and the Lincoln administration in general by the *Argus*'s Democratic editor, J. B. Danforth, Stephen Fleharty transferred his writings to the (Republican) Rock Island *Union*.

Rock Island County Historical Research Library, Moline, Illinois

The five Fleharty brothers. Stephen is standing at right. The other Flehartys were William Lane, Jesse Jackson, John Quincy Adams, and Henry Clay, but it is unknown which of those pictured here was which.

Courtesy of Mrs. Sarah Glass

Stephen F. Fleharty at the time of the Civil War

Courtesy of Mrs. Sarah Glass

William McMurtry, the former lieutenant governor of Illinois
who became the first colonel of the 102d Illinois Infantry

From Albert J. Perry, History of Knox County, Illinois:
Its Cities, Towns, and People *(Chicago, 1912)*

Franklin C. Smith, who succeeded William McMurtry as colonel of the 102d

Illinois State Historical Library, Springfield

J. B. Danforth, editor of the Rock Island *Argus*

From Portrait and Biographical Album of Knox County, Illinois *(Chicago, 1886)*

Myron S. Barnes, editor of the Rock Island *Weekly Union,* where "Jottings from Dixie" appeared after Fleharty's disagreement with Danforth.

From James Grant Wilson, Biographical Sketches of Illinois Officers Engaged in the War Against the Rebellion of 1861 *(Chicago, 1862)*

Top officers of the 3d Division, 20th Corps, as photographed by the famed Mathew Brady. From left: General (and future president) Benjamin Harrison; General W. T. Ward, the division's commander; and Colonels Daniel Dustin and Charles Cogswell.

Library of Congress

Stephen Fleharty, most likely in the 1870s

Courtesy of Mrs. Sarah Glass

Fleharty in Tampa, Florida, where he moved in the early 1880s
in hope that the climate would cure his tuberculosis.

Courtesy of Mrs. Sarah Glass

Fleharty's name is misspelled on his headstone in Waynesville, North Carolina. The family pronounces the name "Fleeharty," with a long *e* sound, and perhaps the stonecutter simply carved it the way he heard it.

Photo by Philip Reyburn

CHAPTER 6

"The Monotony of Camp Life"

∾ No. 25 ∾

Lavergne, Tenn.,
Aug. 25th, 1863.

On the morning of the 19th inst. we received marching orders, and soon our pleasant camp at Stewart's Creek was broken up.—We halted at Lavergne—or rather four companies did—at which place regimental headquarters are established.[1] The other companies have been assigned to as many stockades between Nashville and Murfreesboro. The 102d in fact holds the entire road between the two places, with the aid of about two hundred cavalry, all under command of Col. Smith. The Colonel very facetiously observes that he has "an army almost equal to that of Rosecrans—my right rests near Murfreesboro and my left in the vicinity of Nashville."

Col. Smith is commander of the post, and Lt. Col. Mannon has been appointed Provost Marshal. They are doing a lively business in the way of receiving repentent [*sic*] rebels back into the old Union church. They come in daily, take the oath and give bonds for its faithful observance. An old gentleman who came in to-day, is a fair representative of thousands of Tennesseans. He was old and somewhat decripted [*sic*]—walking with a cane—wore a "bran new" pair of strong, home-made trousers, and the usual butternut suit throughout. The unlettered old man was slightly embarrassed in making his confession, but he made a clean breast of it. He spoke substantially as follows:

"We all have been told that we have to come in and take the oath, and I thought I'd come in to-day. I voted against 'secesh' the first time the question was voted upon in this State, although most all my neighbors were agin me, and some of them were very mad. When the question was voted on next time, I voted 'secesh.' *I had heard some stories about Lincoln,* and thought if he would not do right we would make him do right.—But I was too old to do anything more than vote."

The old man seemed sincerely repentant, and as he was poor, the Colonel permitted him to take the oath without exacting bonds. Here, amidst the ruins of the once beautiful village that was probably his trading point, he had ample opportunities of observing the effect of listening to the malignant and libelous "stories about Lincoln," with which the traitors duped the honest ignorant masses.—Tennessee has tasted the most bitter fruits of rebellion; and all that portion of the State within our lines is thoroughly humbled. I am not sure that the government will have as much difficulty hereafter with this State as with some half-civilized parts of the Northern States.

It seems very strange that, in the midst of unprecedented success; at a time when the destruction of the Confederacy is as fixed as fate; there should be men so fallen, in our own State as to oppose their feeble might against the power of the government. The almost rayless gloom through which we were passing last winter, was a slight pal[l]iation for murmuring at that time. But there can be only one interpretation of the motives of men who presist [*sic*] in their schemes of opposition to the authority of the Government in this hour of almost complete victory. *They are identified heart and soul with the rebellion; and with it they will sink.* The success of the Union arms has torn aside the mask, and they stand before the world convicted traitors. The soldiers feel very bitter toward these men, and have far less charity for them than they have for the deluded followers of Jeff. in the South.

Poor, miserable wretches! it were perhaps magnanimous to let the grave hide their errors, but we have thought that when the Lord in mercy to the rest of mankind, shall take them from earth, it would not be inappropriate to represent on their tombstones, a rebel flag trailed in the dust and a serpent sti[n]ging itself to death, with the inscription.

"Thus be it unto all the enemies of our country."

Perhaps I write too much in the spirit of vindicativeness [*sic*], yet I cannot go so far as to wish that the horrors of civil war may visit the rebellious communities of the North—the result of which could only be the annihilation of all such rebels. Could they but realize the terrible power of that Government which they have insulted and betrayed, as it has been felt here, they would be more tame in their demonstrations of opposition. Another phaze [*sic*] of this question is worthy of attention: How shall the seceded States be received, as members of the old Union, from which they have been nearly three years virtually separated?

There are those who would make the Confederacy a howling wilderness, and reduce the people to the condition of subjects under a provincial government. There are, it is to be hoped, but few of this class.

An opposite policy is more in harmony with our ideas of proper Republican rule.—Let the Old World now learn that, while we fight with most bitter vindictiveness, we settle our difficulties as brothers. Having given the insurgents a demonstration of its irresistable power, let the government exhibit toward them a degree of charity and mercy that will forever annihilate any desire for separation.

But I have dwelt at sufficient length on political topics.

Our New Camp[2]

I should have stated before, that the other regiments of our brigade went to Nashville at the same time we came to this place. Numerous log buildings were left here by those regiments. These buildings have been removed to the vicinity of the fort, and are occupied by the different companies. Tents are discarded. The log huts are about ten feet square, and are arranged in order, forming three streets. There are not less [than] fifty of these rude dwellings, and they are [an] improvement upon the sultry tent. It is [said], however, that we will not long enjoy the fruit [of] our labor, as it is rumored that we will soon [be] sent to Nashville.

We are encamped in the rear of the site where Lavergne was; on the crest of a hill which overlooks an immense valley formed by the confluence of Stone River and the Cumberland. The back ground is a range of bluffs, and fifteen or twenty miles distant. The undulating nature of the ground, comprised in the intermediate space, is well marked by the long swells and depressions in the forests with which it is covered. A beautiful picture is often presented in the early morning; a dense fog covering the low land, leaves here and there, little islands of timber, and away in the dim distance the bold bluffs apparently mark the other shore of the mythical lake.

It is said that under favorable circumstances, a range of the Cumberland mountains—fifty miles distant—may be seen from our fort.

The country in our immediate vicinity is rocky and cavernous. The forest has been cut down in every direction, and the numberless stumps of ruined buildings render the neighborhood of camp, rather uninviting in appearance.

Our Richland Grove friends will be pleased to learn that Co. C is comfortably quartered here, in a long row of log huts which they have with characteristic industry, rendered very pleasant and inviting abodes.

We are having a regular "Norther." My fingers are partially benumbed with cold—an overcoat would be very comfortable, but some rascal has stolen mine. I hear the Colonel enquiring this moment for one. I must go in search of a fire. Good bye, S. F. F.

(Rock Island *Weekly Union*, September 9, 1863, p. 1)

1. While the Army of the Cumberland was making its initial movements in the Chickamauga campaign, Ward's brigade (except the 102d), now part of the 3d Division of the Reserve Corps of Maj. Gen. Gordon Granger, was ordered to Nashville. Colonel Smith was ordered to post six companies of the 102d in several blockhouses along the railroad, and to proceed with the remainder of the regiment to Lavergne and establish his headquarters. When the regiment moved on August 19, Company A was posted to Stockade No. 3 on Mill Creek; Company B was at Smyrna; Company D at Stockade No. 1 on Mill Creek; Company F at Stockade No. 2 near Antioch, also on Mill Creek; Company H at Overall's Creek; and Company K at Stewart's Creek. Companies C, E, G, and I were at Lavergne. The 102d and a 200-man detachment of the 10th Ohio Cavalry were, consequently, responsible for the security of a thirty-mile stretch of track between Nashville and Murfreesboro. Fleharty, *Our Regiment*, 37.

2. Several portions of the text are interrupted by a tear in the paper. Those portions have been enclosed in brackets.

❧ No. 26 ❧

Lavergne (Tenn.) Sept. 29, '63.

The monotony of camp life at times becomes almost intolerable. Our daily duties degenerate into a dull routine. We have long hours to while away, and after the daily paper is read, and every correspondent has been delighted with a letter, the question frequently arises: in what new mode can we relieve the tedious hours? Such may be said to have been our situation when we were aroused from our life of lethargy by the arrival of friends from home. First came Capt. John A. Jordan, and two days later our esteemed friends, Messrs. John Rhodenbaugh and Major McMullen.[1]

All were loaded with a miscellaneous assortment of articles sent by friends at home to their appreciating friends and relatives in company C. The stock included were [*sic*] a quantity of sweetmeats,—the excellent quality of which was acknowledged by our mess, which naturally came in for a share of some good things prepared by Capt. Jordan's estimable lady.

Excursions and Observations.

The practiced pen of Capt. Jordan has doubtless ere this sketched the incidents attending our excursions through the country,—our visit to Signal Hill and Stone River Battle Ground, and if, in the brief observations following, I trespass upon the topics of his letters, he will, I am assured, magnanimously pardon the offense. Signal Hill is an unusual elevation about two miles from our camp, and nearly equi-distant between Nashville and Murfreesboro. On the summit of the hill a platform has been prepared, about thirty feet from the ground, amidst the branches of a large tree. From this observatory the view is sublimely beautiful. The locality of Nashville is well marked; the dome of the State House towers above the intervening hills; in the opposite direction the outlines of Murfreesboro are visible, and yet encircling both cities, far beyond them in the dim hazy distance, long ranges of forest-crowned hills and bold bluffs or mounds are visible. The vast scene, enclosing territory that must ever possess a deep historic interest, forms a picture that will live in the recollections of those who view it while memory lasts. After the occupation of Murfreesboro by our forces, Gen. Rosecrans established a signal post on this eminence, and also on a similar hill near Tri[u]ne. By means of these, information was flashed from Nashville to Murfreesboro, and *vice versa*, in telegraphic time.

Near the foot of Signal Hill resides an aged gentleman who served as soldier [*sic*] in the war of 1812, under Gen. Andrew Jackson. We were considerably interested in the opinions of the old man in regard to the war. One would suppose that a veteran of Old Hickory's army would be unconditionally loyal, and such he stoutly claimed to be, yet his loyalty, in common with that of citizens generally in this vicinity is, to say the least, questionable[.] A majority of those citizens who have remained at home have a very extensive *property interest* in the welfare of the Federal Government, which, during the occupation of the country by our forces, operates as a strong bond of Union. The old man expressed a high degree of respect for the Constitution and Washington's

Farewell Address, which latter document he allowed was a "powerful piece."

In connection with our ride to the Stone River Battle Ground, an unintentional joke was perpetrated at the expense of our friends, Capt. John A. Jordan and Mr. John Rhodenbaugh, which is considered worth recording. In addition to these gentlemen there were eight or ten others in the party, among whom may be named Lieut. Col. Mannon, Adjutant J. H. Snyder, Lieut. Byron Jordan, Orderly Sargeant [sic] G. W. Gregg and Isiah [sic] Rhodenbaugh, of company C,—forming a squad that might readily have been mistaken for a scouting party.[2] Our visiting friends were of course clad in unmistakeable citizens' clothes. As we approached Stewart's Creek we met a number of citizens, one of whom, looking significantly at Capt. J. and Mr. R. remarked to some one in the rear: "Aha! got a couple of *Bushwhackers* have you?" The supposed captives and captors richly enjoyed the mistake of the travelers.

At the battle-ground we busied ourselves for an hour or more gathering mementoes.—The heavy growth of weeds and the constant attendance of curiosity seekers, render the acquisition of such articles much more difficult than I found it three months ago.

Having satisfied our propensity for battle-field relics, we repaired to the house of a citizen and supplied the pressing wants of the inner man, by disposing of a rough but palatable dinner. The landlady evidently furnished her table with the best available articles, but the physiological character of the pork placed before us remains to this time a problem unexplained. The thin slices appeared to be lean on the part that we would term the outside, and fleshy on the opposite part. Whether, by some strange process, his porkship had, during his probationary career, suffered a violent reversal of the order of nature, by having the internal surface of its organization exposed to the outer world, we did not determine; but we did reach the conclusion that said porker must have been an anomaly in the animal creation.

This family was in the midst of very severe fighting during the battle— their premises being occupied alternately by Union and rebel soldiers. A young lady of the family was standing in the doorway at one time when a shell, with uncourteous familiarity, clipped off a number of shingles from the roof above her head.

But I must not occupy your space with details of our pleasant excursions and happy hours of reunion with old friends, which would be mainly a reproduction of scenes and experiences represented in previous letters. We deeply regret that our visiting friends must soon leave us.

The War News.

The events transpiring in the vicinity of Chattanooga have intensely interested all minds. We have seen numbers who were engaged in the great battle, and all concur in the declaration that it was one of the most desperate contests of the war. The battle of Stone river, terrible as it was, has been styled a skirmish in comparison with the bloody field of Chickamauga.³ The strength of the Confederacy was thrown against Rosecrans, with the intention of utterly annihilating his army, and nothing but unconquerable courage, endurance and generalship averted the calamity. But the whirlwind has spent its force, and the army of the Cumberland remains, with thinned but determined ranks, confronting the enemy. The friends at home may rest assured that the hour of danger is now past. The rebels will not immediately venture an attack upon the Union lines, and from personal knowledge, we are satisfied that Gen. Rosecrans is being rapidly placed in a condition to assume the offensive. It is thought the rebels will soon retreat to Atlanta. Twelve hundred prisoners, principally from Longstreet's corps, have been sent to Nashville. Our men acknowledge that this corps fought with the most determined bravery, but the result shows that their dash and daring was overmatched by the cool courage of the Western boys. The terrible punishment inflicted upon this flower of the rebel army adds new laurels to the army of the Cumberland.⁴

We mourn the loss of many noble patriots, but have felt most deeply pained to learn that Capt. Edgar Trego, of the 8th Kansas, is fallen.⁵ Capt. Trego was long known to the people of Mercer and Rock Island counties as an estimable citizen, in his sphere as such, and finally as a gallant and accomplished soldier, in the service of his country. He nobly fell while obeying the impulse of a generous nature—having been picked off by a sharp-shooter while caring for his wounded, after the heavy fighting was over.

S. F. F.

(Rock Island *Union*, October 14, 1863, p. 1)

1. John Rhodenbaugh, father of Pvt. Isaiah Rhodenbaugh, was a farmer living in Richland Grove Township. Rhodenbaugh and his wife, Polly, were the parents of nine children, including their youngest, a son born in 1859, and named Stephen A. Douglas Rhodenbaugh. McMullen (whose first name was Major) had enlisted in Company C of the 102d in August 1862 and had been discharged because of disability on January 14, 1863. 1860 manuscript census of Mercer County, Illinois [microfilm], 297; *Adj. Gen. Rep.,* V, 599.

2. Second Lt. Byron Jordan of Coal Valley, 1st Sgt. George W. Gregg of Berlin, and Pvt. Isaiah Rhodenbaugh of Richland Grove were all members of Company C.

3. Fleharty was correct that Chickamauga (fought September 19–20 in northwestern Georgia) was a bloodier affair than Stones River, at least in terms of total casualties. At Chickamauga the total Union loss was 16,170, and the Confederate loss was 18,454. At Stones River, the North lost 12,906 men and the South lost 11,739. But the loss in terms of the total number of men engaged was greater at Stones River. At Chickamauga, both sides lost about 28 percent of the number of soldiers who participated. At Stones River, however, the Union army lost 31 percent and the Confederate army about 34 percent. Boatner, *Civil War Dictionary*, 152, 808.

4. On September 8, 1863, largely in response to Bragg's continued pleas for reinforcements, two divisions of Longstreet's First Corps, Army of Northern Virginia, began boarding trains for transfer to the West. The Federal army had cut the most direct route, through east Tennessee, and Longstreet's men were forced to take the more circuitous southern route through the Carolinas, a distance of more than 700 miles. By the evening of September 12, the first of Longstreet's men had reached Atlanta. But of the eight infantry brigades transferred west, only four had arrived and deployed in time to see action at Chickamauga. Nevertheless, the transfer of nearly twelve thousand men over such a distance, using the lines of six different railroads, and all in less than a week, ranks as perhaps the greatest logistical feat of the war. For a full account of this difficult movement, see Robert C. Black III, *The Railroads of the Confederacy* (Chapel Hill, 1952), 184–91.

Longstreet's official report of the action claims that his left wing captured no fewer than 3,000 prisoners, 40 pieces of artillery, 10 regimental standards, and 393,000 rounds of small arms ammunition. *OR*, Vol. XXX, Pt. 2, p. 290.

5. Capt. Edgar Poe Trego was born April 1, 1838, in Bucks County, Pennsylvania, and was related to the various Tregos in Fleharty's company. Paul Raymond Kendall (1822–97), president of Lombard University in Galesburg, who had been so instrumental in recruiting the 102d, had also recruited men in and around Mercer County for the 8th Kansas. Lutz, *The Trago/Trego Family*, 22.

ᗛ No. 27 ᗕ

Lavergne, Tenn., Nov. 15th, 1863.

Last Monday Col. Smith received an order to march with his available mounted force to Lebanon. It was understood that General Paine would meet us there with a detachment from Gallatin. Parties from other points were to unite with us in an attempt to catch and shoot a number of bushwhackers, who have long been a terror to the loyal portion of Wilson county. According to an order recently issued these men are "not entitled to the privileges of prisoners of war, but shall be treated summarily as highway robbers and pirates."

The four companies of our regiment stationed here had just been furnished with the Spencer rifle—a seven-shooter, and one of the best species of fire-arms in the service.[1]—In addition to a Spencer rifle each man carries one of Colt's or Remington's revolvers. They were anxious to try their new weapons, but as the sequel will show only a few of them were permitted to try their range with a bushwhacker as a target.

We left camp at four o'clock in the evening, crossed Stone river at dark, and struck into the cedar brakes. Our guide was slightly intoxicated; a fact which had not been observed before we commenced our march.—However, he picked his way remarkably well, through the dense cedars, over ground so rough that we were obliged to march in single file.

"No one but a drunken man could find his way through this place," says our philosophical surgeon, who ventures a remark perchance once in two hours, and drives on over the rocks in his taciturn mood, as if half oblivious of all terrestrial affairs. At length we emerge into the Murfreesboro and Lebanon Pike and finally halt at the plantation of an old citizen, about ten miles from camp.

The old man was considerably alarmed by the unexpected arrival of the Yankees, and evidently supposed his entire stock of forage and provisions would be utterly consumed.—And the manner in which the boys invaded his graneries [sic] was not likely to remove this impression. The boys were hungry, and I am assured by one who viewed the scene that a few moments after our arrival, something less than a dozen chickens were, like so many tops, simultaneously spinning around in the front yard of a negro hut—minus their heads. Before leaving, however, a receipt for forage was given which was sufficiently liberal to cover all the losses sustained. With a friend from Co. C as bed-fellow, I slept comfortably on our blankets before the old man's fire.

The old gentleman kept a few negroes about him, and they were his sole companions. Everything about the premises was of a decidedly primitive style. Oddly colored dishes were placed on the table—such as were common twenty years ago. A triangular cup board stood in one corner of the main room. The culinary operations were carried on in a building near by. The biscuit[s] were baked in an old-fashioned skillet—a mode of baking which furnishes better biscuit[s] than can be baked in the modern style. Preparatory to placing the dishes upon the table, one of the colored women proceeded to wash them very carefully in a vessel which was placed upon the floor in the middle of the room. Notwithstanding the slovenly movements of the colored cooks, everything appeared neat at the breakfast table; and the hot biscuit, hard butter and fresh beef were highly relished by a limited number of the command—the majority of the detachment having been divided into squads, visited neighboring "plantations," and thus every man was furnished with a good breakfast.

A ride of seventeen miles over rocky country, and through the ever-present cedars brought us to Lebanon, the county seat of Wilson county, and the prettiest village I have seen in the South. There is still an unusual air of neatness about the place. Before the war broke out there were no less than four public institutions of learning in operation, viz: a college for gentlemen, a seminary for ladies, a law school, and a theological school.² The average number of students in attendance was estimated at five hundred. The Southern people speak of the village as the "Athens of America." There are many elegant private residences. The institutions of learning are having a long vacation, and in the meantime have been occupied as barracks alternatively by rebel and Federal soldiers. The citizens were not a little astonished by the sudden influx of troops, and were no doubt much annoyed by our visit, as we were out of rations, and were compelled for a time to depend upon them for subsistence.

The manner in which some of our soldiers compel weak and defenseless women to furnish them with food and lodging is a burning disgrace to the Federal arms. Although there are unprincipled soldiers in all regiments, it appears that there is a larger proportion of such characters in regiments from the Border Slave States than in those from the Free States. The citizens have an unbounded degree of hatred for the "homemade" Yankees as they are pleased to term the loyal Tennessee soldiers; and I must admit that some of them have a very ruffianly and lawless appearance. I have seen and conversed with numbers of East Tennesseans who were perfect gentlemen in every respect. I would not classify these with the above mentioned characters.

I was informed by ladies of the highest class that it is no unfrequent occurrence for soldiers to enter their premises, armed and equipped, and in the most profane language order them to prepare food and lodging.—"Give me the regular down-east Yank—from away down in Maine, rather than these Tennessee blue coats," said a Lebanon lady while in conversation on this subject.

The profession of a soldier is not inconsistent with the character of a gentleman, and I believe a majority of the Union soldiers are worthy representatives of a noble cause,—but there are some sad exceptions.

At Lebanon our command was divided—eighty men were sent out under four commissioned officers, to act in concert with other detachments in a scout up the Cumberland. The remainder of the command garrisoned the town during their absence. On the morning following the day of our arrival General Paine, with a small escort, rode into town and established his headquarters at an elegant private residence. Col. Smith continued in command of the Post.

In my next I will give some additional items concerning our short occupation of Lebanon; for the present I must close, as it is very nearly mail time. S. F. F.

(Rock Island *Union*, November 25, 1863, p. 2)

1. Col. Smith had procured 225 Spencer repeating rifles and an equal number of Colt navy revolvers for the four companies. The soldier equipped with a Spencer repeating rifle could fire seven .52-caliber rounds without reloading his weapon. The cartridges were fed into the breech from a tubular magazine that was inserted through the butt of the piece. The rifle weighed only ten pounds, was forty-seven inches long, and took the regulation triangular bayonet. The soldier could carry up to ten extra magazines with him in a special box, allowing him to fire up to seventy-seven rounds with great rapidity. The Spencer added considerable punch to the offensive and defensive capabilities of any unit fortunate enough to be armed with it. See Boatner, *Civil War Dictionary*, 782; Francis A. Lord, *Civil War Collector's Encyclopedia* (Harrisburg, Pa., 1965), 253; Harold L. Peterson, ed., *Encyclopedia of Firearms* (New York, 1964), 308.

2. The "college for gentlemen" was Cumberland University, founded in 1842 by the Cumberland Presbyterian Church. The "seminary for ladies" was the Abbe Female Institute, founded by Miss Harriet Abbe in the 1830s. In 1856, Alexander P. Stewart (who served as a lieutenant general in Johnston's army in 1864) was its principal. The "law school" and the "theological school" were both part of Cumberland University. James Victor Miller of Lebanon, Tennessee, to the authors, May 3, 1996.

ᴓ— No. 28 —ᴓ

Lavergne, Tenn., Nov. 15th, 1863.

At the close of my last letter I had referred to our arrival at Lebanon. I will now append some additional items.

Col. Smith established his headquarters in the Register's office at the Court House. The scene presented when the doors were thrown open was somewhat novel. The spiders had apparently, for a long time, held undisputed possession; and the office chairs were literally enveloped in a system of cobwebs. A venerable gentleman of a sun-dried appearance, furnished the keys of the room, and was very solicitous for the safety of the voluminous books of record in his keeping. He stated with a self-complacent smile that he had held the office of Register for eighteen years.[1] The vicinity of the Court House presented a scene of activity during our occupation, such as has not been witnessed in that locality for many long days. The butternuts poured in by dozens to get passes. Among others a man dressed in ordinary butternut clothes, came in, and, addressing the Colonel, requested a pass.

"Have you taken the oath," inquired the Colonel.

Citizen—"No sir, I have not."

Colonel—"Then we cannot give you a pass."

The man retired, but in a few moments returned and said:

"I am a slave man, Colonel, but my master has taken the oath."

We then, for the first time, observed that the man was faintly tinged with the contraband color. We had given passes to white men who were no whiter than him, and doubtless fully as ignorant of the duties and obligations assumed in taking the oath of allegiance. His master had taken the oath, however, and according to the military rule in such cases he was entitled to a pass.[2]

Gen. Paine and the Whiskey Seller.

We were permitted to hear one of General Paine's peculiarly scathing off-hand lectures, which have so often made offending citizens tremble in their boots when brought into his presence. A citizen who had been guilty of selling whiskey, was brought before him, when the following conversation took place:

General—"I understand you have been selling this infernal tangle-foot, which puts the d——l into the minds of peaceable citizens, and causes them to rob and murder their neighbors.["]

Culprit—I have been selling whiskey, General, but only to citizens. I have sold none to soldiers of either army.

General—It is just as bad to sell to citizens as the rebel soldiers,—for whiskey turns out more hell-born rebel soldiers than all other causes put together. Now I will tell you what you must do,—take a hatchet, go into your doggery, burst in the head of every whiskey barrel you have, and pour the infernal stuff upon the ground. Leave not a drop—not a spoonful about your premises! Perhaps you think I am not in earnest?

Culprit—I have no reason to think so, General.

General—I mean every word I say, and more: if I learn hereafter that you have been selling whiskey (and I will know it if you do) I will make a bonfire of your business house, and I will tie you up by the thumbs and feed you on bread and water for forty-eight hours. You will have cause then to remember me to the latest day of your life. I will dry up this infernal traffic even if I am compelled to resort to fire-brands and hempen ropes.

Culprit—(in a husky, choking voice, as he retired from the room) I will do as you have ordered, General.

And I do not doubt that he did.

Influence of Love in the Cause of Rebellion.

The tenacity with which many of the ladies cling to the hope of a Confederacy is really surprising. The young ladies are almost universally allied to the rebel cause,—allied too, by the closest possible ties—they have lovers in the Southern army. While conversing with a number of these fair rebels, one of our boys asked the question, whether they would, in the event of the final overthrow of the Confederacy, be content to live under the old government? "Oh! no! no! that can never, *never* be! The Confederacy cannot be overthrown until the last man is hilled up." ["]We will not admit of any such supposition as that!" exclaimed the defiant beauties with flashing eye and haughty mien. An elderly lady declared that "this war will never end until there is a Southern Confederacy." The feeling among the men is not so intensely Southern, or, if they have the same sentiments in their hearts, policy dictates silence on the subject.

A Straw Bed—Lebanon Hospitality, Etc.

My first night in Lebanon was passed in a bed of straw on the upper floor of a barn.—The following night I was more fortunate. Happening to meet with a citizen friend from the vicinity of Gallatin, he invited me to the house of an acquaintance (Dr. Harrington) whom I found to be a perfect gentleman. I cannot soon forget the hospitable manner in which we were entertained by the Doctor and his excellent lady. Whatever may have been the former sentiments of the Doctor he believes the cause of the rebellion hopeless. He expressed surprise at the wonderful resources of the Federal Government, and commented upon the great prosperity of the North, in comparison with the poverty, destitution and bankruptcy of the South. His son has but recently returned from the rebel army. He is a hearty robust boy, and must have been a hardy soldier.[3] He stated that he had been in the rebel service nearly two years. Was in Virginia—at the battle of Bull Run and in the seven days' fight before Richmond—was discharged from the service in consequence of being a minor—came home—remained sometime, and was pressed into the service again by conscript agents.[4]—About the time of the great battle of Chicka-mauga he availed himself of a favorable opportunity—came into our lines—surrendered himself—was paroled, and says he intends to do no more fighting in this war.

Dr. Harrington stated that Gen. John H. Morgan was almost idolized by the ladies of Lebanon. As the rebel chief rode through the streets they literally blocked his way in their efforts to express their unbounded admiration of his person and qualities. Many of them actually took out their scissors and clipped portions of the mane from the neck of a beautiful mare that he rode—intending to preserve the locks of horse hair as mementoes of their beloved General.

While in Lebanon we looked upon the dead bodies of two bushwhackers. They had been captured and shot by the 4th Middle Tennessee Cavalry.[5] It is said that the guerrillas killed four of these Tennessee cavalry boys after capturing them, and these were but two of forty bushwhackers who should be caught and shot ere the account would be balanced.

On the third day of our "occupation" the scouting parties came in. The general result of the combined scout may be summed up in a few words—about twelve bushwhackers were shot, and twenty armed rebels captured and taken to Gallatin.

At noon of the same day we set out for our camp at Lavergne, which we reached at eight in the evening—not a little tired you may rest assured, as the road to camp was the most rocky of any I have ever traveled in Dixie. We approached camp by what was called a "near cut," through cedars so dense that it seemed we had plunged into a mid[-]summer forest.

It appears that our "raid" into Wilson county has had a salutary effect upon the inhabitants of that section, as the citizens of said county are coming in daily to swear allegiance to the Government of their fathers. Twenty-five came in and took the oath to-day.

S. F. F.

(Rock Island *Union*, December 2, 1863, p. 1)

1. Allen W. Vick was register of Wilson County from 1846 to 1876.

2. The administration of loyalty oaths in Tennessee under Rosecrans and Gov. Andrew Johnson was especially severe. Special commissioners were appointed to the Army of the Cumberland to administer the oath to civilians in occupied areas. Any person refusing to take the oath risked imprisonment. Even those who had remained loyal to the Union were not exempt from the requirement. This latter class particularly objected to being required to subscribe to the same oath as those sympathizing with the Confederacy. General Rosecrans also required aliens residing within his jurisdiction to take the oath. Those refusing were made to post a $5,000 bond to guarantee good behavior. Failure to comply led to expulsion from the Union lines. When foreign diplomats complained of the severity of these measures, the Lincoln administration intervened on behalf of the aliens, mitigating somewhat the harshness of Rosecrans' requirements. See Harold M. Hyman, *Era of the Oath: Northern Loyalty Tests During the Civil War and Reconstruction* (Philadelphia, 1954), 39–40.

3. There was no physician named Harrington in Wilson County at this time. However, there was a grocer living in Lebanon named Thomas (or Truman) Harrington. This man had a son named Alpheus (who was eighteen years old in 1861) who had been a member of the 7th Tennessee Infantry of the Army of Northern Virginia. James Victor Miller of Lebanon, Tennessee, to the authors, May 3, 1996.

4. At the time Fleharty wrote this letter, the Confederacy had operated under two conscription laws. The first went into effect April 16, 1862. It allowed the drafting of all white males between eighteen and thirty-five for a period of three years or the duration of the war. The long list of exempted occupations, however, soon stirred up a great deal of controversy. Particularly offensive to poorer southerners was the clause that exempted one white male for every plantation with twenty or more slaves. This was generally, if incorrectly, interpreted to be a way for the slaveholding class to escape the draft. Equally objectionable was the provision allowing a man to hire a substitute to meet his service obligation. Once again the poorer southerner saw what appeared to be favoritism toward the upper classes. The second conscription law (effective September 27, 1862) attempted to solve some of the problems of the first, with little success. Under its terms all white males between eighteen and forty-five were eligible for service, the hated substitution clause remained, and the list of exemptions actually grew. Resistance to the draft, especially in eastern Tennessee, North Carolina, Alabama, and Mississippi, intensified as the war progressed. See Jennifer Lund, "Conscription," in Richard N. Current, ed., *Encyclopedia of the Confederacy* (New York, 1993), I, 396–99.

5. Fleharty is mistaken in his identification of the Tennessee cavalry regiment, there being no such unit as the 4th Middle Tennessee Cavalry. The unit was most likely the 5th Tennessee Cavalry (also known as the 1st Middle Tennessee). Until November 1863 it formed part of the 3d Brigade, 2d Division, Cavalry Corps, Department of the Cumberland. Dyer, *Compendium of the War of the Rebellion*, 1638–39.

๑— No. 29 —๑

Lavergne, Tenn., Dec. 22, '63.

Our camp has been the scene of intense excitement to-day in consequence of a desperate encounter between two of our officers and a band of guerrillas last night. I will give you the particulars of the adventure as narrated to me by one of the actors in the deadly affray—Capt. Wm. K. [*sic*] Wilson of Aledo, Mercer county, Ills. His companion in arms was Dr. T. S. Stanway, Assistant Surgeon of our regiment—formerly of New Boston, Mercer county.[1] Those who are acquainted with these gentlemen will readily conclude that they are not the men to surrender without resistence [*sic*], even when attacked by overwhelming numbers.

The Captain and the Doctor had been visiting a stockade, at which Co. D of this regiment is stationed, about ten miles from this place.[2] About dusk they set out for camp. It was a bright moonlight night, and the adventurers anticipated a pleasant ride,—little apprehending that more than a score of villains were lying in wait to capture or kill them. When about six miles from camp, as they were riding leisurly [*sic*] along, under the shade of dense cedars that line the pike, and engaged in a somewhat animated conversation, they found themselves confronted by four men on horseback, who presented revolvers to their heads with the words:

"Surrender—you are our prisoners."

Quick as lightning the Doctor had whipped out his pistol, and his first shot was fired simultaneously with their first volley. Unluckily Capt. Wilson's pistols were buckled in the holsters in such a way that valuable time was lost in getting them out. The combattants [*sic*] were so close together that their horsesheads almost touched each other when the affray commenced. At the Doctor[']s first fire one of the scoundrels threw up his arms and exclaimed, "I'm hit," and retired from the arena. Meanwhile the bullets of the guerrillas whistled about the heads of our brave officers. One clipped the handsome whiskers of the Captain—another grazed his temple. Others of the guerrilla party who had been stationed at the sides of the road, and where they had passed, now closed in upon them. The Doctor continued to blaze away at the villains, and the Captain was now "letting fly" at them in good earnest, when a most desperate hand to hand conflict took place. One of the gurrillas [*sic*] and the Doctor engaged each other at arms length. The Reb leveled his revolver in the Doctor[']s face, and the Doctor struck down the pistol with his own, an instant before it was discharged, the ball however, entered his right leg and shattered it above the knee. Still he endeavored to escape, but the wound was too severe. He felt that he was falling and steadied himself to the ground. He was riding a favorite mare and, with remarkable presence of mind balanced himself an instance upon his wounded leg, and with the other gave the animal a desperate "dig" in the side to induce her to escape.

Seeing the Doctor fall, and knowing it would be madness to contend alone with a dozen men, the Captain—being mounted upon a very fleet animal— dashed away down the pike, the balls of the enemy whistling about his ears every instant. The Doctor's mare followed after and was not captured. For at least two miles the desperate race continued, and for a time the guerrillas,— riding on a parallel line at the side of the road—were but a rod or two distant. The Captain fired repeatedly at his pursuers as his noble steed flew along the pike. At length he began to gain upon them very perceptibly, when a shot struck his horse in the thigh inflicting a severe flesh wound—still, for a time he increased the distance that separated him from his pursuers, and was so far ahead that he could not see them, when the animal, faltering and staggering, it became apparent that he could ride no further. Dismounting, he hurriedly relieved the saddle, and taking his brace of pistols plunged into the thick cedars. A peaceable citizen whom he met the moment his horse failed, went with him into the cedars, and seemed equally desirous of avoiding the guerril- las. It is probable that he had money in his possession, and feared being robbed. They proceeded some distance and halted. The rebs followed, carefully searching the cedars in their immediate vicinity—then retired—all was still— they ventured to change their position—again the rebs approached—they lay low and "breathe light," as the Captain expressed it. Nearer they come, and circle around them,—cursing their luck in losing their game. The Captain had given his companion one of his pistols, as he said be determined to "sell out" as dearly as possible if discovered. Again their retiring footsteps are heard. After waiting a long time the Captain and his companion again changed their position. Once more the scoundrels are heard approaching. They search long and carefully in their immediate vicinity, but finally retire, and their horses hoofs are soon heard upon the pike, as they gallop away.

Then the Captain realized that he was safe, and endeavored to reach a stockade about two miles distant; but he had become bewildered among the cedars, and after proceeding a short distance and finding himself utterly lost, abandoned the attempt, and remained in the woods until morning, when he came into camp.

Our poor friend, Dr. Stanway, did not fare so well. The guerrillas robbed him of everything valuable. Fortunately he had but little money with him. On leaving camp in the morning he handed his pocket book to Lieut. Col. Mannon, with the remark that he "did not want the confounded bushwhackers to get his money if they should get him."

They took from him his overcoat, dress-coat, watch and vest—told him he ought to be shot for being so fool-hardy as to contend against so many, and left him lying helpless in the road.

Citizens living near heard the firing and repaired to the place to ascertain the cause. The Doctor was taken to a neighboring house where he yet remains—his wound being so severe that he cannot be removed. He is a universal favorite with the regiment, and the boys "breathe not loud but deep" vows of vengeance against those who have injured him.

You can bet your life, Mr. Editor, that they will "make the fur fly" if they ever get them within range of their Spencer rifles.

It may seem strange, but it is nevertheless true, that we learned nothing of the affair until the following morning. If we were among friends such information would not be long withheld, but we are among citizens who have "taken the oath," but feel in their hearts that they owe nominal allegiance to the Government. There are a few exceptions—a few genuine, noble-hearted Union men, but in our humble opinion four-fifths of all who have sworn allegiance acknowledge permanent allegiance to the rebel Government.

It is hoped that it will not be necessary to amputate Dr. Stanway's wounded limb, but we fear it will be a long time before he recovers. S. F. F.
(Rock Island *Union,* December 30, 1863, p. 2)

1. Capt. William A. Wilson joined the regiment in September 1862 as first lieutenant of Company K. He was promoted captain in March 1863 and resigned his commission on October 20, 1864. First Assistant Surgeon Thomas S. Stanway joined in December 1862 as Second Assistant Surgeon. He was promoted in July 1863 and resigned August 13, 1864. *Adj. Gen. Rep.,* V, 593, 610–11.

2. Company D had been posted to a stockade on Mill Creek about ten miles from Lavergne. Fleharty, *Our Regiment,* 37, 42.

✑ No. 30 ✑

Lavergne, Tenn., Feb. 6, 1864.

Yesterday was a glorious day. The sky was almost cloudless; the rays of the sun were tempered by a refreshing breeze, otherwise the heat would have been immoderate. It was a propitious day for a ride into the country, and we improved it by visiting the "Hermitage." The party consisted of fifteen persons, including Lieut. Col. Mannon, and his excellent lady.

The "Hermitage" is twelve miles east of Nashville, on the Lebanon pike. Our visit was necessarily short, "as the exigencies of the service" required that we should return to camp the same day.

A ride of four hours brought us to the far-famed earthly home, and final resting-place of Andrew Jackson—yet we failed to discover its locality until we had passed three-fourths of a mile beyond the place. We had inquired of every white man and every negro that we met for some time before reaching the vicinity of the Hermitage. Some directed us in one way, some in another, and all seemed lamentably ignorant of its whereabouts. The Hermitage Mansion is about one eighth of a mile from the pike. It is a stately and tastefully finished structure, and has a somewhat venerable appearance. The building is approached through a long arch of deep green cedars, and near it interspersed with the cedars, are a number of beautiful pines.

We were met by Andrew Jackson, Jr.[1]—the adopted son of the General. He was calling his hounds, I suppose to have a fox hunt, but relinquished his purpose, and very kindly inviting us into the mansion, exhibited to us a variety of relics of Old Hickory. Among other things was a hickory vase, about the size of an ordinary water pitcher, and having a handle that was formed by a small limb which grew out of the tree, and into it again, not more than four inches above the place where it sprouted. A silver tablet on one side of the vase bore this inscription:

"A sprout shooting from a hickory stump whose trunk was severed during the Revolutionary war—on Long Island—disclosed to Wm. W. Lyon, 1824, by whom it is presented, wrought into a vase (as a fit emblem) to the man who fills the measure of his Country's Glory."

The furniture of the building is principally the same that was used by its former illustrious owner. Two fine paintings upon the walls represent him respectively in his prime, and in his old age. Busts of different members of his cabinet are in the hall, and near the entrance is a venerable arm-chair, which we were assured was once the office-chair of Geo. Washington. It was covered with cloth—except the elbows of the arms—the object being, I suppose, to protect it from the ravages of time and the vandalism of curiosity-seeking visitors.[2]

The tomb is in a garden adjoining the mansion. The ground was laid off by the General, with the aid of his artist friend, R. E. W. Earl, and is enclosed by a rude fence, made of pickets driven into the ground. The tomb, also, was constructed under the superintendence of the General and the artist. It is an unassuming structure, and is almost hidden by surrounding trees.[3]

The brave old hero of New Orleans rests by the side of his beloved wife, and a plain slab covering the vault, bears this inscription:

GENERAL
ANDREW JACKSON,
BORN MARCH 18TH, 1767,
DIED JUNE 8TH, 1845.

The slab which marks the resting place of his wife has a more lengthy inscription, portraying her many virtues. Beautiful magnolias (as green now as in summer), weeping willows, all planted by the General's own hand, grow near the tomb.

A short distance from the tomb is a small monument bearing this testimonial of friendship:

In Memory of
R. E. W. EARL, Artist,
Friend and Companion of
Gen. Andrew Jackson—
Who died at the Hermitage, the 16th of
Sept. 1837.

It is exceedingly difficult to secure suitable mementoes of the place. However, we succeeded in obtaining hickory canes from a venerable darkey, who cuts and trims them roughly, and keeps a supply of them constantly on hand for visitors. The old man evidently realizes quite a large income from this service as visitors generally pay him liberally for the rough hickory sticks which they carry away as mementoes of Old Hickory.

The old negro is 75 years of age, and his wife is 80. They revere the name of "Old Massa," as they call General Jackson. His picture—half obliterated by the ravages of time—hangs on the wall of their hut, and beneath it is another—calm, resolute face, bearing the impress of indomitable determination—the portrait of Abraham Lincoln.

"That is Old Massa Linkum," said the old woman; "he seems to be doing *great things*, but some says *not*, yet I likes him mighty well."

"Do you like the master you have now as well as you liked old Master Jackson," asked one of the party.

"Ah! Lor' bress your soul," replied the old woman, "it[']s mighty hard to find a better 'Massa' than 'Old Massa' was; and our Massa what we has now don't think the blacks is free, either."

Thereupon the old man straightened himself up and declared:

"As for dis chile, I'se g'wine to stay where I is de balance ob my days. Dese niggahs what's runnin' away from der Massas had better stay at home."

The old woman did not argue the case but her remarks showed plainly that her mind was imbued with that vague desire which impels these poor creatures to leave their comfortable [*sic*] homes in pursuit of a phantom—for the negro's dream of liberty will never be realized in this country.

There has apparently been no innovating improvements or changes on any part of the premises since the General died—The small gates—one on each side of the main entrance—have a time worn appearance—indeed, seem gradually crumbling to dust. It would be sacreligious [*sic*] to replace them by new ones.

After passing a pleasant hour at the Hermitage we mounted and set out for camp.

About sunset the party halted for supper. With three others I called upon 'Squire Bender, who claims to be a "good Union man," and asked for supper, when something like the following conversation ensued:

Squire B.—"You call at a very poor place for supper. I have nothing to eat. I feed [*sic*] the soldiers whenever they called, as long as I could stand it but 'self-preservation is the first law of nature.' I must look out for myself now."

Hungry Soldier—"But we intend to pay for our suppers."

S. B.—"I never took pay from a soldier in my life, and never will." (Straitening [*sic*] himself up, with offended dignity.)

H. S.—"If you would take money of them—which they would, in most cases, gladly give—you would be able to feed them without loss to yourself."

S. B.—"That is not my way of doing; if I can't feed them for nothing, I will not feed them at all."

H. S.—"This then is a specimen of your hospitality—you would starve men because you cannot feed them gratuitously—'I can't see it.'"

The squire is an old man, and we did not like to be harsh with him, therefore we mounted and proceeded on our way hungering. To enable the reader to realize the destitute condition of the old squire, I will state that he has at least one thousand bushels of excellent husked corn in his granary.

At the next house I secured a supper of coffee, warm bread, pork, and molasses—for 50 cents.

An hour after dark we reached camp—having rode at least thirty-two miles. Mrs. Col. Mannon seemed less fatigued than some others of the party at the close of the ride.[4] When within a mile or two of camp she led off in a gallop, apparently as unconscious of fatigue as when we started in the morning. The ride, though fatiguing, was a pleasant one, and will be long remembered as an agreeable episode in the history of our sojourn in Tennessee. S. F. F.

(Rock Island *Union*, February 17, 1864, p. 1)

1. Andrew Jackson Jr. (1808 or 1809–65) was the son of Mrs. Jackson's brother, Severn Donelson, and his wife Elizabeth. He was one of twin brothers, who, because of his mother's frail health, was adopted by the Jacksons and renamed. The young man proved to be a spendthrift whose wasteful ways caused a number of financial problems for the president that remained unresolved at the time of his death in 1845. Early in the war, Jackson had commanded a battery of Tennessee heavy artillery. See Robert V. Remini, *Andrew Jackson and the Course of American Empire, 1767–1821* (New York, 1977), 161; and *Andrew Jackson and the Course of American Freedom, 1822–1832* (New York, 1981), 3 and 395, note 6, for more on the relationship of the two.

2. When President Jackson died in 1845 the Hermitage continued to be occupied by Andrew Jr., his wife Sarah York Jackson, and their children. In 1856 Jackson sold the five-hundred-acre Hermitage Farm to the state of Tennessee for $48,000 and moved away with his family. Four years later, however, the governor of Tennessee persuaded the Jacksons to return to care for the property until a final disposition could be made. The Hermitage was offered to the federal government for use as a branch of the U.S. Military Academy, but the Civil War intervened before anything came of this proposal. The Jacksons remained at the Hermitage throughout the war. To protect the famous property from ruin at the hands of scavengers and sightseers, Gen. George H. Thomas ordered a guard posted there. After Andrew Jackson Jr.'s death in 1865, his widow was allowed by the state to live at the Hermitage for the remainder of her life; she died in 1888. See Mary C. Dorris, comp., *The Hermitage: Home*

of General Andrew Jackson, Seventh President of the United States (Rev. ed.; Hermitage, Tenn., 1957), 19–20.

3. Ralph E. W. Earle (sometimes sp. "Earl") was born in England about 1785 while his father was there studying art. The younger Earle studied in London and Paris before returning to the United States. In 1817 he arrived at the Hermitage to do Jackson's portrait. In a short time the young artist married Mrs. Jackson's niece and moved into the mansion. Until his death, Earle remained close to the president, becoming one of his warmest friends (he referred to himself as "the King's Painter"), and a traveling companion. He accompanied Jackson to Washington in 1829 and returned to the Hermitage at the close of the president's second term. See Robert V. Remini, *Andrew Jackson and the Course of American Democracy, 1833–1845* (New York, 1984), 448–49, for a brief discussion of the relationship between Earle and Jackson.

4. Sarah J. Moore was married to Lieutenant Colonel Mannon in 1859, sixteen months after the death of his first wife, Rebecca. Aledo *Democrat*, May 28, 1901, p. 1.

CHAPTER 7

"Wretched Mismanagement at Camp Butler"

ᴗ No. 31 ᴗ

Camp Butler, Ill.,
Feb. 20th, 1864.

On the 12th instant, an order was received at regimental headquarters, detailing a commissioned officer and four enlisted men (including the undersigned), for the purpose of proceeding to Illinois to take charge of recruits for the regiment. It was supposed we would be permitted to pass a few weeks at home recruiting. But this anticipation will not be realized. Friends of the regiment who entrusted articles of value with us, will please be patient, as we will probably be enabled to make a flying visit there in a few days. But more of this anon.

I will not detail incidents of our humorous ride, but will indulge in a few generalities. The weather, when we left Lavergne, on the 13th, was as glorious as summer. We could not realize that we would soon be plunged into the midst of winter, but such was our fate, for when we left the cars at Indianapolis, the bitter cold blast made us shiver in every limb, and, for my part, I could hardly breathe the icy atmosphere—my lungs seemed suddenly collapsed, and as the result of the transition from summer to winter, I have a severe cold. The burden of our songs have been, "Oh, take me back to Tennessee," and, "I wish I was in Dixie." Really, I have been in a measure alienated from my native State—though not from her people. Men who are of the type of the sturdy oak may live in Illinois, but feebler constitutions will find a climate like that of Tennessee more conducive to health and long life. It has been said that the rugged climate of our State, toughens men; and in support of the proposition, examples are given, wherein the hardy Westerner becomes inured to every exposure, and seems endowed with a constitution of iron. But it occurs to me that these men are the favored few, who have been provided by nature with strong powers of physical endurance. However, this is somewhat foreign to my subject, and I will resume the general thread of my sketch.

The number of soldiers returning home was unusually large. At every ticket-office, eating-house, or hotel, the crowds blocked all progress. At Cave City, Ky., when the train stopped, it was announced that we should be allowed twenty minutes for dinner, and there was a universal rush from the cars into the depot hotel. In a moment we found ourselves at a dead-lock in the midst of the throng, which was crowding their way to the dinner-table. We could not go backwards; we could not go forwards! "I don't want any dinner," exclaims a slim-looking gentleman with straps; "Let me out; let me out," cries a portly gentleman; "if I get any dinner, I can't keep it down!" But there was no alternative. The crowd slowly commenced moving forward, carrying the lean man, and the portly gentleman into the dining-hall.

At Jeffersonville, Indiana, the crowd was even more annoying, and the train was filled before half of the soldiers could procure tickets. The guard, at the entrance to the depot, would admit none without tickets, and we experienced the pleasure of watching the train glide out of the depot—leaving us to wait a more favorable opportunity; that opportunity occurred twenty hours after-wards. At Lafayette, Indiana, we endured a still greater pressure. We reached this place about 2 a. m., Feb. 16th—beds at the hotel all full. With about thirty others, I enjoyed the luxury of siting [*sic*] around the bar-room stove until daylight. Ate a good breakfast, and repaired to the depot about ten o'clock in the morning—train delayed. Depot building filled to overflowing with soldiers—many of them drunk; nearly all hilarious. And thus for two mortal hours, amid unparalleled cursing, swearing, and drinking, we awaited the train. It came at length; there was a wild shriek, a terrible rush, and the cars were almost instantly filled. Happily, we secured seats; the train rolled away, and ere long we were sweeping over the bleak prairies of Illinois.

At Springfield, Ill., the pressure was less heavy. We secured good lodging, and, for the first time, after leaving Lavergne, enjoyed a night's sound sleep.

Soon after reaching Springfield, we learned that any further advance home-ward must be indefinitely postponed. Our commanding officer, Capt. Ed. H. Conger, of Galesburg, Ill., has been placed in command of Barracks No. 4, Camp Butler.[1]

We have been in camp now two days, but those days have been weeks to us. For the lovely climate of Tennessee, we have, in exchange, bitter cold winter. Instead of our pleasant little log houses, with their cheerful fire places in Lavergne, we have board barracks, indifferently heated with coal stoves.

We had always supposed Camp Butler a model military camp, but it is the reverse.[2]—There has been criminal mismanagement somewhere. Near the capital of our State, and almost under the eye of our Governor, many soldiers are suffering—and I believe many are dying—from exposure and inattention.

The hospitals are filled with sick, and men may be found in the barracks dangerously ill; having but one or two blankets between their bodies and their hard board bunks; and with equally insufficient covering. Add to this the ceaseless uproar in a room containing over a hundred raw recruits, and you will realize, in a measure, what many poor fellows have suffered at Camp Butler. The proper authorities may be able to show exterminating [sic][3] circumstances, but the stern fact is undeniable,—there has been and still is, wretched mismanagement at Camp Butler. Our individual experience has been similar to that of all others who have been so unfortunate as to sojourn here. We have as yet failed to secure straw for our bunks, and all the sharp angles of our physical structure have been well worn by the rough boards upon which we have slept. We expect, however, to obtain straw this evening, and in that case, will have a glorious sleep to-night. You cannot censure us I know, if, as we sleep, we dream of the Sunny South, and the pleasant times we were having at Lavergne. The military authorities may have supposed that we would like to soldier awhile at Camp Butler for the privilege of going home a few days, but we can assure them that it is *no accommodation to us.* However, we enlisted "for better or worse," and will not falter in the discharge of the duties assigned us.

Yet we have not been utterly miserable, for we have met old friends— veterans of various regiments who have won for themselves unfading laurels, and are going in again.

Recruits and veterans are constantly coming in, and the mustering and disbursing officers have heavy work on their hands.

The scene on the beautiful drill-ground, revives our first experience at Knoxville. The old familiar command is heard—"left!" "left!" "left!"—as the recruits are initiated into the first principles of soldiering.

Many of the recruits are mere boys. Yet experience has proven that the majority of them will make good soldiers. There are many lads now in the field bravely bearing the hardships of war, and winning the honors which full grown men have not the manhood to seek. I met a bright little fellow on the cars, who had been in the service nearly two years, and was then but 18 years of age. He had just re-enlisted. His first service had been in the navy. He re-enlisted in a cavalry regiment. There were about a dozen boy-recruits with him. If they abstain from the vices of camp, they will make for themselves a glorious record.

Providence and the Post Commander permitting I will, ere long, pass a few days at home, and if there are any who wish to enter the service, in one of the best regiments in the field, I will be happy to have them return with me.[4] The 102d is being mounted as fast as horses can be obtained. Five companies, and part of the sixth, are already mounted and equipped, and are armed with the Spencer rifle—the best rifle in the service.[5] In addition to the rifle they have Colt's army pistol, and in an engagement every man can fire 13 times before re-loading.

Col. Smith, our commander, is using every means in his power to insure the effectiveness of his regiment, and persons joining his command can depend upon having an able leader. I could with propriety extend these laudatory remarks, first, because every word I have written is true, and secondly, because we are not permitted to keep a representative at home in the recruiting service, but the length of this letter warns me that I must close. S.F.F.
(Rock Island *Union*, March 2, 1864, p. 1)

1. Capt. Edwin H. Conger (1843–1907) of Galesburg had perhaps the most distinguished postwar career of any member of the 102d. After graduating from Lombard University in Galesburg in 1862, he joined the 102d as 1st lieutenant of Company I. In 1863 he was promoted captain, and he held that rank at the war's end. After the war he studied law and moved to Iowa, where he held county office before being twice elected state treasurer. He was a member of Congress from 1885 to 1890, when he resigned to accept an appointment as U.S. minister to Brazil. He served there for three years, until a change in administrations at home resulted in his replacement. In 1897, President McKinley reappointed him to Brazil. Less than a year later Conger was transferred to China, where he represented the United States during the trying days of the Boxer Rebellion. After serving for a short time as minister to Mexico, he retired from public life in 1905. See *Dictionary of American Biography*, IV, 344–45.

2. Camp Butler was established in August 1861 on Clear Lake, about six miles east of Springfield. By December of that year, the War Department had ordered that all temporary rendezvous camps in the state be abandoned; Camps Butler and Douglas (in Chicago) would

henceforth serve as the general rendezvous for Illinois. Camp Butler continued to process the muster-in and muster-out of Illinois regiments throughout the war. With the arrival, in February 1862, of Confederate prisoners captured at Fort Donelson, Camp Butler began to function as a prison camp as well. See Helen Edith Sheppley, "Camp Butler in the Civil War Days," *Journal of the Illinois State Historical Society* XXV (January 1933), 285–317.

3. The text at this point should undoubtedly read "extenuating."

4. Lt. Col. George R. Clarke of the 113th Illinois Infantry was commandant of Camp Butler at this time.

5. In October 1863 the 102d began to "press horses from the disloyal for the purpose of mounting themselves." By the end of November, four companies (C, E, G, and I) were mounted and armed with Spencer rifles. But the mounting and arming of infantry regiments, such as the 102d, with repeating rifles had taken some months to accomplish.

Raids by John Morgan and local guerrilla outfits on his lines of supply and communication led General Rosecrans to diligently seek the addition of mounted units to the Army of the Cumberland. Early in 1863 he sent Gen. Lovell H. Rousseau, a Kentucky Unionist and one of his division commanders, to Washington to seek permission to mount some of his infantry units. Rousseau met with Lincoln and argued that raiders such as Morgan could be dealt with most effectively by mounted infantry armed with breech-loading, repeating rifles. Lincoln was convinced and supported the idea. By mid-April the Ordnance Department notified Rosecrans that two thousand Spencers would be shipped to him within a few months.

Undoubtedly the most notable and distinguished mounted infantry unit of the war was Col. John T. Wilder's "Lightning Brigade" in the Army of the Cumberland. This famous unit consisted of the 17th and 72d Indiana, and the 92d, 98th, and 123d Illinois Infantry regiments. See *History of Mercer County,* 395–96; Robert V. Bruce, *Lincoln and the Tools of War* (Indianapolis, 1956), 253–56.

◦— No. 32 —◦

Camp Butler, Ill., March 11th, '64.

What I write in this communication is intended mainly for the perusal of the *boys* I left behind me in Tennessee. If others find anything herein to interest them, I assure them they are at liberty to read. My comrades in the "102d," who have been on a long and weary march since I left them, may wish to know something of passing events at home, and I will give them the benefit of a few notes taken during a visit of ten days in the counties where our regiment was raised.

Taking the evening train for Springfield on the 24th ultimo, with glad hearts we bade adieu to Camp Butler. In the morning, when the sun peered above the horizon, our train was dashing along over the beautiful prairie land near Macomb. The rays of the sun glistened over a frosty plain; the air was crisp and cutting, yet that prairie scene was a beautiful picture, and we thought the brilliant morning an auspicious beginning of our ten days at home.

Galesburg.

The sun had mounted but a few degrees in the heavens when we caught sight of the spires and minarets that marked the locality of the College city. Old Lombard loomed up grandly on the right, and classic Knox was visible on the left.[1] We felt that we were at home, and a few minutes later received a joyous welcome beneath the paternal roof.

Time seems to make but few changes in the appearance of Galesburg. The only public building erected since we were last there, is the Universalist Church, which is by far the most beautiful church edifice in town. A number of very good private residences are in process of erection, but the city has grown very slowly since the war broke out.

In passing through the streets we were frequently reminded of a remark made years ago, by a friend on visiting the place for the first time. Said he: "In geographical parlance Galesburg is remarkable for two things,—its many beautiful girls and its numerous niggers."[2]

The superior educational advantages of the place have populated it with bevies of young ladies from all parts of the State, and they are almost universally pretty.—[W]e were told that a soldier possessed superior advantages in cultivating the good will of the fair ones of Galesburg; and friends in Dixie will readily apprehend that we felt ourselves completely at the mercy of bright eyes and bewitching curls, and we attribute our escape from immolation upon the altar of matrimony to the fact that no one of the fair damsels had the audacity to propose[.]

We like Galesburg. Its citizens have received a high standard as an educated community, and to live in its precincts is to become imbued with a more refined appreciation of the beautiful in art and nature.

Pond Creek Station.[3]

After passing three days in Galesburg we boarded the morning train on the C., B. & Q. R. R. for Rock Island. Reached Wyanet (near the junction of the above named road with the Chicago and Rock Island road) about 11 o'clock, a. m.[4]—Proceeded thence to the above mentioned station, which we only mention in this connection to announce that it is the most lonely place to wait for a train, that has ever been found by the most unfortunate traveler. We remained there three hours and if all the hours of our furlough had been as long as these, our ten days would have been lengthened to twenty. But the train came at last and we were soon landed in

Rock Island.

We were but slightly acquainted in the city, and on the streets looked in vain for a familiar face. Ere we left, however, we found one or two old-time friends and also made the acquaintance of a portly, good-natured, elderly gentleman who is widely known in the literary world, as the presiding genius of the Rock Island UNION. May his extensive shadow never grow less.

We confidently anticipate a brilliant future for the city of Rock Island. Fast as the city has grown—and although some may imagine that it has almost attained its full growth—we predict that twenty-five years hence the city would not be recognized in the daguerreotype that may fairly represent it now. The life of Rock Island is derived from the great natural and artificial arteries which connect it with the commercial world, and while the immense piles of brick and mortar of which it is built, have not the neat and cleanly appearance that makes some of our prairie, wooden-built towns so beautiful, we knew that the soot which settles down from immense smoke pipes, and the dust that is whirled up from the thronged streets are an index to the strong, healthy business life which makes the city what it is.

The cities of Rock Island, Moline and Davenport, as a common center of business in the Northwest, are one in their interests and destiny. The delightful locality in which these cities are situated, derives something of a romantic interest from the associations that cluster around the early history of that section. As the scene of stirring events in connection with the Black Hawk war, and pioneer life in the west, it will furnish many graphic pages in history and romance.—The scenery is such as would enchant the eye of a poet, and the great natural advantages of the locality for business operations cause the tradesman, the artisan, and the manufacturer, who seek a new theatre of action, to halt, ponder and finally invest their capital.

While at Rock Island we visited the island of that name, opposite the city.—Our object was to visit prisoners whose relatives in Tennessee had sent letters and money with us to be delivered to them. We applied at Col. Johnson's

Headquarters for a pass, but were told that it could not be granted—that they were not authorized to admit any person into the prison barracks.[5] We then asked the Adjutant to bring the prisoners to his headquarters, this too was refused. The failure to see the prisoners was a cause of much regret to us, as their relatives in Tennessee are persons of the best reputation, and although doubtless involved with a strong sympathy for the south, they have ever acted an honorable part towards the Federals who have been stationed near them[.]

The officials at headquarters on the island were courteous and kind, and we believe they obeyed the instructions received by them *to the letter*, in refusing admittance; yet we could but regret the stringency of the order relative to intercourse with the prisoners.

The prisoners appear to suffer much from the severity of our climate, and while the military authorities have taken special care to provide them with comfortable quarters, the numbers that have died of pneumonia indicates the effect of the bitter cold weather that has visited that section since their arrival.[6]

We left our letters and money with the obliging and attentive Commissary of Prisoners (who seemed up to his ears in work), and turned our face again southward.

A ride by stage over a portion of Rock Island and Mercer counties furnished us with evidence of the continued prosperity of our people. Farmers are busily at work preparing everything for an early commencement of their spring labors, and the general air of thrift does not indicate that so large a proportion of the population are in the army.

It may interest the boys of Co. C, 102d Ill. Vols., to know that we took a look at the little school house, where the company was organized eighteen months ago. Instead of the boisterous group of soldiers there were a number of school children about the door, and a pretty girl with shy glances watched the passing soldier, as if the presence of a blue coat was an anomalous occurrence in that locality.

The next place that we visited was

Berlin.

Antiquated Berlin! A village of about one hundred and sixty inhabitants—twenty miles south of Rock Island and said to be precisely twenty miles from every place. It is the centre of a heavy rural population, and on rainy days and Sundays the streets are as full of life as Illinois street in Rock Island.

Berlin would evidently have been a city if it had not been doomed to remain a village. For the many virtues of its citizens we love the place. The secondary strata of the town may occasionally get up a street row—and what rural community is exempt from these visitations? and for that matter wherein is poor fallen human nature to blame if a group of canines initiate a street fight and thereby involve the entire fighting population.—

Yet, even in bellicose Berlin all are not devoted to the pleasures of pugilism, and there we have, in years gone by, found many strong friends, and there we passed many pleasant days ere the cloud of war darkened over our land.

To those who wish to escape the noise and bustle of city life we would say, by all means, visit Berlin; and while you sojourn there make your headquarters at the hotel of our friend, P. F. Shackle, who keeps one of the best rural hotels in the State of Illinois.

But this letter is already so long that we will not proceed farther than Berlin until our next.

S. F. F.

(Rock Island *Union*, March 16, 1864, p. 2)

1. Knox College, originally called Knox Manual Labor College, was founded in 1837 by the Rev. George W. Gale, a Presbyterian clergyman. Both the school and Galesburg itself were the fruit of Gale's plan to establish a colony and an institution of higher learning in the West. Lombard University, started by Universalists in 1851, numbered among its graduates several of the 102d's officers.

2. In 1860 there were about ninety blacks living in Galesburg, twelve of whom enlisted in the noted 54th Massachusetts Infantry in 1863. See Hermann R. Muelder, *A Hero Home from the War: Among the Black Citizens of Galesburg, Illinois, 1860–1880* (Galesburg, 1987), 3, 5.

3. Pond Creek Station was in Bureau County, Illinois, near Wyanet, on the Chicago, Rock Island, and Pacific Railroad.

4. Wyanet, Bureau County, Illinois, is on the Chicago, Burlington, and Quincy Railroad (now the Burlington Northern), about fifty miles northeast of Galesburg.

5. Construction of the prison camp, situated on Rock Island in the Mississippi River, commenced in the summer of 1863. The first prisoners, captured at Lookout Mountain, arrived in early December. By March 1864, at the time of Fleharty's visit, the number of prisoners had swelled to more than seven thousand. The commandant at this time was Col. Adolphus J. Johnson, formerly of the 8th New Jersey Infantry. See Otis Bryan England, *A Short History of the Rock Island Prison Barracks* (Rev. ed.; Rock Island, Ill., 1985), 1, 5, 27, 42.

6. During the month of March, 288 of the more than 7,200 prisoners confined at Rock Island died. There had been 350 deaths the previous month. England, *Rock Island Prison Barracks*, 42.

⌒ No. 33 ⌒

Camp Butler, Ill.,
March 14, '64

I will not weary the reader with details concerning the numerous little towns visited after leaving Berlin; yet must dwell somewhat upon my ride through Henry county, which was personally, not a little interesting. The county is very sparsely timbered, and traveling in winter over her bleak prairies is about as pleasant as it would be in the Arctic regions. Fortunately the weather was not excessively cold; yet it was a capricious March day, and while we were crossing the baldest of bald prairies, the clouds which had been loweri ıg all morning, suddenly filled the atmosphere with dense volumes of snow. ſ snow storm upon the prairie is a wild scene. How completely the storm spi ıt here asserts his sway, and as if rolicking [*sic*] and joyous, in conscious suɟ ːemacy, the snow-waves sweep fantastically on their way. All animate life di appears. The farmers' stock seek shelter on the leeward side of every availa ɔle wind-breaker, and the storm howls spitefully around the bleak houses of t'ıe farmers, as if angered by the security and comfort of the inmates. Our snow storm was, however, of short duration. The March clouds soon broke awɛy, leaving a light, fleecy covering upon the earth.

It was the fourth day of the month, and I noticed that numerous fields had already been sown with wheat. I am of the opinion that those who sowed their grain at that unseasonable time, have shown more enterprise than discretion.

A great many of the citizens of these counties which I visited, are making preparations to go to Idaho, as soon as the weather will render a forward movement practicable.[1] In some localities the fever runs very high. I noticed a party of rugged looking men on the cars en route for Quincy and St. Joseph; their ultimate destination being the new found land of gold. They were well equipped, and each carried one of Smith and Wesson's breechloading rifles. Many of these men are doubtless induced to leave the country by the dread of a coming draft. I predict that Idaho will be well stocked with Copperheads. Though I trust there will be enough of the loyal element, to prevent them from uniting with Brigham Young, and setting up a Deseret Confederacy.[2]

During my home visit I have marked an extraordinary prevalence of contagious diseases. Indeed I may say that such has been my experience everywhere during the past six weeks. At Lavergne the negroes had the small-pox. It is also among the prisoners at the Rock Island Barracks, and almost every village I visited was afflicted with measles, mumps, or whooping-cough. Probably about all of the diseases that appear in the medical calendar, are contracted by the soldiers at Camp Butler.

In reference to the prevalence of these diseases, and their fatal effects, it may well be said:

Death rides on every passing breeze,
And lurks in every flower.[3]

Since returning to Camp Butler we have been principally engaged in contriving methods to kill time.

The tedium of our Northern camp-life is occasionally relieved by a visit to Springfield. Our State capital has a decided military apperanc [sic]. The national blue is constantly visible on the streets. Officers of almost every grade may be seen. Commissioned and non-commissioned officers seem almost as numerous as privates. It is probable that this is owing to a somewhat indiscriminate appropriation of Uncle Sam's badges of honor by some of his unscrupulous nephews. It is becoming a mark of distinction to appear in a plain, neat suit of blue.

Recently, in company with a friend, I stepped into the Chenery House, and mingling with the crowd, which was as usual somewhat dense, my friend suddenly exclaimed, in a low tone—"Hold, or you will run over General White." Sure enough, there was the General in plain citizens suit; without anything whatever to indicate his rank. The General is evidently an unassuming man, and deems it his mission to work, rather than—(to use an army phrase)—"put on style."[4]

The constant arrival and departure of veterans and recruits makes much work for the government officials, and it is to be regretted that the corps of workers has not been sufficiently large to hurry the recruits more expeditiously into the field.

There are now twenty-nine hundred recruits in Camp Butler. There has been, however, a marked diminution in the number of recruits arriving at Springfield per day, and unless there is a new call, our camp must in a few weeks present a deserted appearance.

About one-half of the 30th Illinois Volunteers reached this camp last Saturday. They came direct from Vicksburg. The regiment was with Sherman on his expedition to Meridian.[5]

The boys whom I saw were healthy, robust fellows, and seemed not at all worn down by their recent severe march into the heart of the Confederacy. They were evidently allowed a great deal of liberty while on that march and were not a little disconcerted when they found their freedom limited to the space within the wooden enclosure of Camp Butler. "The unsophisticated blockheads,"—say they, in reference to the guards, who are new recruits,— "they do not know their business, and stand at the entrance, audaciously denying a soldier's right to go where he pleases!"

The regiment is commanded by Col. Warren Shedd, of Mercer county. Two companies of the regiment were raised in Mercer.[6] The boys have re-enlisted and were all happy in anticipation of the thirty-days furlough which they are soon to receive, and which they have nobly earned. This regiment under its gallant colonel has done some of the hardest fighting of the war. If General Sherman's entire army is composed of as good material, it is no longer a wonder that he is enabled to move with so much celerity and effect.

The boys represent that everything was laid waste upon their recent march and they literally subsisted upon the enemy. Bacon and hams were found in abundance and except during the two last days of this return march, they lived on the fat of the land.

Praying that my next may be written from the land of cotton, and from my army home, in the bosom of the 102d, I remain.

S. F. F.

(Rock Island *Union,* March 23, 1864, p. 2)

1. In 1860 gold was discovered on Orofino Creek in what was then Washington Territory. Other discoveries during the next two years sent droves of prospectors and settlers to the region (the population had reached seventy thousand by 1863). Consequently Congress established Idaho Territory on March 3, 1863.

2. Although no friend of the North, at whose hands Young and his fellow believers had suffered greatly in the 1830s and 1840s, and an ardent opponent of emancipation, Young had no dreams of a "Deseret Confederacy." The closest he could be said to have come to such an idea was his prediction that northerners and southerners alike would flee their desolated homelands and head west. Then, he said, the saints "will forget all your sins against us, and give you a home." Stanley P. Hirshson, *The Lion of the Lord: A Biography of Brigham Young* (New York, 1969), 259.

3. Fleharty is quoting from a poem entitled "At a Funeral," by the English churchman and author Reginald Heber (1783–1826).

4. Brig. Gen. Julius White (1816–90), formerly colonel of the 37th Illinois Infantry, was

commanding the general rendezvous for drafted men and volunteers at Springfield at the time of Fleharty's visit.

5. On February 3, 1864, Sherman left Vicksburg with about twenty-five thousand men of the 16th and 17th Corps (commanded by Maj. Gen. Stephen A. Hurlbut and Maj. Gen. James B. McPherson respectively), destined for Meridian, Mississippi. His immediate objective was to strengthen the Union hold on Vicksburg by further destruction of Confederate supplies and transportation in central Mississippi. Sherman's force entered Meridian on February 14 after encountering only light resistance. After remaining in Meridian for five days, doing his work of destruction, Sherman withdrew toward Vicksburg, arriving there on March 5. The entire expedition had cost the Union only about one hundred and seventy casualties. The 30th Illinois participated in the raid as part of the 3d Brigade of the 3d Division of McPherson's Corps. See Sherman's report of the expedition in *OR*, XXXII, Pt. 1, pp. 173–79. Also see Boatner, *Civil War Dictionary*, 543–44.

6. Col. Warren Shedd (1821–81), a native of New Hampshire and brother of Capt. Frank Shedd of Fleharty's company, had been the Democratic treasurer of Mercer County from 1859 to 1861. Companies A and G of the 30th Illinois were raised primarily in Mercer County.

ᴑ— No. 34 —ᴑ

Camp Butler, Ill.,
March 19, '64.

I intend to make this mainly a political letter, and therefore give your readers due warning, that they may not struggle through it only to wish that they had halted at the close of the first paragraph.

Without assuming to decide whether it is profitable or expedient to devite [*sic*] my attention to this subject, I grant to the reader as much liberty in passing judgment upon what I may say, as I assume in deciding to write upon a subject which is foreign to those topics which have heretofore engaged my attention.

The ensuing Presidential campaign will be one of momentous importance in its results, and the people in choosing their Chief Magistrate become responsible for the future fate of our country. It is to be deplored that the wild excitement that has attended all previous campaigns must enter into this; which should be a cool, calm expression of the judgment of an intelligent people.

The great interests of free Governments are to be, for the time being, placed entirely in the hands of the people. The previous coin of liberty is to be returned to the mint to receive the impression of the age.

If the people are qualified by proper education and their judgment is not rendered subservient to a whirlwind of party strife we may expect a happy result, but in the existing state of society there is much to be feared.

It seems to me that the friends of the Union should at the outset define their position fairly and fully upon the questions at issue, and should enter the contest with an eye single to the good of our country.

In diffusing correct political principles, calm reasoning, rather than noisy declamation should be relied upon; and especially in the coming contest this should be our most trusted weapon. It would seem strange that in such times as these any portion of our people should make their patriotism subservient to party interests: yet we may confidently anticipate such political servility, and it will be the proper work of patriots to unfold to such party-blind citizens, the duties which they owe to the Government of their fathers—to the present generation and to posterity, at this hour of national peril.

And we may anticipate dissensions, of more or less consequence among those who have been avowedly the most earnest supporters of the Government. The ultra men will in all probability fail to secure the adoption of a platform that will accord with their progressive ideas, and the over-conservative may find much in the Union platform distasteful to them. (I speak here of the Union platform *per excellence.* There will be other platforms professedly and really devoted to the interests of the Union, but that upon which patriots must rally, will primarily seek the restoration of the Union upon principles honorable to the Government and just toward the rebels.)

The chances are indeed, that men who take medium grounds upon the questions at issue, will occupy the central planks of the platform, and as the majority of men, unprejudiced by political excitement, are actuated by common sense, in exercising the right of suffrage, we may expect that genuinely conservative principles will be triumphant, if dispassionately examined by our voting population.

It may be too that a candidate will be chosen who is obnoxious to many friends of the Union. These considerations render it apparrent [*sic*] that the business of selecting a Chief Magistrate for the ensuing four years will be one of extreme peril to the Government.

It is of the utmost importance, therefore, that our prime movers on the political chess-board be actuated by honesty of purpose, and profound judgment in the discharge of their duties.

What the platform of principles should be I will not presume to suggest, but I will say, 1st. That it should be a platform upon which Abraham Lincoln can stand; and 2d. Abraham Lincoln should stand upon it as the candidate of the Union party for re-election to the Presidency.[1]

The verdict of the people as to his fitness has already been given. Coming into power untried, and even distrusted by many of his own party; and having sustained unparalleled persecutions while administering the Government during a period of civil disorder that has scarcely a parallel in history, at the close of the third year of his administration we have unquestionable evidence that he is considered, by nearly all who are not traitors, as the only man who can be implicitly relied upon to carry us safely through our National difficulties. Three years of his administration have won for him the hearts of all unprejudiced, honest men.

The world has not witnessed a more sublime spectacle than that presented by the present triumphant position of the President. Jeered, ridiculed, cursed by his foes; sneered at by all snobdom—he yet remained ever unmoved. Good hard sense has thus far carried him through. His friends who have anxiously watched his career, can now feel assured that his name will be revered and loved, when his most powerful opponents and revilers have slumbered for ages in unremembered toombs [sic].

I have, it is true, at various times objected to the policy of the President in conducting the war, yet at no time have I doubted his honesty of purpose; while some of his measures may not accord with our ideas of conservatism, it is apparent that he habitually holds a tight rein upon all the extremists. While his policy upon the "vexed question," may not have been entirely satisfactory, we know precisely what to depend upon in the future, and it will be a long step towards civil concord to be assured that we are not again to drift rudderless on the sea of uncertainty in reference to the policy of the Government upon this question.

The slavery question will hardly assume a new phaze [sic] during the war, and when the war closes who will be so competent to deal justly with master and slave as our humorous and enlightened Chief Magistrate? Who so well qualified as he to fulfill the requirments [sic] of the Constitution in re-establishing the authority of the Government, while jealously guarding the great interests of human liberty?

These declarations are certainly not dictated by a hero-worshiping enthusiasm—a species of idolatry which I have ever deprecated, and which has always awakened in my mind emotions of disgust. In the honest exercise of the best faculties of my mind, however much I may err, I, with all due modesty, announce Abraham Lincoln as *my* candidate for the Presidential term; and with a platform upon which he can stand, having received the nomination of the Union party, I have no fears for the result.

S. F. F.

(Rock Island *Union*, March 30, 1864, p. 1)

1. The Union Party, a coalition of Republicans and proadministration—or "War"—Democrats, met in convention at Baltimore in June and renominated Lincoln. Tennessee Democrat Andrew Johnson was chosen to be Lincoln's running mate.

No. 35

Camp Butler, Ill.,
March 21, '64

"That's what the '11th' brought up with them from Vicksburg!"

"What?"

"Why, that machine on wheels, there," and one of the two soldiers whose remarks I have quoted pointed to a beautiful brass field-piece—a rifled nine-pounder—which is "planted" a few feet from the door of our barracks. The "11th" (cavalry) came into camp last Thursday night, 450 strong.[1] They have re-enlisted. The gun alluded to was captured by them while out with Sherman in his great raid. It is to be presented to Governor Yates.[2] Companies C and G, of Mercer county, participated in the charge that resulted in its capture, and are chiefly entitled to the honor of securing so brilliant a trophy for our State.

Company C is commanded by our young friend Capt. George W. Greenwood.[3] I knew George well, years ago. He was then a sober, deacon-like boy, with a little *down* upon his chin, and gravity enough in his nature to fit him for a Judge of the Supreme Court. Thus he appeared when the war broke out. Little did I think then, or years before, when we played as neighbor boys together, that George would so soon, at the head of veteran soldiers, win laurels on the field of battle. But George has won them, and wears them with the modesty becoming the brave soldier that he is.

Mercer county has reason to be proud of the noble soldiers she has furnished for the army of the Union.

The boys received their thirty days' furlough last Saturday evening.[4] They appeared remarkably healthy, and in this respect as well as in their general bearing there was a strong contrast between them and the *camp-sick*, undisciplined recruits in Camp Butler.

But hark! Do you hear the deep swelling tones of a Martial Band, playing,

We will rally 'round the flag, boys,
Rally once again,[5]

and do you hear that steady, unmistakable,—tramp—tramp—tramp, which tells you that veterans keep time to the music? Oh! yes, and we of course tumble out in double-quick time at the risk of breaking our necks over benches, boxes and stovewood, to take a look at the boys.

Ah! it is a rich treat to witness their triumphal entry! How prettily those bayonets gleam in the morning sun, and how they sway with one motion,— a slight undulating motion,—corresponding with their steady tramp as they march on, apparently unconscious that so many curious eyes are fixed upon them. And they bear a faded silken flag, which the wind seems vainly endeavoring to unfurl. Ah! there is a reason why it will not spread its ample folds! The blue field is almost gone—but few of the stars remain. The huge rent in that part of it was made by grape shot. There is hardly a square foot of its surface free of bullet-holes. The marks of 103 balls are visible in the flag and flag-staff. The staff is shivered in two or three places, and will hardly support the tattered flag.

"But what regiment is it?" you are asking. Well, excuse me,—my enthusiasm is playing the mischief with my rhetoric—it is the *Twentieth Illinois* Veteran Volunteers,—which declaration by the way, reminds me of a remark made by an officer the other day.[6] Said he: "The Illinois boys are proud of their State—or, rather, I should say, of the proud name they have given it— wherever I have been in Dixie I have noticed this fact—when one of our boys is asked, by a soldier from another State, what regiment he belongs to, he (giving the number of his regiment where I place a dash) invariably yells out: "—— Illinois!" with a heavy emphasis—a *proud* emphasis, I may say, on the last syllable—evidently esteeming it a privilege to shout the name of his State to friend or foe at the top of his voice.["]

The 20th left Vicksburg on the 12th inst., and came in to-day. One hundred and ninety men of this regiment have re-enlisted, which number comprises a majority of those fit for duty.

The boys, like all the returned veterans whom I have seen are robust, rugged and rosy-cheeked. They express their disapprobation of our inhospitable climate with more force than elegance: —"Everything was coming out green, when we left Vicksburg, but here we meet with a confounded chilling reception, that makes our marrow bones rattle and our teeth chatter, which they never did in the presence of the enemy."

I sought out the color bearer of the regiment, Sergt. Martin Mohrle, and requested him to exhibit the battle-torn flag.[7] It was deeply interesting to see the boys gather around, as the Sergeant, a sturdy, vivacious little German, unrolled the precious memento of their battles and victories.

"Carefully, carefully, it will not bear rough usage," they would say to the Sergeant, who needed, however, not a word of warning.

"I picked it up from the dust at Shiloh," said the veteran, his eye sparkling with honest pride—"and it was the only flag planted upon the enemy's fortress, when our forces made that desperate assault, on the memorable 22d of May, at Vicksburg."[8] "Yes," said another, "and the staff was shattered here, and here, at the very moment he was planting it on the enemy's works."

This regiment was raised in the vicinity of Joliet and is commanded by Lieut. Col. Bradly.[9] It has been sadly decimated by disease, and battle, yet when it returns with recruited ranks, will do good service in the work of finishing the rebellion.

Thank heaven, and the War Department for the privilege of meeting and conversing with the returning veteran volunteers. Without the pleasant little episodes attending their arrival and departure, life would hardly be endurable in this place. S. F. F.

(Rock Island *Union,* April 6, 1864, p. 1)

1. The 11th Illinois Cavalry was raised in the counties of west central Illinois in the latter part of 1861. Its original commander was Col. Robert G. Ingersoll of Peoria, who would later become famous as the "Great Agnostic."

2. Richard Yates (1815–73), of Jacksonville, was governor of Illinois from 1861 to 1865.

3. Capt. George W. Greenwood (Company C) of Pope Creek in Mercer County originally enlisted as 1st Sergeant. He was mustered out December 19, 1864. *Adj. Gen. Rep.,* VIII, 291.

4. In an effort to get veteran soldiers to reenlist, the government paid any man with at

least two years' service $402 for signing up again. If a majority of a particular regiment reenlisted, the unit was given a thirty-day furlough and was allowed to attach the title "veteran" to its unit designation. Thus the 11th Illinois Veteran Volunteer Cavalry was in Springfield on its thirty-day leave while Fleharty was visiting. See James W. Geary, *We Need Men: The Union Draft in the Civil War* (DeKalb, Ill., 1991), 112; and *Adj. Gen. Rep.*, VIII, 331.

5. "The Battle Cry of Freedom," one of the North's favorites, was the work of prolific songwriter George F. Root. The song appeared in two versions, "the battle song" and "the rallying song." It is also possible that Fleharty refers to the less well-known piece by James T. Fields and William B. Bradbury, "Rally 'Round the Flag." See Willard A. Heaps and Porter W. Heaps, *The Singing Sixties: The Spirit of the Civil War Days Drawn from the Music of the Times* (Norman, Okla., 1960), 69–72.

6. The 20th Illinois Infantry was recruited and organized in east central Illinois in the spring of 1861. It had seen action at Fort Donelson, Shiloh, Port Gibson, Raymond, Champion Hill, Vicksburg, and the Meridian expedition. It was in Springfield on its veteran furlough. *Adj. Gen. Rep.*, II, 182–84.

7. Sgt. Martin Moreley of Clinton, DeWitt County, Illinois, originally enlisted in the 20th in June 1861. During a charge at Champion Hill (May 16, 1863), according to a member of the regiment, Sergeant Moreley "ran so fast with the colors that we had hard work to keep up with him, and keep any kind of order." Moreley reenlisted as a veteran in January 1864 and was killed on July 21 near Atlanta. Ira Blanchard, *I Marched with Sherman: Civil War Memoirs of the 20th Illinois Volunteer Infantry* (San Francisco, 1992), 92; *Adj. Gen. Rep.*, II, 164.

8. On May 22, 1863, General Grant, wanting to avoid a siege and hoping to take the city before reinforcements could arrive, ordered a second frontal assault on the defenses of Vicksburg. (The first, on May 19, had been repulsed.) Having underestimated the enemy's strength, Grant was again unsuccessful, this time at a cost of 3,200 men. Boatner, *Civil War Dictionary*, 876.

9. Lt. Col. Daniel Bradley of Champaign, Illinois.

᠊ᢒ᠊ No. 36 ᠊ᢒ᠊

Camp Butler, April 8, 1864.

Since writing my last letter for The Union, I have passed a few days at home, under circumstances that will ever render the recollection of the visit one of the most sorrowful of my memories of home,—alas it is home no longer— while there I listened to the dying words of a friend who has ever been true to me,—*my mother*.[1] Her spirit has winged its flight over the valley and through the shadows of death. What greater loss could be suffered? The long years of her labor in behalf of her children; the hours of happiness; made happy by her presence; are yet present in memory. But I must not dwell upon this subject, even though it is ever present in my mind,—the busy world thinks not the second time of bereavements that cast the deepest shadows over the pathway of individuals.

To-morrow! Oh! how wild and uninviting the prospect! To-morrow *will dawn*, relentlessly as time rolls on, burying deeper in the bosom of the past the happiness and the hopes of other years.

To morrow brings another change; and the beginning of a long ride into the heart of the South. We are ordered to proceed to Vicksburg, Miss. with recruits. The ride in itself cannot be unpleasant, and although not in the mood for catering to the tastes of the reading public, the readers of The Union may anticipate the occasional appearance of a letter from

S. F. F.

(Rock Island *Union*, April 20, 1864, p. 1)

1. Mrs. Amelia W. Fleharty died March 22, 1864, in Galesburg. Unlike death notices of most ordinary citizens, her obituary appeared, with a headline set in bold type, on the first page of the April 6, 1864, edition of the *Union*. One must suspect that her grieving son had a hand in its composition if not in its placement in the paper.

CHAPTER 8

"Upon the Broad Bosom of the Mississippi"

◦⟋ No. 37 ⟍◦

Benton Barracks, Mo.,
April 11th, 1864.

I must condense the account of our journey southward, to this point, into a very brief letter. Our detachment of recruits, between six hundred and seven hundred strong, left Camp Butler on the morning of the 9th inst.

The recruits were all highly elated with the prospect of joining their regiments, and, the guard being light, some of them managed to get some whisky on board the train. As a result, I presume, of the introduction of the whisky we lost one man. The train being near Carlinsville [*sic*], the engineer checked it for the purpose of leaving it outside the limits of the town, while taking the engine into the city to replenish his supply of wood and water.[1] One of the soldiers had climbed upon the tender, and, an instant after the engine was detached from the train—both being in rapid motion—attempted to spring over the increasing space between the tender and the first car in the rear.— He failed to reach the car and fell just ahead of it. The train halted and on all sides was heard the cry, "man killed[.]" Glancing at the rail beneath our car steps as we passed out we observed that it was covered with gore. Beneath the car just ahead, was the mangled trunk of a man's body, almost in a nude state. Ten or fifteen feet from it lay the head of the man. It was a sickening sight, and as I turned hastily from it then, so I will not torture the reader with further details. I have not yet learned the name of the unfortunate man.

A few miles further on, another accident befel [*sic*] us which resulted in detaining us for sometime. A portion of the engine gave way, and it was so much weakened by the accident that we surmounted the "grades" with the utmost difficulty. A few miles from Alton we reached a heavier grade than any we had passed over. "If we can pass this we are all right," said one, "for it is down grade beyond, all the way to the city." Slowly the engine approached the summit of the grade, and is strained until it seems to quiver upon the track, but it continues to move more slowly, and finally stops fifty yards from the summit. Then the weight in the rear draws it helplessly backwards. Stones are placed in the rear of the wheels to check the retrograde movement,—they are ground to powder. Then the engine apparently like a thing of life renews the struggle, and moves slowly forward fifteen or twenty feet; then helplessly backward again. This vibratory movement is kept up for some time, but at length after the track has been well sounded and the utmost power of the crippled locomotive has been brought into play, the grade is surmounted and we run quickly into Alton. Late in the evening we reached Illinoistown, opposite St. Louis. It was fully dark when we landed in St. Louis. The officers in command then went in search of quarters for the men. In vain they called at the head-quarters of the military men in the city. They were generally absent, or if any were in their offices they appeared to have no authority in the premises. It seems that no preparations had been made for us, and those whose duty it was to provide us with a place to pass the night, conducted themselves as if entirely ignorant of our coming. An hour or two we waited on the levee. At length the cheering order to move forward was caught up along our impatient line. I asked one of the Captains in command if he had secured a place for the men. He said "I think we have, although I am not sure that we will get into the place promised us; a Sergeant at Gen. Rosecrans' headquarters will take us to the Turners' Hall.[2] The Sergeant has taken upon himself the responsibility of opening the hall for us." We arrived at the hall but our Teutonic friends had full possession and were in the midst of a brilliant ball. As a last resort the Mayor of the city was appealed to and after having waited three hours or more, we were, through his kind efforts permitted to occupy the basement of the Turners' Hall.[3] It was almost midnight when the recruits had all stretched themselves upon their blankets. All slept upon the floor, and every available foot of space in the large room was taken up. It was a curious spectacle—that mass of reposing humanity[.] I was fortunate enough to secure a few hours rest at a hotel near by, and can assure you that those hours of rest, from midnight until five o'clock in the morning, were well improved[.]—From the hall we took up the line of march for Benton Barracks, which we reached at one o'clock, on the day following our arrival in the city.[4] I regret that I must give so many instances of mismanagement and inattention on the part of our military officials. I wish indeed, that I could introduce only pleasant topics into my letters. The character of a habitual grumbler is certainly to be avoided, but I propose to give truthful sketches of experience, and when I must censure, endeavor to do so in as mild terms as I can use. It is apparent to most unsophisticated military men, that six hundred recruits who had just received a liberal supply of greenbacks, should not have been conducted to St. Louis, and left for hours on the streets, with but thirty guards to prevent their escape under cover of darkness. The result of this carelessness will undoubtedly be the loss of quite a number of men in this instance—temporarily, at least.

It is pleasant to be able to say that there have been and still are military men at Benton Barracks who have endeavored to do their duty. It is really a "soldiers' home." There is every convenience about the camp that could be asked for by any reasonable men. If my recollection serve [sic] me right we are principally indebted to Gen. J. C. Fremont for the excellent arrangement and accommodations of this camp. Although I do not want him for President, it is a pleasure to give him due credit for the good work that he accomplished here.

It is probable that I have falsified the declaration made at the commencement of this letter, that I would write very briefly, if so I cannot perpetuate my error as limited time will not permit me to write more to-day. I will say, however, for the satisfaction of any who may be interested in our future movements that we will probably start down the river to-morrow.

S. F. F.

(Rock Island *Union*, April 20, 1864, p. 2)

1. Carlinville, seat of Macoupin County, is located about forty miles southwest of Springfield.

2. After being relieved of command of the Army of the Cumberland, General Rosecrans had been named to command the Department of Missouri.

Turner societies (from the German *Turnerbund*, or "gymnastic society") were brought to America by young Germans migrating after the 1848 revolution. They "blended nationalism, anticlericalism, and utopian socialism. As part of their program of universal education to prepare men for political and social democracy, the Turner groups placed great emphasis on gymnastic training and sponsored competitions of athletic skill." The Turner Hall in St. Louis was one of the largest and most impressive in the country. See Elliott J. Gorn, "Sports Through the

Nineteenth Century," in Mary Kupiec Cayton et al., eds., *Encyclopedia of American Social History* (New York, 1993), III, 1627–41.

3. Chauncey I. Filley was mayor of St. Louis on April 9, 1864.

4. Benton Barracks, a Federal camp of instruction, was opened in 1861 by Maj. Gen. John C. Frémont on land rented for $150 a year. It was west of the fairgrounds at the northwestern corner of the city.

ᠥ— No. 38 —ᠥ

On Board Steamer Constitution,
April 13, 1864.

About 11 o'clock a. m. yesterday, we boarded the splendid steamer named above and at three p. m. were under way for Vicksburg. As the vessel moved out from the landing we had a fine view of the city. The long line of smoke stacks at the levee—the masses of humanity hurrying to and fro and the immense buildings looming up in the back ground indicated to us the great commercial importance of St. Louis.

While viewing such a scene one is naturally impressed with the greatness of man, and is at the same time obliged to acknowledge the *insignificance* of his race. Men move among the magnificent [*sic*] creations of their own hands, like the little ants among the hills they have created. About the levee of such a city the very scum of the human race are constantly congregated. They grow up from childhood in such localities, and the adults may be termed full grown wharf rats. They contract thieving habits as naturally as if they received initiatory lessons from those unscrupulous animals. And there are others who, though depending upon labor for a livilihood [*sic*] are the slaves of commercial power—and devote the days of their lives to the meanest drudgery. The gigantic machinery of commerce must move and the wretched, toiling, sweating deck hands and wharf men must furnish the primary motive power.

But I must not take up too much time in philosophising upon this subject. There is nothing in the world so difficult to understand as human nature; it is full of excellences—and yet how fallible is man—full of nobility, and yet how wretched and depraved he may become.

If in the course of my rambles I occasionally wander into fields of speculation connected with a subject like this somewhat "foreign to the occasion," the reader will, I hope, attribute my eccentric style to the strong impressions which are received under favorable auspices for obtaining new views of men and things.

Any one who is curious to observe a variety of phases in human nature should, by all means, have the privilege of accompanying a detachment of recruits on an expedition like this. The majority of them have never seen service, and are as impatient and dependent as unweened [*sic*] children. Poor fellows, they are going a long way from home, and it is not surprising that they feel much solicitude for their future fates. We are nevertheless provoked to laughter when listening to their innumerable questions; and woe betide the unlucky individual who has been in the field—for it is taken for granted that there is little worth knowing which he does not know.

They must pass through a rough school. Many of them will come back improved by the lessons to be learned; while others will sink beneath the severities of the service[.] One cannot but reflect when looking upon such a crowd of uninitiated soldiers, that each must pass through many vicissitudes ere he returns again to his home. Each one may be said to have his destiny. Many must perish far away in an enemy's land. Others will return perhaps maimed for life; others forever morally ruined; and there will be homes made happy by the return of noble, true men.

But we are in sight of Cairo, where I must mail this letter, and I have told you nothing of our glorio's [*sic*] ride thus far down the river. I wish I had time to picture, in my imperfect way, the beautiful scenery that we have looked upon to-day.—The noble river—the lovely islands—the bold bluffs—the grand combinations of picturesque scenery must all go undescribed.

S. F. F.

(Rock Island *Union*, April 20, 1864, p. 3)

⌒ No. 39 ⌒

Cairo, Ill., April 16th, 1864.

Few towns in the Union have been more perseveringly abused by travelers than this—and I might add that few are more deserving of abuse. Notwithstanding all the diatribes of traveling bohemians, the revilers of the city have however, failed to sink it; the place is still above water—barely. In conveying my impressions of the appearance of Cairo I feel inclined to liken it unto a country town which has suddenly become an important business point and has not had time to assume becoming dignity. The place has a chronic dilapidated appearance. The buildings are generally of an inferior order; the sidewalks are most wretched, and everything seems to indicate that the inhabitants have held themselves in readiness to evacuate the town at a moment's warning. The resident population does not exceed five thousand. Probably for every individual in the place there may be numbered fully five hundred rats. It is astonishing to go on shore in the evening and witness the numbers and audacity of these little marauders. It is more surprising that such sagacious animals will select such a miserable locality as a place of residence. It is said that they follow civilization, but I am inclined to think that they scented the wrong track in this instance.

As a business point, Cairo, at this time, presents a lively appearance. Business men are reaping a harvest of wealth from the soldiers who are constantly landing at, and embarking from this point. Aside from the desire to accumulate wealth there is nothing in the world to impel a man to emigrate to Cairo.[1]

Our opportunities for making observations about the city have been very good—far better indeed than we could have wished. The fall of Fort Pillow compelled our Captain to tie up his boat, and here we remain from day to day, as impatient as seamen becalmed upon the ocean.[2]

I have observed no formidable defenses in or about Cairo. There are some heavy guns mounted on an earthwork near the point of land formed by the conjunction of the Ohio and Mississippi rivers; and it may be gratifying to loyal Illinoisans to know that we found one of Uncle Samuel's nephews, with his bayonet gleaming in the sun, standing picket on the last foot of terra firma that forms the southern terminus of our State.

The levee is crowded with boats awaiting the issue of events below. We are anxiously anticipating the order for a forward movement, and the majority of those on board would doubtless vote to run the blockade at night, in order to get away from Cairo. But the hours do not pass heavily with all on board our boat. As I write, a number of the devotees of Terpsichore are preparing to "trip the light fantastic toes," in the ladies' cabin.[3] As a consequence the end of the cabin in which I write is fast becoming deserted. The music begins, and my friend, Captain E. H. C., who is a model dancer, sits so uneasily at my side, that it seems painful to him, not to join in the mazes of the dance. The book that he has been reading with such interest is closed in his hand—he will go directly. A very worthy looking minister who sits near by looks uneasily in the direction of the music, as though his moral feelings were grievously outraged. Now he takes his pen, arranges his paper, and will probably launch some heavy arguments against this popular amusement. But it is no war of mine, and I acknowledge but little interest in arguments pro or con on this mooted moral question. The dance goes on brilliantly, as dances will without doubt continue to go on as long as human nature is what it is.

We get very little news from the seat of war in Kentucky and Western Tenn. What items we obtain indicate that the rebels are having everything their own way in those sections. The territory will of course be reclaimed ere long, but will have been stripped of horses, money, provisions and men. If any better result is reached by our military men they will exceed our anticipations. Meanwhile we will wait the issue of events with as much patience as we can command, hoping that the embargo upon travel at least will soon be removed.

S. F. F.

(Rock Island *Union*, April 27, 1864, p. 4)

1. Located at the confluence of the Ohio and Mississippi Rivers, and at the terminus of the Illinois Central Railroad, Cairo was a strategic riverport and depot throughout the war. On April 19, 1861, Secretary of War Simon Cameron requested that Illinois governor Richard Yates dispatch troops to the town. The first companies and batteries arrived on April 23 and began the process of fortification. By August the ships that were to become the navy's western flotilla were assembling there. From this base, Union forces launched the campaigns that reopened the western waterways; consequently, Union troops passed through the city traveling to and from various theaters of operation during the balance of the conflict.

But the location had its flaws, and Fleharty was not alone in his opinion of the place. "Fever, dysentery, a plague of mosquitoes, and hordes of rats," noted one historian, made Cairo both an unhealthy and an unpleasant place to stay or visit. Dead animals floating in the river and garbage thrown in the streets combined to make Cairo quite a foul-smelling place. Adding to these discomforts, the levees and pumps built to control the great rivers often failed. All factors taken together made Cairo highly forgettable to many soldiers, sailors, and civilians. See James Merrill, "Cairo, Illinois: Strategic Civil War River Port," *Journal of the Illinois State Historical Society* LXXVI (1983), 242–43, 256; *Adj. Gen. Rep.*, I, 7–10; Nancy Anderson and Dwight Anderson, *The Generals: Ulysses S. Grant and Robert E. Lee* (New York, 1988), 204.

2. On April 12, 1864, Fort Pillow, which was garrisoned by 262 black and 295 white soldiers, was surrounded by Confederates under the command of Nathan Bedford Forrest. Refusing a surrender demand, the defenders were easily overrun and lost 231 killed, 100 seriously wounded, and 226 captured (58 of them black). Federal accounts maintain that the defenders, seeing the fort about to be overrun, attempted to surrender but were cut down in cold blood

by the Confederates (especially the black soldiers). News of the massacre quickly spread throughout the North. Boatner, *Civil War Dictionary*, 295–96.

3. In Greek mythology, Terpsichore was the muse of dancing and choral singing. The quotation is a slightly inaccurate rendering of lines 33 and 34 of Milton's "L'Allegro" (1631).

᠊ᢒ᠆ No. 40 ᠆ᢒ᠊

On Board Steamer Constitution.
April 17th, 1864.

Late in the afternoon yesterday, a steamer with news from below rounded to at Cairo, and our long suspense was over. No rebels had been seen at Fort Pillow or anywhere along the river. Our good boat soon had steam up and just as the sombre shadows of evening were beginning to envelop the city we glided away from the levee. Standing upon the hurricane deck, away from the noise of the engines, and watching the waters, glinting by in the feeble light of the young moon, one could hardly resist the impression that the lovely scene was the work of enchantment[.] For a time half regretfully our eyes followed the receding point of land that was dear to us as a portion of our State. Farther and farther it is left in the dim distance, and the low bank on the right with its ragged fores[t], and the deep dark woods on the left bank of the great river seem converging as the outlines of our own State become invisible. The scene was surpassingly beautiful, and we (my good friend E H C & I) remained on deck until a late hour unwilling to forego the enjoyment of its loveliness. About nine o'clock we approached Columbus, Ky. The bold bluffs which seem to surround it as great natural works of defense, loomed up grandly in the dim moonlight. Opposite the bluffs and the city could be seen the outline of the woods in which occurred the sanguinary battle of Belmont.[1] The river is comparatively narrow opposite Columbus, and the rebel batteries on the bluffs near the town must have played upon our forces with great effect. Our boat landed for a few moments and then continued on. We passed Island No. 10, and New Madrid ere morning, but did not see those places.[2]

Less than an hour ago we passed Fort Pillow. We had been running all day between low banks; and but for the occasional islands the scenery would have become monotonous[.] At length in the far distance down the river, the Tennessee bank assumed a more broken appearance, and the bluffs, rising like huge battlements, seemed as if thrown up expressly to command the river. All were anxious to view the scene of the late terrible tragedy, and the decks were crowded long before we reached the locality. The fort is located on the first of the high bluffs referred to, and appears to be an insignificant earthwork. Its great strength may be attributed to natural advantages and not to any superiority in its construction. We were within short cannon range of the fort before its outlines became visible to us. A few persons—citizens or negroes—were hanging about the place. In the vicinity of the fort could be seen the charred and blackened remains of the houses which were occupied by the garrison. I noticed that the flag staff had been left unmolested. There was no flag up. Everything in the vicinity of the fort has a lonely, deserted appearance—save the green trees, which I almost fancied were hastening to put on full robes, that they may throw a shadowy mantle around a spot so foully cursed by "man's inhumanity to man."

The forests which line the river banks appear more green as we proceed southward, and a grateful aroma of budding trees and blossoming flowers comes from the islands and the mainland.

S. F. F.

LATER—9 P. M. We are landing at Memphis.

S. F. F.

(Rock Island *Union*, April 27, 1864, p. 1)

1. U. S. Grant's first major action in the war took place at Belmont, Missouri, on November 7, 1861. Fleharty was indeed correct that Belmont had been a bloody affair. Grant, ordered by Gen. John C. Frémont to demonstrate against Confederate forces at Columbus, Kentucky, chose to attack the rebels camped across the river at Belmont. Initially successful, and flushed with victory, Grant's little army suddenly found itself trapped and cut off from its transports and covering gunboats. With Grant in the lead, the Federals cut their way back to the boats, reembarked, and steamed back up the river to Cairo. The northern press, especially in Illinois, were in a furor over Grant's handling of the expedition, and were especially critical of his losses. Of 3,114 engaged, 607 were casualties (roughly 20 percent). The Confederates lost 642 of about 4,000 that saw action. See Boatner, *Civil War Dictionary*, 57–58; Bruce Catton, *Terrible Swift Sword* (Garden City, N.Y., 1963), 63–64; Hicken, *Illinois in the Civil War*, 19–24; and Long, *Civil War Almanac*, 136.

2. Confederate Mississippi River forts at New Madrid, Missouri, and Island No. 10 were taken by the combined army and navy forces under Brig. Gen. John Pope and Flag Officer Andrew H. Foote. After a ten-day siege, rebel forces evacuated New Madrid on March 14, 1862. On April 8 the garrison on Island No. 10 capitulated, opening the middle Mississippi to Union river traffic. See Boatner, *Civil War Dictionary*, 587–88; Long, *Civil War Almanac*, 184–85; Catton, *Terrible Swift Sword*, 238–46.

⌒ No. 41 ⌒

On Board Steamer Constitution,
April 19, 1864.

Our boat is taking on wood at a Mississippi landing and we have just returned from an exploring expedition on shore.—The forests along the river are very dense yet there are few varieties of timber. Cottonwood and willows predominate. The woods here appear as green as our own in early summer. From the leafless forests and brown prairies of the North, we have been quickly transported to a land of blooming flowers and leafy groves. Viewed from an aesthetical stand-point the change is exhilirating [*sic*], but considered with reference to the effect upon our physical natures, we must acknowledge that it is decidedly debilitating.

The river scenery below Cairo cannot be compared with that of the Upper Mississippi. The banks are uniformly low, and in many places the plantations are below high water mark. They were once protected by levees from overflow, but these are now in a dilapidated condition.

But I am anticipating the thread of my sketch and must return to the time of landing at Memphis, where I concluded my last letter. We remained at that place about two hours and then continued on down the river. As it was night, I failed to get a good view of the city. We ran all night, and yesterday morning landed at Helena, Ark. This is a very pretty little town, and has a lively business appearance. There is a high range of fortified bluffs in the rear of the place, and it is apparent that Gen. Prentiss was in a good position to meet the assaults made upon his works there, on the 4th of July last. Brig. Gen. Buford now commands the post. But few white troops are stationed there. The place is garrisoned mainly by negro soldiers, of whom there are nearly three thousand.[1]

Below Helena we landed at an island where a company of Iowa negro soldiers are stationed.[2] They have been placed there to protect a party of Union refugees who are cutting wood for Government use. The blacks have built very comfortable cabins on the island and have thrown up breastworks about their camp. They say that if attacked they will die before they will surrender. A very sensible conclusion, methinks, in view of the sad fate of so many colored comrades in arms. They assembled at the landing and amused us with a number of songs—done in good Ethiopian style. "Old John Brown" and "Kingdom Coming" seemed to be the favorites with them.[3] Song books, testaments, &

c., were thrown to them by our boys, and were received by the negroes with many expressions of gratitude.

I am told that black soldiers from Northern and Border States, are much superior to those from the Cotton States. The latter are less spirited and do not exhibit an equal degree of soldierly pride. This is doubtless owing to the more servile condition in which they were held previous to the war.

An hour ago we passed the town of Lake Providence—seventy-six miles above Vicksburg. It is a small place, but contains some neat buildings.

The plantations which we have passed today are much finer than any we have previously seen. Yet they have a deserted appearance. Below Cairo the shores of the Mississippi present few indications of that vigorous life which is indicated by the neat farms and flourishing villages that line her shores above that point. Hour after hour at times, we have moved along without observing a human habitation, or anything to indicate the presence of human beings. Then perhaps we would discover a lone hut, and perchance at intervals a series of forsaken plantations. Outside of the cities, I remember seeing but two or three representatives of labor during the last two days. One of these representatives was a lazy looking mule, and another was a negro woman holding the plow to which the mule was attached.

We are more than ever impressed with the importance of the Mississippi as a commercial outlet for the products of the Northwest. The free navigation of this river is essential to our existence as a Nation. The Northwest cannot do without it—the Nation cannot live without it[.] As we sail upon its broad bosom, upon which no rebel craft now dare make its appearance, we feel impelled to urge our countrymen to make a more solemn vow that it shall be forever free to them. Better at once yield up our birthright of liberty; disown our National record; discard the flag of the free; and be remembered only in history. Yet we can trust the people of the North. They understand the issue[.] They know that, divested of all political sophistries, it is simply a question of National life or death, and they will prove themselves able to finish the great work devolving upon them.

So long as we have a good fleet of gun-boats on the Mississippi, it is next to impossible for the rebels to regain a foothold. There are but few vulnerable points, this side of Memphis, and to retain any point on the river, the rebels must be supported by an immense land force. This support cannot be given, unless they succeed in winning one or more brilliant campaigns in the west.

4 o'clock p. m.—We have just left the landing at Milliken's Bend, twenty-

five miles above Vicksburg; will reach the latter place about two hours hence. We remained but a few moments at the Bend, but during the interval, I improved the opportunity to tread the sacred soil of another of the so-called Confederate States—Louisiana. I was actuated by a bit of vanity in going ashore, for I was enabled to say on returning to the boat, that I had been in every State that borders upon the Mississippi River, from its source to its mouth.

If I can find time I will write my next letter in Vicksburg.

S. F. F.

(Rock Island *Union*, May 4, 1864, p. 2)

1. In a belated attempt to relieve Grant's pressure on Vicksburg, Lt. Gen. Theophilus H. Holmes, commanding the Confederate District of Arkansas, launched a badly handled assault on Helena on the Fourth of July (the day Vicksburg surrendered). The bungled affair cost the southern cause 1,600 casualties, while inflicting more than 200 on the victorious Federal defenders. At the time of the attack, the post was commanded by Maj. Gen. Benjamin M. Prentiss (1819–1901), one of the heroes of Shiloh. Prentiss was succeeded in command at Helena by Brig. Gen. Napoleon B. Buford (1807–83), originally colonel of the 27th Illinois and a resident of Rock Island. Boatner, *Civil War Dictionary*, 98, 393, 668.

2. Most of the soldiers belonging to the 900-man 60th U.S. Colored Infantry were recruited in Iowa, which contained a population of only about one thousand blacks in 1860. Six of the companies rendezvoused at Keokuk and were mustered during October 1863. The remaining four companies entered the service at St. Louis by year's end. The regiment was commanded by Col. John G. Hudson. For details about the regiment see S. H. M. Byers, *Iowa in War Times* (Des Moines, 1888), 568, and Lurton D. Ingersoll, *Iowa and the Rebellion* (Philadelphia, 1866), 706–707.

3. "Old John Brown" probably refers to a later parody of the more familiar "John Brown's Body." The first line of the later version runs thus: "Old John Brown's body lies a mouldering in the grave." The composer is unknown, but the tune is identical to its more popular predecessor. See Silber, *Songs of the Civil War*, 11, 24, for the origin of the John Brown songs and for the words of the later version. "Kingdom Coming" was written by abolitionist songwriter Henry Clay Work and first performed by the Christy Minstrels on April 23, 1862. The song became immensely popular in the North among both whites and blacks. For an interesting account of the publisher's unique advertising campaign preceding the song's introduction, see Silber, 306.

ᴑ— No. 42 —ᴑ

Vicksburg, Miss., April 20, '64

At eleven o'clock last night we landed at Vicksburg. The night was exquisitely beautiful. The moon shone brightly and [t]he light zephyrs scarcely ruffled the silvery surface of the river. The city was wrapped in repose, but we could see enough of the place even at that hour, to convince us that it is pleasantly located, and presents many evidences of taste and refinement.

Our recruits were this morning delivered up to the Post Commander, and since disposing of them we have been exploring the city and the battlefields of Vicksburg. Commencing at or near the right of the rebel line of defense, we traced their works around the city as far as Fort Hill, which appeared to be about two miles from the extreme left of this line.[1] The operations of the two armies in the rear of the city have given it the appearance of a great mining country. An immense amount of labor has been accomplished here. The main rebel line of defense—a trench with occasional heavy breastworks—runs in a zig-zag course, forming an irregular semicircle, eleven miles in length. Confronting this line, and at various distances beyond, may be seen occasional earthworks, trenches and rifle pits. They indicate where our brave boys approached the rebel strong-hold. The defenses thrown up by our soldiers have been with few exceptions leveled to the ground—the object being to prevent the rebels from using them in case they should attack the city.

I despair of conveying a correct idea of the physical appearance of the country in the rear of Vicksburg. It is not inaptly represented by the pictures of the moon which appear in works of astronomy. The city itself is located upon the face and summit of a series of bluffs which rise boldly up from the water's edge.—These bluffs are isolated from each other by deep ravines, which seem to diverge inland from the city. In the rear of the place, instead of uniform hills and valleys, thousands of steep little hills, thrown promiscuously together, in chaotic confusion, meet the eye. Let the readers select the most uneven surface of land in the State of Illinois, and then let him fancy it thoroughly upheaved and broken up by an earthquake, and I fancy he will have an imperfect understanding of the appearance of the country in the rear of Vicksburg. The rebels selected their line of defense with great skill. The trenches, following an irregular ridge, are easily approached from the city. The nature of the ground was such that large bodies of rebels could be marched from the city into the works, or from one portion of them into another without attracting the attention of our commanders. The great strength of Vicksburg is not to be attributed to the skill, industry or energy of the rebels, but to the handiwork of a higher power. Any one at first sight is ready to declare that the position is impregnable. And it is questionable whether it would have fallen to this day, had the rebels been well supplied with food, clothing and ammunition.

There are still remaining numerous evidences of the perseverance and bravery of the Union soldiers during that memorable siege. Within a very short distance of the heaviest rebel works may be seen the Yankee rifle-pits.

I well remember the day when the news of the humiliating defeat at Bull Run, electrified and horrified the North, and I well remember how we walked with bowed heads for a long time after that great disaster, but if no other fields had vindicated the character of the Northern armies, Vicksburg alone would have wiped out the disgrace of the Manassas rout. The battlefield must be seen, and the nature of the ground studied, before the importance of the Napoleonic achievement of Grant, in capturing this strong-hold, can be fully comprehended.

Along the entire line of rebel works visited by us, the ground is strewn with musket balls, buck shot, grape shot, cannon balls, shells and fragments of shells. Within the space of a square yard we could have counted dozens of these missiles.

A line of pickets is extended along the vacated rebel works. About half of them are negroes. Negro soldiers are quite numerous in Vicksburg, and those on duty in town make a fine military appearance. We noticed one fellow pacing to and fro on his beat in front of a Colonel's headquarters, and must confess, that we have never seen a white soldier conduct himself more faithfully while on duty.—Nor have we seen any white soldier surpass him in the military precision which characterized all his movements. He evidently felt that he held a dignified position, and wished to fill it according to a contraband's idea of "becoming dignity."

At a short distance from the city of Vicksburg, no one could discover that it has passed through a destructive siege; but a close inspection reveals the terrible nature of the conflict that for so long a time compelled the citizens to burrow into the earth for protection. These "rat holes" may be seen in every hillside, and the numerous rents, where shot and shell tore their way through private dwellings and public buildings, demonstrate that this precaution was necessary to their safety. Many stories of the siege are related by citizens. One secesh gentleman proposed, one day, during the bombardment, to have a mess of peas for his dinner. Taking a vessel in his hand he went into his garden, but at the moment he approached his pea patch, a huge shell fell in the midst of them and exploded. He was not hurt, but obtained no peas for his dinner, as none were visible after the dust, caused by the explosion, had passed away. Almost every house in town was struck by one or more balls or shells.—The damaged buildings have in most cases been repaired, yet the patchwork shows very well where Gen. Grant left his mark.

The weather here is as hot as August weather at home. The streets are very dusty, and great clouds of dust are constantly flying through the city. Our walk over the battlefields was quite exhausting. My fellow traveler,[2] mentioned in previous letters, breathed like a porpoise, and we were both glad to avail ourselves of an occasional rest beneath the leafy trees.—We had walked as much as eight miles when we reached Fort Hill, and were weak and faint, yet the long return walk was before us . But fortune was propitious. At that moment, a soldier with an army wagon approached us. We solicited a ride, he cheerily granted our request, and amid clouds of dust we rolled away towards Vicksburg. It was a pleasant transition, from the fatigues of a march to that rude conveyance, and forcibly reminded me of a time in my Kentucky experience as a soldier, when exhausted by a long march, I was permitted to enjoy the luxury of riding in a heavy, jostling army wagon.

While returning to the city we observed large numbers of negroes at work upon fortifications. Very strong defensive works are being erected immediately around the place.

Gen. J. McArthur is in command here and, judging from the nature of the defenses in process of construction, I apprehend that he entertains no idea of relinquishing his command at the bidding of the enemy.[3]

But my letter is already sufficiently long. I will improve the first favorable opportunity to write again.

S. F. F.

(Rock Island *Union,* May 4, 1864, p. 2)

1. Fort Hill, situated on a bluff north of Vicksburg, was undermined and blown up by Grant's men on June 25, 1863. Confederate resistance continued there, however, necessitating the explosion of a second mine on July 1.

2. Capt. E. H. Conger.

3. Brig. Gen. John McArthur (1826–1906), a native of Scotland, had originally commanded the 12th Illinois Infantry. Elevated to command of a brigade and subsequently a division, he served at the capture of Forts Henry and Donelson, at Shiloh, at Iuka, and at Vicksburg. He commanded the garrison of that city until August 1864, when he joined Sherman in front of Atlanta. See Warner, *Generals in Blue,* 288–89.

◦— No. 43 —◦

On Board Steamer Lancaster,
April 22, 1864.

We are again upon the broad bosom of the Mississippi and the prow of our vessel is turned northward. We left the city of Vicksburg yesterday afternoon and are now far up the river on our return voyage.

I must, however, devote a few more paragraphs to Vicksburg and vicinity.— While there we obtained a fine view of Young's Point, from Castle Battery, south of the city. It will be remembered that this is the point which Grant proposed to isolate from the mainland, and thus make an inland city of Vicksburg.[1] The plan certainly was a feasible one, and under more favorable circumstances, must have succeeded[.] After coming around the Point on our way up we obtained a view of this celebrated work. The city may be plainly seen from a point in the river opposite the canal, yet it is at such a distance that our troops could not have been greatly annoyed by their batteries.

From the deck of our vessel, as we moved up the river, the view of the city was very fine. As a place of residence, I would select Vicksburg in preference to any town that I have visited below Cairo—unless I may except Memphis, which I have not seen by daylight; of course I do not except Cairo!

Our return ride thus far has not been, in its general features, unlike our downward trip. Our vessel is, however, much inferior to the "Constitution." While in the cabin of that vessel, we could hardly discover, by any sound, or by a quiver of her timbers, that she was in motion, but this one moves with such a vibratory motion, that I can scarcely write a legible hand. The motion of the boat is communicated to my pen, and the consequence is, my "crow tracks" indicate an exceedingly nervous style.

While coming up the river to day, our emotions of the ludicrous, and our emotions of pity were successively awakened by incidents that I will sketch somewhat in detail. Somewhere above Vicksburg a party of contrabands were taken on board; their destination being a landing about one hundred miles above. On arriving at the landing, one of them failed to go ashore, but was not discovered until the vessel was well under way again. The fellow evidently wished to remain on board, but the Captain of the boat discovering him, "rounded to" about a mile above the landing. A strong wind was blowing, and when the boat landed, it was necessary for Sambo to "walk the plank" with some celerity, as the vessel commenced wheeling and gradually receding from the shore. But Sambo was in no hurry; reluctantly, and at a snail's pace, he moved towards the plank. Forcibly seizing him, the deck hands urged him along[.] He made some slight resistance and fell from the plank, but caught hold of something on the bank, and with the aid of three or four of the deck hands—one of whom made an application of boot leather which was more forcible than elegant—he reached dry land, minus one shoe which fell into the river. He was certainly the laziest darkey that I ever saw, and we all concluded that it would have been to him an especial accommodation to have allowed him to tumble into the river.

The case that awakened our pity was this: A short distance above the place where we landed the lazy contraband, we observed an unfortunate calf standing upon a portion of the bank which had slipped half way to the water's edge. By stepping a foot forward or backward, it would be precipitated into the surging flood below, and as if instinctively aware of this, it remained perfectly quiet. Our boat, of course, moved relentlessly on, but I felt that if I had been running a vessel as large as the Great Eastern, I could have halted it to rescue the innocent little creature.

We have on board, a soldier who was captured by the rebels during the Sherman expedition. He effected his escape from a rebel prison at Cahaba, Alabama, about three weeks ago.[2] He furnished me with some interesting items concerning the state of affairs in that part of Rebeldom. There is much disaffection among the soldiers of the Southern army, and in conversing privately with individuals he discovered that many of them would avail themselves of a favorable opportunity to come into our lines. In Jones county, Miss., two regiments of rebel troops were endeavoring to suppress an insurrection that had been inaugurated by deserters from their army, but the deserters were so well prepared to meet them that they made but slight progress in quelling the little counter rebellion.[3] He stated further that prominent rebels remarked to him that they will endeavor to "worry through" Lincoln's Administration, and that they would be "all right" if McClellan should be elected President, for he would recognize the Confederacy. He assured all such hopeful rebs that we will re-elect Uncle Abe. The rebels have been dilligently [sic] at work repairing the portions of the railroad torn up by Sherman's army. The Mobile & Ohio R. R. is again in running order south of Meridan [sic], and the road from Meridan to Jackson, Miss., will probably be in running order within one month from this date.—My informant states that they have already finished it to a point ten miles west of Meridan.[4] The rails that were torn up by our troops, are in most cases used in re-constructing the road. The attempt to render them unserviceable, by simply bending them was a failure. A portion of the rails were twisted or "kinked" when torn up, and the rebs can make no use of these.

There are, according to the statement of this escaped prisoner, about ten thousand of the Vicksburg paroled rebel prisoners at Demopolis, Ala. It is thought that they will soon be furnished arms, and assigned to active duty. Many of them declare, however, that they will never take up arms until regularly exchanged.[5]

In view of the activity of the rebels in the rear of Vicksburg, and at various points along the river, I think in [*sic*] not improbable that they intend to make a strong effort to re-establish a blockade of the Mississippi this summer. And I cannot resist the impression that this great thoroughfare is held with too light a grasp by our Government. We pass along over its bosom for hours without seeing a soldier or a gunboat. It is true, as I have said before, that the rebels must meet with great success in the field in order to sustain such a blockade, yet it would be wise policy to strengthen our hold upon the river to such an extent that it would be impossible for them under any circumstances to regain a foothold. The continued possession of the Mississippi guarantees the final suppression of the rebellion. Would it not be wise to forego further trans Mississippi expeditions, and use the men and means liable to be sacrificed in such affairs as that at Shreveport, to render the continued navigation of the river no longer an uncertainty.[6] Such are the impressions made upon me by observations during this trip, and while I admit that our distinguished Generals should know precisely the state of affairs along the river, and understand what measures are necessary to keep it open, I yet claim the right to express my humble opinions upon the subject. Of course the Administration and Military Chieftains will not consider themselves obliged to follow the line of policy indicated in the above remarks!

April 23d.—We will reach Memphis to-night, and probably will remain there one day.

S. F. F.

(Rock Island *Union*, May 4, 1864, p. 2)

1. One of Grant's early plans for getting his army south of Vicksburg and across the Mississippi to the east side where maneuvers would be significantly easier, was the completion of a canal across the base of the peninsula formed by the river's sharp bend at Vicksburg. The

canal had been started in the summer of 1862, before Grant assumed command, using soldiers and slaves to do the digging. But by the early months of 1863 the ground had become too swampy, and Grant abandoned the plan.

2. The Confederate prison at Cahaba, Alabama, was established in 1863 as a temporary facility. Circumstances, however, forced its continued use until the end of the war. At one time as many as two thousand prisoners were confined there. See William O. Bryant, *Cahaba Prison and the Sultana Disaster* (Tuscaloosa, Ala., 1990), and Frank L. Byrne, "Prisons," in *Encyclopedia of the Confederacy*, III, 1265–68.

3. In 1864, according to tradition, the pro-Union citizens of Jones County, Mississippi, seceded from the state and from the Confederacy and established the "Republic of Jones," which remained a separate political entity until the end of the war. The facts, however, are somewhat less romantic. Because of the remoteness of its location, Jones County became a haven for Confederate deserters and vagabonds who committed acts of plunder and violence upon its citizens. When Federal troops entered the area, the perpetrators attempted to represent their depredations as political in nature and directed against the Confederate government. When the Confederacy attempted to stop the activities of the Jones County outlaws in mid-1864, its action was taken by some in the North as repression of political dissidents. The legend has persisted to the present day. See Rudy H. Leverett, "Jones County, Mississippi," *Encyclopedia of the Confederacy*, II, 870; and Leverett, *Legend of the Free State of Jones* (Jackson, Miss., 1984).

4. This was track that had been torn up by Sherman's men on his Meridian expedition two months earlier.

5. Earlier in the war, prisoners captured in battle would have been paroled in a matter of days and sent back to their own lines. Once there they would await formal exchange, which would take place once an equivalent number of parolees had been received on the other side. By the early months of 1864, however, disputes between the U.S. and Confederate governments had arisen over the status of captured black soldiers. This, along with changing attitudes toward the exchange system itself, led to an almost complete cessation of exchanges. Indeed, the new Federal general-in-chief, U. S. Grant, believed the system as it had been functioning, led to easy surrender and even desertion to the enemy. Once the system broke down, the backlog of prisoners on both sides inevitably led to the establishment of such prison camps as those at Andersonville and Elmira. See Frank L. Byrne, "Prisoners of War," *Encyclopedia of the Confederacy*, III, 1256–64.

6. Shreveport had been an objective of Maj. Gen. N. P. Banks's Red River campaign, which had begun early in March. On April 8, however, at Sabine Crossroads, the Union army had suffered a disastrous defeat and then been forced to fight again the next day at Pleasant Hill. Following these bloody actions, and in view of the fact that part of his army was due to return to Sherman, Banks gave up his efforts at taking Shreveport. Boatner, *Civil War Dictionary*, 655, 685–89.

◌— No. 44 —◌

On Board Steamer Belle Memphis,
April 26, 1864.

When I closed my last letter we were a short distance below Memphis. We reached that place some time during the night of the 23d—the precise time I can not tell, as I was then making a voyage far away into the realms of dreamland.—It was Sunday morning when we went ashore, and the city wore a quiet Sabbath day appearance. Memphis is a lovely city. One may pass many pleasant hours, viewing the beautifully ornamented grounds in which are embowered the elegant dwellings of her wealthy citizens[.] I have nowhere seen more tastefully or more richly ornamented grounds. The City Park, known as Court Square, is a lovely little spot near the levee, and has been reserved from the business portion of the city, as a place of resort for those who could not well spare the time necessary to rusticate in the fields and groves beyond the limits of the city. It is beautifully ornamented with trees and shrubbery, and among the attractions of the place are a number of tame squirrels, which seem as much at home there as in their native forests. They evidently obtain a rich livelihood from visitors who delight to feed them with filberts and other nuts. The pretty little animals are not at all afraid to take the proffered nuts from the hand, and they frisk away with them to bury them for future use; or perhaps perch upon some limb, and satisfy the immediate demands of their appetites.

Do you think, Mr. Editor, that I take up too much space in writing about such insignificant creatures as squirrels? It may be that I do, yet I delight to dwell upon the many manifestations of a love for the beautiful in nature, as exhibited by the citizens of Memphis. It is impossible to entertain an unfavorable impression of those who can throw aside the cares of business and devote their energies to beautifying their homes and their city by the introduction of the choicest ornamental trees and such playful, innocent little city pets.

Two domesticated wild (?) geese were cropping the herbage of the park.

In the centre [*sic*] of the park, surrounded by an iron railing, is a neat monument erected in honor of Andrew Jackson. It is surmounted by a bust of the General. One side of the monument bears this inscription: "The Federal Union: it must be preserved,"—and, let it be recorded, to the eternal disgrace of the rebel arms, that the traitors endeavored to obliterate the noble inscription. The words of Jackson were a standing rebuke to them, and some sacreligious [sic] secession wretch, apparently with a bayonet, partially disfigured every letter in the first two words of the inscription and also the "U" in the word "Union." Whether a guilty conscience or the proximity of Federal gunboats induced him to suspend his dastardly work, I cannot say, but I wish the scoundrel could have confronted for one instant, the living author of those immortal words. I imagine his punishment would have been complete.

We remained from Sunday morning until Monday evening in Memphis, and of course had ample time to explore the city. Memphis bears few marks of the desolating war that has ravaged the South, and in passing through her thronged streets, nothing but the ubiquitous [sic] blue uniform, flitting here, there and everywhere, indicates the proximity of an enemy. The landing was crowded with steamers, and the scene on the levee reminded me of the hurrying, jostling crowd that I looked upon at the St. Louis levee as we left that place on our downward trip. From the observatory of a five story block I obtained a fine view of the city, which lay spread out below like a life-size picture. Noble business blocks; lovely little cottages; elegant private residences, and the hovels of the poor, blend in a scene that has in it more of beauty than deformity; that is, more suggestive of happiness than wretchedness.

Our sojourn in Memphis was in every respect exceedingly pleasant, and that which tended mainly to make it agreeable to us was the generous reception we met with at the Soldiers' Home; and the Soldiers' Home at Memphis is not improperly designated a home for the soldier—The building was at one time the property of Wm Richardson Hunt—according to the plate on the door.[1] He is now a rebel Colonel, and while he is faithfully serving the Confederacy his commodious dwelling and ornamental grounds are found to be very servicable [sic] as a pleasant home for his enemies. The arbors and the ornamental shrubbery deserve more attention than they receive at this time, and it is to be regretted that the absconding Colonel left some of the rooms with rather ancient paper upon the walls, yet we have derived much benefit from his labors—and must not complain that he did not prepare everything to suit our taste and contribute to our comfort, when he "went and runned away."

I wish every reader of THE UNION could visit that lovely "Home." Each visitor, methinks, would come away with an enlarged faith in humanity and with a better assurance of the righteousness of that cause which enlists, in addition to our military strength, all the generous feelings of our home population.

The institution is sustained mainly by the Western Sanitary Commission.[2] Uncle Sam furnishes a limited share of the rations, but the soldier is indebted to the noble organization just named, for the luxuries of the table; for nice clean beds, with snowy sheets and feather pillows; for the books, magazines and newspapers in the reading room, and for the thousand little home comforts that I cannot enumerate here. The Home is a model of neatness and order. Everything about the kitchen has a cleanly appearance.—The long pine tables are guiltless of grease spots or dinginess. A sunshine of happiness seemed to throw its light around the locality, and leave its impress upon the features of all who sojourned there. Even the uncomely features of the Irish cook who poured out our coffee, seemed lighted up with the sunshine of gladness.

And now good reader do you wish to know how you can render such "homes" more happy? I will tell you: when you finish reading your newspapers and magazines fold them up, and mail them to some one of the Soldiers' Homes. Address them, for instance, thus: "Soldiers' Home, Memphis, Tenn.," and they will be received by the Superintendent, and deposited in the reading room of that institution. It would cost but a few cents per month to make such contributions, and many hearts would be made happy thereby. Another plan is this: order your favorite newspaper or magazines sent to one of these homes for three, six, nine or twelve months, from the office of publication. You may rest assured that in doing so, your kindness will be appreciated[.]

Mr. O. E. Waters—a discharged soldier—is the Superintendent of the Memphis Home, and his heart throbs with generous sympathy for the wayfaring men in blue, who claim the hospitalities extended by our noble Northern friends, through his instrumentality. I trust that his pleasant "Home" may continue, during the war, to be, as it seemed to us, an oasis in life of the soldier sojourning there[.][3]

April 27th—We are now about one hundred miles above Cairo, and I will briefly recapitulate the prominent incidents of our ride from Memphis to this point. We left Memphis at sunset, April 25th—passed Fort Pillow the following night, and during the succeeding day passed New Madrid, Island No. 10, Hickman and Columbus. On the levee at the last named place I noticed three heavy pieces of artillery, and near them, immense pyramids of shot and huge piles of shell[.] The military authorities are evidently preparing to place the city in a better state of defense.

At dark yesterday evening we landed at Cairo, left that place at 10 o'clock p. m., and expect to arrive at St. Louis to-night.

S. F. F.

(Rock Island *Union*, May 4, 1864, p. 2)

1. William Richardson Hunt served throughout the war in the Confederate Ordnance Bureau, first as an ordnance officer in Memphis, and later in charge of the Bureau's iron and mining operations in Alabama, Georgia, Tennessee, Mississippi, and South Carolina. See *OR*, Ser. IV, Vol. I, p. 965; Vol. II, p. 778, and Vol. III, p. 702.

2. The Western Sanitary Commission was created September 5, 1861, by Gen. John C. Frémont and was composed of several St. Louis businessmen and philanthropists. For most of the war the commission had exclusive charge of relief activities for the western armies. It established hospitals, furnished medical supplies, assigned nurses, set up soldiers' homes, and performed countless other humanitarian functions. This organization should not be confused with the United States Sanitary Commission, an entirely separate entity. The Memphis Soldiers' Home was opened to receive guests on February 13, 1863. After being confiscated by the Union army, the house had served as headquarters for General Grant, and for the commander of the 16th Corps, before being turned over to the Sanitary Commission. See Jacob G. Forman, *The Western Sanitary Commission: A Sketch. . .with Incidents of Hospital Life* (St. Louis, 1864), 80–83; and William Quentin Maxwell, *Lincoln's Fifth Wheel: The Political History of the United States Sanitary Commission* (New York, 1956), 98–100.

3. Orrin E. Waters, agent of the Western Sanitary Commission, served as superintendent of the colored public schools in Memphis after the war. See *House Reports*, 39th Cong., 1st Sess., No. 101, p. 259.

CHAPTER 9

"The Buried Hopes of Many"

⌒ No. 45 ⌒

In the Woods near Dalton, Ga.,
May 8th, 1864.

When I mailed my last letter at St. Louis, Mo., I hardly supposed that my next would be written in the wild woods of Georgia. But here I am, soldiering again in the old fashioned style—living on hard tack, coffee and pork; sleeping among lizards and spiders, and listening occasionally to the picket firing in the immediate front.

I will briefly sketch the prominent incidents of my recent journey southward—my time being very much limited, I cannot enter into details.

We reached Springfield on the 28th ultimo, from Vicksburg. On the 2d day of May I set out to rejoin the regiment. In thirty four hours arrived at Nashville. Stopped at Lavergne one day. Thursday, May 5th, left Lavergne and had a long wearisome ride to Chattanooga. Distance 130 miles. Made the trip in twenty-four hours. The weather was very warm.—During the ride there was a great demand for water, and at Tullahoma some little boys came 'round selling "Adams ale"[1] at five cents a glass. I invested that amount, philosophically concluding that it was a better investment than might have been made in procuring a more exhilirating [*sic*] beverage.

Friday, at noon, May 6th, arrived at Chattanooga. I wish I had time to delineate the grand scenery along the route, between Stevenson, Ala., and Chattanooga, but must defer the pleasant task until I have a more favorable opportunity. I may say here however, that it is worth a ride from the North,— to view the lovely Tennessee winding among the mountains and above all (!)

noble old Lookout—towering up into the regions of the clouds—its sides and summit covered with a dense growth of timber—in the midst of which, in beautiful contrast, may be seen dark clumps of pine. The railroad runs around the base of the mountain,—which in many places presents a perpendicular wall hundreds of feet in height.

I had, previous to reaching Chattanooga, learned that the regiment was "somewhere in the front." After remaining in the city two hours, during which time I succeeded in obtaining a second-rate dinner for the sum of one dollar, I took up the line of march for the front, in the direction that I was told had been taken by the 102d. Marched eight or ten miles that afternoon and night. Found an officer, with a brigade that I had overtaken, who had a brother in my regiment. He treated me with every kindness, gave me a bed in his tent[,] also supper and breakfast. Next day (yesterday) I trudged on—taking the Lafayette pike, beyond Rossville. The 15th Army Corps was advancing on that road, and the 20th Corps, to which my regiment belongs, was said to be in advance of it.[2] After proceeding five miles on this road I learned that the 20th Corps had followed a road that turned off to the left, at Gorden's [*sic*] and Lee's mill.[3] Not wishing to take the back track I took a by-road across the country. A Pennsylvania boy was with me. We wandered about three miles and struck the road referred to. Halted at a house—made coffee—fried our meat—ate dinner (?) and then pushed on. At length overtook the rear Brigade of the Corps. I marched until ten o'clock last night, still the regiment was "somewhere in the front."—Found a very gentlemanly officer of a Potomac regiment who shared his hard tack, his coffee and his bed with me. This morning was told that I would find the regiment about two miles ahead. After proceeding about that distance, I found a part of the Brigade, but the 102d was still "just a little ahead." I was informed that it was on picket duty at the right of the road, and after proceeding a short distance further I plunged into the thick woods in search of the regiment. To a final inquiry, a German soldier said, "more to the right, a little more," and, changing my course, "more to the right[,] a little more," I soon found myself in the midst of the boys. The meeting in the wilderness was a happy one to me.[4]

We are about ten miles southwest of Dalton. The enemy are near by and countless in force. We will probably have a fight to-morrow. There has been considerable firing to-day, but I think there has been no heavy engagement. A stupendous movement is being made. We have an immense force, and the line is so long that the fighting must consist of a series of battles. The troops are all confident of success. Ere you receive this you will probably hear of a great battle, and of the fall of Dalton.

The boys of the 102d are healthy, rugged, and hopeful. But it has become so dark that I cannot see to write. Good night.

S. F. F.

(Rock Island *Union*, May 18, 1864, p. 2)

1. The only beverage available to the father of the human race: water.

2. The 15th Corps (Army of the Tennessee) was commanded by Maj. Gen. John A. Logan and the 20th Corps (Army of the Cumberland) by Maj. Gen. Joseph Hooker. In September 1863, the 11th and 12th Corps of the Army of the Potomac were transferred west, under Hooker's command, to aid Grant in his campaign against Chattanooga. On April 14, 1864, the two corps were consolidated to form the new 20th Corps under Hooker. The 102d Illinois was assigned to the 11th Corps from January 1864 until its consolidation in April. See Frank J. Welcher, *The Union Army, 1861–1865: Organization and Operations* (Bloomington, Ind., 1989–93), II, 325, for details of the corps' creation; and Dyer, *Compendium of the War of the Rebellion*, 455.

3. Lee and Gordon's Mill stood at the point at which the LaFayette Road, a main thoroughfare out of Chattanooga, crossed Chickamauga Creek. Here began the concentration of Union and Confederate forces that led to the battle of Chickamauga on September 19 and 20, 1863.

4. This soldier was quite possibly a member of the old 11th Corps (now part of the 20th). Because of the large number of German-speaking units that went into its makeup, the 11th Corps had been known in the Army of the Potomac as "the German Corps." Boatner, *Civil War Dictionary*, 193.

⌒ No. 46 ⌒

Chattoogata Mountains, Ga.,
May 12, 1864.

Since my last letter was written we have marched twelve miles southward, yet we are still in the woods. Our present camp is in a romantic locality. We are in Snake Creek Gap—a narrow pass between lofty ranges of the Chattoogata Mountains.[1] Thousands of troops are camped in the valley, and thousands are passing by. The tent in which I write is pitched on the side of a mountain which commands an extensive view of the busy scene below. Rearward the mountain rises hundreds of feet above us.

The mountains and the valleys are covered with heavy forests. I notice many

strange varieties of timber and shrubbery. Upon the mountain sides the pine
and the laurel are abundant.

To-day, in company with a friend who is an ardent lover of the beautiful,
I proceeded far up the mountain side, and we collected fine bouquets of wild
flowers.

"But what are you doing in Snake Creek Gap," methinks I hear you ask.
Well, this is a question that is more easily asked than answered, yet I may
safely say that if you could observe the ant like industry exhibited in all the
movements of the army you would not conclude that we are idle. It is, however,
utterly impossible for an individual to comprehend or anticipate the general
movements of our troops unless he is permitted to visit all parts of the extensive
field of operations, or unless he can communicate with the different corps
headquarters. We are stationed temporarily in a mountain gap and can only
imagine what is being done miles away on the right and on the left of our
position. It is true that our imagination is materially aided by the occasional
booming of cannon in other parts of the field. The troops in this Gap are
busily at work. New roads are being cut through the woods, and a portion of our
corps is throwing up fortifications. It is thought that the rebels may endeavor to
retreat in this direction from Dalton. If they do they will find us ready to
receive them—as our prisoners.

I wish the reader could have stood with me on the mountain side last
evening, and viewed the romantic scene that met my eyes. It was a picture
that represented some of the most striking features of life in the army. The
white tents of the soldiers dotted the narrow valley, and their fires gleamed
through the foliage of intervening trees. Night was settling over the earth, and
the surrounding hills were dimly outlined amidst the gathering gloom. Dusky
forms could be seen flitting to and fro about the camp fires, and the hum of
voices struck upon our ears, in a monotonous sound, that grew less audible as
the night advanced. Above the hum of voices could be heard the constant
rumbling of wagon trains, which continued to move about without cessation
during the night. At length the clear notes of a bugle is [*sic*] heard playing
"ta[t]too," and ere it has finished, others take up the strain, and then comes
the crashing roll of the drums; while the surrounding hills repeat the inspiring
martial airs with many variations.

You would term this romantic—and it is. But do not conclude too hastily
that ours is a romantic life. The soldiers who are preparing to lie down to rest

in those diminutive tents, in the valley below, have even recently passed through severe privations—severe at least, they would be to inexperienced men. They have thrown away everything that could possibly be spared to lighten their loads. Some have thrown away their blankets. They sleep beneath their shelter tents and upon a rubber blanket—never removing their clothing before retiring. And their fare is such as soldiers usually have upon the march. All this may be termed romantic by some, and it *has* in it a vein of romance, that materially cheers the soldier in the discharge of his duties. There is, however, a feeling of confidence in the eventual success of our arms—and the soldiers seem to feel instinctively that the day of final success is not far distant, and they work with strong hearts and willing hands. Privations which once would have caused them to murmur, are considered mere trifles now. It is the hope of final victory which buoys them up more than all else.

But before I branch off too far from my pen picture of mountain scenery, I must give you another sketch. Some of your readers may remember my old friend E, whom I mentioned in a former letter as being incorrigibly *unmilitary.* "Uncle George," as he is familiarly called, has found a new and more appropriate sphere.[2] He has charge of pack mules and as he trudges along leading his heavily laden mules over the mountains, furnishes a picture that excites our admiration as well as our risibilities. His careless apparel; his heavy, uncombed beard and bushy head of black hair, give him such a wild appearance that a stranger would readily suppose him to be a native of these rugged regions. The illussrated [*sic*] newspapers should send a special artist to make a sketch of him, and it should bear the heading, "A Mountain Muleteer." However Uncle George has such a kind heart beneath his rough exterior that I must not abuse him with further criticisms—besides he might threaten me with vengeance, and his huge, rough fists are not to be despised.

Another Picture and Another March.

Since I commenced this article I have, in company with Adjutant I [*sic*] H. Snyder, ascended the mountain opposite the one upon which we had pitched our tent, and since returning we have marched about five miles. We ascended one of the highest peaks of the range, and looked down into the valley of the Oostananla river, in which valley the city of Dalton is situated. The city could not be seen. However, the extensive view of the valley amply repaid us for the fatigueing [*sic*] march up hill. A signal station is located upon the summit of the mountain, and one of the corps was busily at work repeating the cabalistic figures received from another station. We felt, as our eyes wandered over the extensive plain below, that we were viewing the land of the Rebs. Miles away eastward could be seen a number of army wagons—in park. We were at first puzzled to know whether they belonged to rebels or Federals. But an incident which occurred a moment later settled the question quite satisfactorily. A Union soldier who had wandered to the foot of the mountains, in that direction, came running back, and, after recovering his breath, announced that he had been chased by about ten rebels. He evaded his pursuers by dodging into a ravine.

We observed occasional "clearings" in the valley and connected with these were dwelling houses which appeared in the distance like ordinary tents. Everything was represented in miniature. The use of a field glass enabled us to obtain a very distinct view of the range of mountains beyond the valley, and the mountains far away southward and westward. The lofty ranges rise, hill above hill in beautiful succession and at various points culminate in solitary peaks.

We returned to camp and found our regiment in line, ready to move. This we thought was more than we bargained for, but there was no alternative, and we marched away without obtaining rest for our weary limbs.

We have simply taken up a new position at the mouth of Snake Creek Gap.

Our Generals are active and it is encouraging to know that Gen. Sherman visits the different parts of the field in person. He passed near our camp a few moments ago. Gen. Thomas is also in this part of the field. Gen. Hooker rode along our lines yesterday. The General is a fine looking man, but exhibits a degree of vanity that does not seem warrantable in any General. Major Gen. Sickles was riding with Hooker's staff, and when passing the troops, Gen. Hooker invariably motioned him and others to the rear, and rode about twenty feet in advance, to receive the plaudits of his soldiers.[3]

There is heavy fighting to day in the vicinity of Dalton. At short intervals we hear the angry "boom" of belliggerent [sic] cannon. The sound comes from a point almost due north of us. How strange the thought that there are thousands of battling rebel hosts between us and our peaceful homes in the North!—The tide of battle may roll in this direction at almost any moment. We hope and pray for a decisive victory.[4]

S. F. F.

(Rock Island *Union*, June 1, 1864, p. 2)

1. To get around Joseph E. Johnston's defensive line extending from Buzzard's Roost Gap down Rocky Face Ridge, Sherman sent McPherson's Army of the Tennessee through Snake Creek Gap in the Chattooga Mountains. When McPherson's troops emerged near Resaca on May 9, the outflanked Johnston fell back to defend Resaca and the important Western and Atlantic Railroad. On May 11, Sherman ordered the 14th and 20th Corps of the Army of the Cumberland to proceed through the gap and reinforce McPherson. See William R. Scaife, *The Campaign for Atlanta* (Saline, Mich., 1993), 15–26; Albert Castel, *Decision in the West: The Atlanta Campaign of 1864* (Lawrence, Kans., 1992), 121–22.

2. Fleharty probably refers to George Eckley of Company C.

3. Maj. Gen. George H. Thomas (1816–70) had succeeded Rosecrans as commander of the Army of the Cumberland in October 1863. Maj. Gen. Daniel E. Sickles (1825–1914) had commanded the 3d Corps, Army of the Potomac, at Gettysburg, where his right leg had been smashed by a solid shot and later amputated just above the knee. A politician by trade, Sickles was now engaged in a political mission on behalf of the president. On February 15, 1864, Lincoln had written to Sickles asking him to make a tour, "principally for observation and information," of Memphis, Helena, Vicksburg, New Orleans, Pensacola, Key West, Charleston, and any other points the general deemed important. Specifically, Sickles was to find out at each point visited "what is being done, if anything, for reconstruction—how the Amnesty proclamation works, if at all—what practical hitches, if any ther[e] are about it—whether deserters come in from the enemy, what number has come in at each point since the Amnesty, and whether the ratio of their arrival is any greater since than before the Amnesty—what deserters report generally, and particularly, whether, and to what extent, the Amnesty is known within the rebel lines. Also learn what you can as to the colored people—how they get along as soldiers, as laborers in our service, on leased plantations, and as hired laborers with their old masters, if there be such cases. Also learn what you can about the colored people within the rebel lines. Also get any other information you may consider interesting, and, from time to time, send me what you may deem important to be known here at once, and be ready to make a general report on your return." See Basler, ed., *Collected Works of Abraham Lincoln*, VII, 185, for the complete letter.

4. The fighting Fleharty heard was likely the encounter between Joseph Wheeler's Confederate cavalry and T. C. Hindman's infantry with George Stoneman's Federal cavalry and elements of O. O. Howard's 4th Corps in Crow Valley north of Snake Creek Gap. Castel, *Decision in the West*, 148–49.

FROM THE 102D ILLINOIS VOLUNTEERS

List of Casualties in the Battle of May 15th, 1864.

Headqr's, 102d Ills. Vols.,
Near Cassvill., Ga, May 20.

Editor of the Rock Island Union:

We have had severe marches and desperate fighting. I cannot now give details;

must first have some rest. I append a list of casualties in our regiment, most of which occurred at Reseca [*sic*], Sunday, May 15th, during a charge upon a rebel battery, which we captured. We mourn the loss, of many noble comrades who fell in that desperate charge.

S. F. F.

Co. A.—KILLED—Privates Arthur F. Sabin, Albert P. Cooper.

WOUNDED—Corp. Hugh Butterfield, mortally (since died).

Private J. L. Nash, head.

Orderly Sergeant, John Morrison, flesh wound through both hips.

Serg't Wm. H. Brown, hand and breast.

Private George Crosby, flesh wound left breast; Nealy Daggett, in foot; Thomas B. Brittingham, forehead; Albert B. Thompson, thigh; Rigdon B. Walker, flesh wound in leg.

Co. B.—KILLED—Serg't Joshua M. Kellogg.

Private Stephen Cousins.

WOUNDED.—Serg't. J. J. Armstrong, in hand; corp. Ezra D. Bugbee, left hand; Privates: John Walton, in hand; Wm. H. Rees, sever[e]ly in arm; James Donnelly, sever[e]ly, in left leg.

Co. C.—KILLED—Francis M. Freeman, Edmond Kinsey.

WOUNDED.—Sergts. R. C. Manning, in hand; Henry Bridgford, slightly, in head; Color-Sergeant, R. L. Carver, in mouth.—Privates: H. G. Cooper, thigh; Albion Nichols, sever[e]ly, hip; Peter Olson, arm; Henry Suter, arm; Wm. E. Wallace, hand; J. M. Beardsley, hand, slight; Freeman Merryman, head, by a spent ball; J. Littlefield, slightly, in thigh.

Co. D.—KILLED—Serg't E. E. Champlain.

WOUNDED.—Corp. Silas Area, thigh. Privates: James D. Sprague, mortally; Dan. T. Page, face and neck; Josiah Spencer, in wrist, slight.

Co. E.—KILLED—Private Peter F. Cook.

WOUNDED.—PRIVATES.—J. P. Morrison, leg; Michael Oswatt, knee; Gilbert Zend, temple, slight; R. M. Russ, leg, flesh wound; Wm. Altman, slight wound in foot; R. W. Wiley, shoulder; John H. McCutchen, severel[y].

Co. F.—KILLED.—None.

WOUNDED.—James Cubbage, in hand; Fred Stegael, leg; Thomas Welch, arm; Corpl. L. L. Maxson, arm. Privates—A. V. Firkins, hand; Richard Maxwell, leg; Enoch Rush, finger; Isaac C. Durden, breast; Swan Erickson, leg; Caleb Green, face.

Co. G.—KILLED.—Corpl. John Gibson; Private J. W. Hibbs; Sergt. R. H. Cabeen; Corpl. J. Y. Harris; —Harvey.

WOUNDED.—John Dunn, thigh, severely; J. S. Burnett, severely in thigh; Wm. P. Irvan, severely in thigh; Wm. M. Bunting, severely in shoulder; John B. Felton, severely in leg; Sergt. L. S. Guffey, leg; Sergt. R. B. Seaton, slightly in foot. Privates Geo. H. Mingles, face; W. P. Pierson, slightly in knee; Wm. T. Todd, thigh. Corporal J. C. Cummings, severely in face. Privates David Walever, slightly; Lucien Murphy, shoulder, severely; Thomas Spence, leg, flesh-wound; Peter Cameron, shoulder, slightly; Geo. W. Thomas, finger shot off; Wm. Gorman, leg; Walter Breun, shoulder, slightly.

Co. H.—KILLED.—Corporal B. H. Baird. Private James Elliot.

WOUNDED.—Corporal P. F. Dillen, breast. Privates E. D. Bullard, leg; H. Parmer, thigh severely; F. Ralph, thigh, severely; C. G. Smith, ankle, slightly; N. Truleson, thigh.

Co. I.—KILLED.—Corporals E. A. Aiken; Wm. Reynolds.

WOUNDED.—John Watson, leg; Andrew Brodine, foot; John Goodheart, arm; O. Hanson, flesh wound; I. Lilpatrick, hand; L. Olson, arm; O. Pierce, face; A. Riley, wrist; H. Swanson, back; Sergeant Wm. Brown, in face; John Whannell, leg; W. D. Lee, leg; A. D. Richards, in head.

Co. K.—KILLED—Corp. P. W. Willets. Private, Moses White.

WOUNDED.—P. O. Pierce, mortally (since died. Privates: Geo. W. Bartlett, dangerously; Elias Pierce, leg broken; Henry Willis, severely, in leg; Otis Alby, leg broken; John Sweartz, slightly, hand; Ezra Fuller, wrist; M. A. Butterford, slightly, in arm and side. Corp. Ambrose Rowe, slightly, in arm. Capt. Wm. A. Wilson, slightly.

(Rock Island *Union,* June 1, 1864, p. 3)

᠀— No. 47[1] —᠀

Camp near Cassville, Ga.,
May 21, 1864.

When I closed my last letter we were encamped at the mouth of Snake Creek Gap. The following morning, May 12th, we moved early in a direction to the right of Resacca [*sic*], around which place the rebels had entrenched themselves and were ready to give us battle.[2] The advance of our forces skirmished quite briskly with the enemy during the day and late in the evening we took up our advanced position near the centre of our line, on the right of the 14th Army Corps.[3] We occupied the slope of a hill—or rather a ravine which ran parallel with the hill—about half way upon its side. Night was well advanced when we got into position. It was a lovely night—too lovely for such cruel scenes as were about to be inaugurated. The rebels were busily at work on the opposite hill. We could hear the click—click—click of their axes as they cut down the timber to construct breastworks. Our skirmishers were thrown out yet there was but little firing during the night. Early next morning the sharpshooters of the enemy began their work. Our skirmishers replied briskly, and there was warm work during the day in the valley below us. We found it extremely dangerous to appear on the rise in front of our line. Those who ventured out to that exposed position were almost invariably reminded of their danger by the whistling of bullets near them. At one time three or four of us advanced cautiously and took up a position overlooking the valley. We supposed that we were sheltered from observation by the intervening foliage but soon discovered our error. A ball from the enemy struck some distance below us. "Perhaps a chance shot," we thought. Another came, much nearer, but fell short. Things began to look suspicious and we were thinking of changing our position when "zip" came another ball over our heads and struck a tree directly in the rear of us. We immediately evacuated that place.

There was heavy skirmishing on our left until two o'clock in the afternoon when that part of our line became hotly engaged.—Then we were ordered to advance a short distance. The moment we appeared on the little elevation in front of our position the sharpshooters of the enemy opened upon us vigorously. One man was killed and three wounded. We were halted and ordered to lie down, which we did most willingly and hugged the earth most affectionately. Until late in the evening we remained in that position listening to the occasional whizzing of bullets above our heads, but more deeply interested in the fierce conflict on our left. The combatants could not be seen, but the perpetual roar of musketry indicated the desperate nature of the contest. At times the sound reminded me of the popping of corn over a hot fire—that is in the frequency of the explosions—without reference to the volume of sounds. Above the incessant rattling of musketry, the deep bass of the artillery reverberated grandly through the woods and was echoed back by the surrounding hills. Patiently as we could, we awaited the issue of the fight, marking the varying sounds of the strife as the waves of battle appeared to advance or recede. The sound at times ran along the line towards us until we thought our corps would also become engaged. A battery about fifty yards to the left of our regiment hammered away at the rebel batteries which were throwing shot and shell into our advancing left. The rebel batteries were however so busy with those in their immediate front that they paid no attention to this battery. Towards evening the sounds of battle died away and finally dwindled down to the irregular firing of the sharpshooters. We retired to our sheltering ravine.

Our skirmishers who went out the evening before came in, and we learned that the loss of our regiment during the day amounted to three killed and nineteen wounded. Some of our skirmishers were in close quarters all day, and were in fact held as prisoners behind stumps within easy range of the enemy, until night. To have left their position would have been certain death. They had taken up their position at night, and when night came again they escaped.

That night we remained in the ravine, and beneath the lovely foliage of the trees we slept sweetly—but ere we slept, we looked up through our leafy covering to the bright stars that twinkled so peacefully in the calm blue sky, and thought of other distant skies of peace, and thought of those far away— as dear to us as life—*and thought of the morrow.* The voices of the little insects were heard when the discordant notes of battle had died away. Nature seemed to rebuke "man's inhumanity to man."

The morning of Sunday, May 15th, dawned luridly upon us. The smoke of innumerable camp fires had enveloped hill and valley in a hazy mantle. It was just such a day as I would have called a "battle-day" when a boy. I remembered that we had such days during the Mexican war, and with other boys at home I inconsiderately attributed the haziness of the atmosphere to the smoke of battle which we believed was borne on the breeze from the far off southern battle fields.

At an early hour in the morning we received orders to move, and immediately marched to a new position about three miles distant and nearer the left of our line of battle.

The rebel line of works formed a semi-circle—the right and left wings resting near the railroad and the front between us and Resacca [*sic*]. Thus after marching three miles from right to left we were probably not more than half

that distance from our former position. We were now on the left of the 4th
Army Corps and very close to the enemy's works.[4] These, however, were not
visible, and there were few indications of an impending battle. Yet everybody
looked thoughtful. At length it was whispered around that we were about to
charge a battery. Our brigade was formed into column by regiments.[5] We were
ordered to fix bayonets, and the ominous "clicks" ran along the line when the
bayonets were being adjusted, the nature of the work before us became apparent. Thought was busy then, and faces all seemed a shade paler. But that was
no evidence of cowardice. Those men knew that their courage would carry
them into positions of extreme danger, and they contemplated all the possible
consequences.

The 102d Illinois Volunteers formed the second line of battle. The lines
were to be thirty paces distant from each other, but owing to the inequelity
[sic] of the ground and the dense growth of young pines, where we formed,
the proper distance was not observed. The distance from the point where we
formed to the enemy's works was about six hundred yards. A valley lay between,
and their works were upon the crest of the hill beyond. A dense growth of
young pines completely obscured their position. At length, at about half past
twelve o'clock, the command "forward" ran along the line, and, down into the
valley then up the hill side we advanced. Our columns were hardly in motion
ere the rebels opened upon us a perfect storm of musketry, grape and canister.
The dense pines alone would have thrown an advancing column into confusion. In less than a minute it was "every man for himself," and our men were
mingled with the men who started in advance of us, but they continued right
on, and the center companies of the regiment rushed pell mell into the earthwork surrounding the battery.[6] This work formed an irregular circle about fifty
feet in diameter and was somewhat in advance of the rebel line of breastworks.
The artillery-men who were not killed hastily retired. The banner of our
regiment was carried into the fort an instant after the flag of the 70th Ind.,
which regiment was in advance of us at the beginning of the charge.—Near
the commencement of the charge, our flag bearer, Serg't R. L. Carver, was
severely wounded in the mouth but he continued right on into the fort. Corporal Dillon who bore the banner was shot through the breast an instant later.[7]
When he fell our gallant Adjutant, J. H. Snyder, caught up the banner and
carried it into the fort. Forty-eight ball holes in the banner and two in the
staff, indicate how fierce was the storm of lead in which it waved. Our men

remained in the fort but a moment. A raking cross fire compelled them to fall back to a point immediately in front of it, where they were protected by the rebel earthwork. An order to retreat was given by some one, and many fell back to the foot of the hill. Others presistently [*sic*] remained and disputed the possession of the fort.—We could not then occupy it—the rebs could not retake it. We were subjected to a constant fire from the sharp shooters during the afternoon. In the squad which held the position, several regiments were represented. If any fresh columns moved up the hill they did not reach us, and towards evening we became fearful that the battery would be retaken.—One by one our men retired notwithstanding the expostulations of those who remained. After dark the enemy opened upon us a sharp fire and we gave them a volley in return which silenced them. Then we cheered heartily, and one of our boys yelled out:—"come over and take your brass field pieces."

Help had been sent for, and at length we heard music in the valley below. It was the music of a brass band, and we thought the strains were the sweetest that we had ever heard. We learned afterwards, however, that the music did not herald the approach of the relieving column, yet relief soon came.—A strong force marched into position immediately in front of the fort. The guns—four in number—were held and brought off that night. They are handsome brass field pieces—twelve pounders. One of them is called "Minnie the Belle of Alabama."

The rebels evacuated their entire line of works that night, and were in full retreat southwest ere morning.

Our regiment has lost 21 killed and 89 wounded, including those killed and wounded in the skirmish previous to the battle, and also including one killed in a skirmish on the 20th inst. I received a slight flesh wound from a musket ball during the engagement of Sunday, May 15th.

I wish it were in my power to represent upon paper all the impressions received during the nine hours that we were under fire. But I cannot command words that will do justice to the subject. Yet in memory the scenes of that day are indelibly fixed. The cheers of the combatants; the roar of musketry; the groans of the wounded; the upturned faces of the ghastly dead can never be forgotten. And those who passed through the fiery ordeal will never forget the peculiar "zip," "zip," "zip," of bullets as they barked the trees and clipped the leaves around them.

And the scene after the battle! how shall I describe it? Were it not better that such description remain unwritten? It is enough for those at home to learn of the loss of dear friends and relatives without hearing aught of the nameless horrors attending the general slaughter? [*sic*]

In a deep trench surrounded by evergreen pines fifty-one of the slain of our brigade were buried.

Among those who sleep in that sacred spot there are no better, no braver boys than Edward [*sic*] Kinsey and Francis M. Freeman, of Co. C, 102d.[8] They were both quiet, innocent young men, and amid all the temptation surrounding them in the army, their characters were unblemished by a deed of which they could be ashamed. And they died as nobly as they had lived. Died for their country, fighting hand to hand with the enemy, within the rebel fort. Their surviving comrades deeply sympathize with the bereaved parents of the fallen heroes.

The scene at the grave of the fifty-one fallen patriots, was deeply impressive when the immense crowd of surviving soldiers gathered around to hear the remarks of an aged Chaplain, ere the forms of their comrades were hidden forever from their view. "Many in one," said the venerable minister, "is the motto borne proudly upon our nation's starry banner. Many in one grave— our fallen brothers rest. And is not the coincidence a fitting one? May not this common grave which contains the buried hopes of many, be cherished with a sacred pride by the relatives of the slain and by all who love our country's flag."

We remained in the vicinity of the battlefield until the evening of the 16th inst. The rebels had left their dead unburied, and the day was occupied in burying the dead of both armies, and in gathering up arms from the field. Some of these had been lost by the rebels, others by our own men.

And here I will close the record of our first battle. Much more might be written. I might award the merit of praise to individuals, but in doing so I might be doing injustice to others no less deserving. This much only will I say: We are not ashamed of the record made by the 102d on that occasion.

Marches and Skirmishes.

In the evening we marched away from the battle-field, and pressed on after the enemy until we reached the vicinity of our present camp yesterday morning.—Here we found the enemy in considerable force and our corps skirmished with them all day. At one time while our regiment was in line of battle in a neck of woods the enemy shelled us quite vigorously. We laid low and the screeching demons passed harmlessly over us. One of our men who was on the skirmish line in advance, was fatally wounded by a piece of shell that exploded near him. He lived but a few hours.[9]

An open field was between our line and the line of battle formed by the enemy, was in the edge of the woods beyond, the rebels could be seen riding to and fro, evidently watching our movements. Their line was at one point in plain view. Towards noon we moved to the right about three miles, and in the afternoon Gen. Hooker advanced his entire corps across the open fields and offered battle. But the rebels retired. I have never observed a more imposing spectacle than that presented by the different divisions as they marched with banners unfurled across the open fields. A strong column of the enemy closed in mass were visible in the edge of the woods beyond a field. Our batteries were quickly posted in a [sic] elevated position near the center of an open field, and one of them commenced throwing shell into the rebel ranks.

The rebel column quickly disappeared and we saw no more of them. While we were in line of battle four rebels came in and gave themselves up. Prisoners agree in stating that their Generals fully intended to give us battle at that time but were unable to prevail upon their men to stand fire. Their army is evidently much demoralized, yet they will probably fight again before they retire to Atlanta.

We are now having a short breathing spell and in a day or two will swing out again in a more extensive campaign. The friends at home may not hear from us again for many days. There are long marches and severe battles ahead, and we hope to win victories that will crush rebellion in the heart of the Confederacy.

(Rock Island *Union,* June 8, 1864, pp. 1–2)

1. Letter No. 46 was the last one numbered correctly by the publisher. Numbers 47, 48, 50, 51, 52, 53, 54, and 55 are not numbered at all, and No. 49 is incorrectly headed "Number Forty-Seven."

2. The Union armies began moving on Saturday, May 7, 1864. Feeling out Johnston's defensive position at Rocky Face Ridge, Sherman sent McPherson's Army of the Tennessee off to the right in a flanking move through undefended Snake Creek Gap to capture Resaca, Georgia. Sherman's intent was to interpose his army between Johnston's men and the vital Western and Atlantic Railroad. At noon on May 9, McPherson notified Sherman that he was five miles from Resaca. By late afternoon Union troops were in front of the Confederate defenses and had reached the railroad. Meeting sporadic resistance, McPherson cautiously pulled back, causing Sherman to remark that McPherson had missed the opportunity of a lifetime.

With his rear in jeopardy, Johnston abandoned Dalton on the night of May 12 and fell back to Resaca. By May 14, Sherman was before Resaca in force and began to probe the Confederate defenses. The 20th Corps (to which the 102d Illinois belonged) held the center of the Union line. On May 15, Sherman continued to press the Confederates while at the same time maneuvering to turn both flanks.

That morning, the 3d Division was moved to the left with orders to attack. The uncoordinated assault began around noon with Ward's 1st Brigade striking a lunette manned by four light twelve-pounders of Van Den Corput's "Cherokee" Georgia Battery. That afternoon and evening the 102d lost twenty-four men killed and mortally wounded, seventy wounded, and one missing. Scaife, *The Campaign for Atlanta*, 21–23, 34–35; Bruce Catton, *This Hallowed Ground: The Story of the Union Side of the Civil War.* (Garden City, N.Y., 1956), 416; McPherson, *Battle Cry of Freedom*, 744–45; Boatner, *Civil War Dictionary*, 691–92; Castel, *Decision in the West*, 136–38; Jim Miles, *Fields of Glory: A History and Tour Guide of the Atlanta Campaign* (Nashville, 1995), 22; *Mercer County History*, 400; *OR,* Vol. XXXVIII, Pt. 2, pp. 322, 352–53.

3. The 14th Corps, part of the Army of the Cumberland, was commanded by Maj. Gen. John M. Palmer.

4. Maj. Gen. Oliver O. Howard's 4th Corps, Army of the Cumberland.

5. To attack in "column by regiment," as Fleharty put it, meant that the regiments making up the brigade were formed in line of battle one behind the other. On May 15 the column of attack formed by Ward's Brigade consisted of five regimental lines: the 70th Indiana, 102d Illinois, 79th Ohio, 129th Illinois, and 105th Illinois (in that order). For Ward's report of the day's action see *OR,* Vol. XXXVIII, Pt. 2, pp. 340–41.

6. Capt. Max Van Den Corput's Georgia battery.

7. Sgt. Redding Carver (Company C) of Preemption, Mercer County, survived his wound. Cpl. Peter H. Dillon (Company H) of Knox County did not. He died on May 27. *Adj. Gen. Rep.,* V, 598, 607.

8. Both Edmond Kinsey and Francis Freeman resided in Richland Grove, Mercer County, and both had enlisted in August 1862. Ibid., 598–99.

9. After withdrawing from his position around Resaca in the face of one of Sherman's famous turning movements, Gen. Joseph E. Johnston had intended to concentrate his forces around Cassville and counterattack. His plans were spoiled, however, when one of his corps commanders misread a Federal movement and pulled his men out of line to meet a threat that did not exist. Johnston was consequently forced to retire toward Allatoona Pass during May 19 and 20. The roster of the 102d, ibid., 608, reports only one man, Pvt. Francis Relph (Company H) of Knoxville, as having died on May 20 of wounds received in action.

CHAPTER 10

"Brave Hearts and Steady Nerves"

⌒ No. 48 ⌒

Battle Field near Dallas, Ga.,
May 28, 1864.

On the morning of the 23d inst., we marched from our camp near Cassville, at which place my last letter was written. The entire army had been concentrated in the vicinity of Kingston and Cassville and had been allowed three days rest. I am unable to give the movements of the different corps, since that time. Suffice it to say that they confront the enemy in an extended line of battle at this point.

Our own corps moved to the Etowah river and camped near it the first night. May 24th we marched about eight miles—the enemy continuing to give way before our advance. The next day, May 25th, after marching about nine miles the rebels seemed disposed to dispute the ground with some obstinacy. The columns were halted—forced into line of battle, and ordered to advance. The first division of our corps soon became hotly engaged. The roll of musketry was incessant and terrific. In the meantime our division (the 3d) was forming on the right and was ordered to make a vigorous attack. It was almost night—we were in thick woods, and as some of the regiments failed to get into position no attack was made.[1] Owing to the darkness and the nature of the country there was more confusion in the movements of our division than should ever be witnessed in an attacking column. The 102d was quite near the rebel line. The shot and shell screeched over us, and the flash of the rebel cannon could be seen directly in our front. Fortunately no one was seriously hurt in our regiment. The sound of the battle now began to die away on the left. The rebels cheered and we were satisfied that the 1st division had suffered severely. Darkness set in and it commenced raining. In the thick woods amid the growing darkness—made more impenetrable by the smoke of battle which hung around the earth—it was almost impossible to reform the division in its proper order.—Pittilessly [*sic*] the rain came down—soaking our clothes through and through. After an hour or more spent in manoeuvering, our brigade was formed , as near as could be in column by regiments. We spread our blankets, and with them for a covering, went supperless to bed. Ere morning came our regiment was ordered to a new position, where we confronted the enemy, less than two hundred yards from his breastworks. A slight breastwork had been thrown up by a detail from the regiment, but it was a very poor protection, and the boys went vigorously to work strengthening it. Company E, of our regiment, was sent out skirmishing, and when day dawned they became warmly engaged. Our Spencers were too much for the rebels however, and most of them soon retired from their breastworks, leaving two pieces of artillery into [*sic*] a very exposed position. In vain they endeavored to take away their guns. Our skirmishers held them in tow—making it almost certain death for the rebs to approach them. Company E remained out some hours and had eight men wounded. A part of Company C went out next. Emmanuel Briggs of this company was severely wounded in the right arm.[2] The others returned unhurt after skirmishing three or four hours. Thus by reliefs from different companies skirmishing was kept up all that day (May 26th) and until four o'clock in the afternoon the day following. Our entire loss during that time was fourteen wounded and one killed. I. N. Stevenson of Co. K was killed.[3] At four o'clock yesterday, May 27th, we were ordered to our present position, which is in the front line of breastworks about half a mile to the right of our former position. The rebel line is further off but they have very good range, and whenever they see our excellent national target—the blue uniform—they "let drive" with astonishing accuracy. Since I commenced writing this a member of Co. F, who was in an exposed position, has been shot though the thigh.

The artillery firing was quite heavy on our part yesterday. Up to the present time today (10 A. M.) the firing has not been so heavy. The rebels occasionally reply.

Far away on our right we heard, this morning, the occasional booming of cannon, supposed to be the guns of McPherson.[4] The grand finale must soon come. Yesterday morning Gens. Sherman and Hooker came out to the position occupied by our regiment—200 yards in front of the enemy and walking along the line. There was a worn, thoughtful expression on the professor-like countenance of General Sherman. I liked the man at first sight.[5]

But I must now close. I hope to be able soon to record a decisive victory here.

S. F. F.

(Rock Island *Union*, June 15, 1864, p. 1)

1. When Johnston abandoned his position at Resaca, he retreated to Allatoona Pass and established a very strong defense there. To avoid an assault on this fortified position, Sherman moved his army to the west in the direction of Dallas in an attempt to envelop the Confederate army. Upon learning of Sherman's movement, Johnston countered by withdrawing his own force to the west to get in front of the Federals. On the morning of May 25, Brig. Gen. John W. Geary's 2d Division, 20th Corps, made contact with Hood's Confederate corps at New Hope Church, northeast of Dallas. Encountering stiff resistance, Geary's advance was halted while General Hooker, commanding the 20th Corps, sent for his two remaining divisions. By 5:00 P.M., Brig. Gen. Alpheus S. Williams' 1st Division, and Maj. Gen. Daniel Butterfield's 3d Division (containing the 102d Illinois), were in position. In the assault that followed, Williams's division (on the right, not the left as Fleharty recalled), bore the brunt of the Confederate fire. By 7:30, rain and oncoming darkness brought an end to the fight. Boatner, *Civil War Dictionary*, 219; Castel, *Decision in the West*, 221–26.

2. Emanuel Briggs was a farmer from Richland Grove, Mercer County. See "Descriptive List of Co. C," Record Group 301, Illinois State Archives.

3. I. N. Stevenson, a shoemaker from Millersburg, Mercer County, died May 27. See "Descriptive List of Co. K," Record Group 301, Illinois State Archives.

4. Maj. Gen. James B. McPherson commanded the Army of the Tennessee. He was killed in battle near Atlanta on July 22.

5. In a letter home, Fleharty described his sighting of the two generals: "I had a good look at the big men. Gen. Sherman looks like a college professor. His face has a worn look." Fleharty to "Dear Brother," May 27, 1864, in possession of Mrs. Sarah E. Glass.

⌁ No. 49 ⌁

In the Field, near Ackworth, Ga.,
June 12th, 1864.

Our immense army is still in the woods of Georgia, north of the Chattahuochie [*sic*] river.—There has been an unexpected delay in our onward movement, and while our pickets confront those of the enemy, neither party appear to be very belligerent. We have passed whole days as quietly as if peace had been proclaimed—scarcely a shot being heard on the picket line. If this state of inactivity was a military necessity at first, it has doubtless been prolonged by the heavy and continued rains that have fallen. Instead of an improvement in the state of the weather we have to-day, a slow, easy, perpetual rain.—However, there has been more firing this afternoon than we have heard during the same length of time, within the last eight days.—The heavy sound of artillery is occasionally heard. It is not thought that a general engagement will take place until the roads are in a better condition.

Jo. Johnson will doubtless make a stubborn resistance this side of the river, but will probably choose a position nearer Atlanta for the decisive struggle.[1]

The difficulties encountered in prosecuting a campaign like this, into the heart of the enemies [*sic*] country can hardly be appreciated by those at a distance from the scene of operations. The country is rugged and heavily timbered, and it requires consumate [*sic*] generalship to move our forces forward in concert.—Then we are moving further and further from our base of supplies. The enemy know every foot of the country, and can have no difficulty in providing themselves with rations, such as they are. We have a superior force, but in every other respect the advantage is with them. It is a delusive idea that they are hard pressed for subsistence. If the Confederacy never dies until the rebel soldiers are starved into submission, the Confederacy will live forever. The growing crops look well—or did when we first took possession of this section. They are annihilated as fast as the army moves. The wheat is used as forage for the horses; the fences are used for fuel; and the corn is trodden down by the invading army. Our boys have made good use of the growing crop of apples, which, though not more than half grown, make an excellent addition to our frugal fare, when well cooked.

The citizens have almost universally forsaken their homes. Many of them, it is said, have joined Johnson.

While on the march previous to our arrival at this place, one of our men conversed with a lady who had for some reason failed to accompany the retiring rebel army. She was nevertheless a genuine rebel, and expressed her opinion of the Yankees in words more forcible than elegant. "You'ns don't fight we'ns fair," said she, "whenever our boys choose a position and get ready to meet you'ns, Hooker *with his regiment* makes a flank movement and comes round in the rear; then we'ns must retreat again."

The campaign thus far has been quite severe upon the troops. Thousands of sick and wounded have been sent back to Chattenooga [*sic*], and many of them to their homes in the north.

Yet the spirit of the army is determined. No one thinks of a retrograde movement[.]—We often hear the men telling "what they will do when they get to Atlanta," with as much assurance as if they were about to commence a simple journey to that place.

Our work is nevertheless very arduous. On but two occasions within the last six weeks have I, when retiring to rest at night, removed my clothing as I would at home. On one of these occasions my trousers were placed in the hands of a contraband with directions to have them washed and dry for me by morning! At times we have slept in our clothes after having them thoroughly saturated by a drenching rain.

Our supply of rations has not been bountiful, yet we have been in no danger of starvation. It is impossible to have well regulated cooking arrangements in our present situation. The cooking utensils are very limited in number; and the variety of articles to be cooked is equally limited.

Speaking of cooking I must here pay a compliment to my friend Adam Maucker, who is regularly installed as cook for what is termed the "Excelsior Mess."[2] Fortunately I am counted in said mess, and speaking from experience, can say that Adam cannot be excelled in his particular line of business. In the camp and in the field, in rain and in sunshine, he is ever with us, when others go hungry Adam comes to us with his solacing cup of coffee, and with a supply of cooked rations prepared in his own indomitable style. He is this moment calling "come out to your suppers," and we obey the summons with alacrity.

Having finished my supper I must announce that limited time compels me to abridge my letter. We are in a wretched condition to write;—indeed if some of our friends at home could view our situation, this rainy, muddy, execrable weather, they would be surprised that we endeavor to write at all. In a campaign like this, soldiers must write short letters.

June 13th.—It rained steadily till last night and still continues. I have no special items of news to add.

S. F. F.

(Rock Island *Union*, June 29, 1864, p. 1)

1. Gen. Joseph E. Johnston (1807–91) graduated in the same class at West Point as Robert E. Lee. He resigned from the U.S. Army in 1861 at the rank of brigadier general and cast his

lot with the South. He led the Confederate army at the first battle of Bull Run and commanded in Virginia during McClellan's Peninsula offensive until wounds forced him to relinquish command to Lee. In November 1862 he was named commander of the Department of the West, overseeing the operations of Bragg's army in Tennessee and Pemberton's in Mississippi. Johnston assumed command of the Army of Tennessee in December 1863 and opposed Sherman's advance on Atlanta until he was relieved on July 17, 1864. See Boatner, *Civil War Dictionary*, 441. See also Gilbert E. Govan, *A Different Valor: The Story of General Joseph E. Johnston, C.S.A.* (Indianapolis, 1956), and Craig L. Symonds, *Joseph E. Johnston: A Civil War Biography* (New York, 1992).

2. Adam Maucker (Company C) a farmer from Richland Grove, Mercer County, enlisted August 11, 1862, and was mustered out June 6, 1865. *Adj. Gen. Rep.*, V, 599; "Descriptive List of Co. C," Record Group 301, Illinois State Archives.

᧤ No. 50 ᧥

In the Field, near Kenesaw
Mountain,
June 18th, 1864.

The temporary suspension of active military operations, was followed by a general movement on the 15th inst. As I have said before, my facilities for obtaining accurate information in regard to the movements of the different Corps and Divisions was too meagre to enable me to give details of general movements. Much of the time only that portion of our line of battle occupied by our own regiment was visible.

It was early in the afternoon when we commenced the advance. The rebels were near by. There had been considerable artillery practice during the day, and the picket firing became more active as our columns moved forward. Having approached sufficiently near the rebel line to comprehend their position, skirmishers were thrown out, and they soon became warmly engaged. Our regiment was detailed to skirmish in front of our brigade. We advanced quickly across the open field and into the edge of a wood, where the enemy's skirmishers stubbornly disputed our further progress. For hours from behind trees our men kept their Spencer rifles playing upon the rebels, and they replied with equal energy. On our right, in the meantime, a short but severe engagement took place. A portion of our brigade was engaged, and lost quite heavily in killed and wounded. No decided advantage was gained in this affair.[1]

At length the rebel skirmishers slowly gave way and our men occupied the crest of a hill upon which they had erected slight breastworks. No further progress was made that evening. During the skirmish Capt. Isaac McManus of Co. G, was shot through the left arm, below the elbow.[2] It is feared that his arm must be amputated, as the bone is broken. The Captain has ever exhibited a degree of bravery that almost amounted to rashness, and his loss will be severely felt by the regiment, during the remainder of the arduous campaign in which we are engaged. Lieut. Trego of Co. C, received a slight wound from a spent ball which struck him on the right hand.[3] Several enlisted men were wounded. I give their names, together with the names of those wounded since that time, at the conclusion of this letter.

The skirmishers commenced their work at an early hour the next morning, and in a short time our Colonel was wounded in the left leg. He had proceeded to the skirmish line to post a number of sharp shooters and as he was about to return was singled out by a rebel sharp shooter, who evidently discovered his rank. The ball struck above the knee and passed through the limb barely missing the bone. The men were intensely excited when the Colonel came in, limping and leaning upon the arm of one of his men. They gathered around him with anxious inquiries,—to all of which he replied: "I am only scratched a little, boys." He was unwilling to admit the serious nature of the wound, and was with difficulty persuaded that it was necessary for him to be taken to the rear. He felt as if he were leaving his own children in an hour of great peril, and the men realized that they were being deprived of a commander who has ever been true to them.

Col. Smith has been traduced by slanderous writers at home, since he assumed command of our regiment. It was represented that he was unpopular with his men. If his cowardly enemies could have witnessed the scene when he bade us good bye, they would have been forever silenced.[4]

As a military man he has won for himself a fine reputation. Calm and cool in action, he handles his regiment on all occasions with masterly skill. Unlike many other commanders he has ever looked upon his men as citizen soldiers, not hirelings. While enforcing proper discipline, he has never been tyranical [sic]. He cannot be with us again during this campaign.

The command now devolves upon Lieut. Col. J. M. Mannon, and in him we have a brave leader, and a good man.

During the forenoon of the 16th, artillery was placed in position along our works. At one o'clock p. m., the guns opened upon the enemy, and kept up a lively cannonading during the remainder of the afternoon. The rebel sharp-shooters continued actively at work, but their fire did not interrupt our artillerymen in serving the guns. At sunset the rebels had failed to reply with artillery. The woods between our works and theirs were so heavy that the effect of our shot could not be ascertained. Through a slight opening, however, one of our shell [*sic*] was seen to strike a log that lay upon the top of their works. The rebels were in confusion from that locality, and our skirmishers took advantage of the occasion to throw a shower of bullets into their midst.

A short time after sunset the rebels commenced to give us a specimen of their skill in artillery firing. All quiet along our line, when suddenly *whiz* came a shell and exploded in the rear of our breastworks,—then another and another, and then—bang—bang—bang—came three or four, almost simultaneously, scattering fire and fragments all around.

They continued to pay us their compliments in this way for about 20 minutes. In the mean time we lay close up to the breastworks, and as far as we could learn not a man was hurt by the shells.

Other regiments were exposed more than ours; being in the woods in the rear of us without any protection. Men were walking about promiscuously—some cooking, others washing in a stream just below us. The artillery horses with the caissons were equally exposed,—yet, though the rebel guns were well aimed they did no damage whatever.—We thought the exhibition rather interesting, but were perfectly satisfied to have it end when it did.

Shortly after the shelling ceased another regiment was sent up to take our place behind the breast works, and we were ordered to fall back and form our line about one hundred yards to the rear. Our boys had built the breastwork in front of them, and when ordered to leave them and take up a position fully exposed to the enemy's shells, their curses were not loud but deep. Fortunately we were not disturbed. The rebels evacuated their line of works ere morning, and fell back to a new position about three miles distant.—In the morning we visited their vacant works. They were much stronger than any one had supposed them to be. The first line was sufficiently strong to resist heavy artillery, and in front of it the rebels had driven stakes, leaving sharpened points for the Yankees to meet in making a charge. A battery had been stationed where it could deliver a raking fire upon an approaching column. There were three lines of breastworks. The place could not have been taken by direct assault without terrible loss. But the rebels were compelled by a flank movement to retire.

At eleven o'clock yesterday we were in motion following them up. Hooker's corps and the 23d corps, forming the right of one long line of battle, swung around and pressed closely upon the enemy.[5] The position yesterday evening, June 17th, was, as near as I can [l]earn, as follows: The rebel line of battle appears to be in the shape of a horse-shoe. Within their line and near the toe of the shoe is Kenesaw Mountain, near which the railroad runs. To the right and left of the mountain their flanks cover the approaches to Atlanta. Our line conforms to theirs, leaving them an outlet only in the direction of Atlanta.

The country is much more open here, and we are enabled in a measure to understand the movements of our troops. The range of hills upon which the rebels are entrenched is heavily timbered.

The cannonading yesterday evening was very heavy on our part. Our division being held in reserve we have a fine opportunity to view the scene. From a hill in front of our camp we could see the guns of the 23d corps playing upon the enemy. From these guns a sheet of fire would burst forth, then white puffs of smoke could be seen coming through the tree tops over the rebels, and after this the sounds of the discharge, and the exploding shells would reach us in quick succession. By noting the time required for the sound to reach us we found that the battery was a mile and a half distant from us. Another battery played upon them from a hill a short distance in front of us, and others yet on the left. The rebels replied only at intervals.

There has been some heavy fighting on the left of our corps this morning notwithstanding a driving rain which has continued without intermission since daylight. The cannonading still continues. General Sherman is pressing the enemy closely on both flanks and in front. Unless the rebels retire there must be a general engagement soon. As I close this letter at half past nine o'clock a. m. the artillery firing becomes more animated. The mail will soon leave, and I am compelled to send this without giving the result of the impending conflict.

The following list comprises the names of those who have been wounded since my last report:

Commissioned Officers.

Col. F. C. Smith, thigh, severe flesh wound.
Capt. Isaac McManus, Co. G, left arm, broken.
Lieut. A. H. Trego, right hand, very slight.

Enlisted Men.

Co. A—Simon Burger, shoulder, severe.

Co. D—Elisha Billings, thigh, severe.

" D.—Franz Maul, head, slight.

" E.—Robert Wilson, thigh, slight.

" F.—Serg't Geo. Plummer, thigh, slight

" F.—Oliver Burton, hand, slight.

" F.—Thomas Dean, right breast, slight.

" F.—Nelson Gokey, head, slight.

" I.—Wm. H. Merritt, hand, severe.

" I.—Orderly Serg't R. F. Beals, leg very slight.

S. F. F.

(Rock Island *Union,* July 6, 1864, p. 1)

1. Slowed by bad weather and supply problems, Sherman was forced into a two-week lull in the drive for Atlanta. On June 15 he resumed the offensive by feeling for the Confederate line that stretched from Pilot Knob to Lost Mountain. In doing so, the Union armies fought several heavy skirmishes. One of the fights was the battle of Gilgal Church.

Hooker's 20th Corps of the Army of the Cumberland moved out at 12:30 on the afternoon of the fifteenth. Butterfield's 3d Division was on the right and Geary's 2d Division on the left. Ward's 1st Brigade led Butterfield's advance. At 2:00 P.M. the brigade halted and the 102d Illinois was deployed as skirmishers. Driving the rebel skirmish line for one and one-half miles, the 102d finally came upon Cleburne's main line of entrenchments at about 5:00 P.M. Taking cover, the regiment, reinforced by the 105th Illinois, continued to exchange fire with the enemy until the rest of the brigade came up. It was now midnight, and the men began constructing breastworks. The next afternoon, while reconnoitering the enemy's position, Col. Franklin C. Smith was wounded. During the two days' fighting around Gilgal Church, the 102d's casualties totaled thirteen wounded.

Butterfield was criticized for attacking head-on and committing his brigades one at a time, resulting in the advance's faltering in front of Cleburne's defenses. Union losses for the 15th were about two hundred. See Hicken, *Illinois in the Civil War,* 250; Dennis Kelly, *Kennesaw Mountain and the Atlanta Campaign* (Marietta, Ga., 1990), 22–23; Scaife, *The Campaign for Atlanta,* 62–63; and *OR,* Vol. XXXVIII, Pt. 2, pp. 324–26 (Ward's report), 354–55 (Smith's report).

2. Capt. Isaac McManus (Company G), of Keithsburg, Mercer County, was promoted major on July 9, 1864. In a letter to a Keithsburg newspaper an anonymous soldier praised the wounded captain and lamented his loss to the regiment: "Brave, generous, noble, patriotic, he cannot well be spared, when *men* are so much needed. He is one of those men that a little position does not inflate or puff up like a mushroom of a night's growth." While home convalescing, McManus campaigned for Lincoln and the Union ticket. He did not return to active duty until the last month of the war. After the war, McManus served a single term (1868–70) in the Illinois Senate. Keithsburg *Observer,* July 28, 1864, p. 1; *History of Mercer County,* 423–24.

3. First Lt. Alfred H. Trego was a student at the time of his enlistment. See "Descriptive List of Co. C," Record Group 301, Illinois State Archives.

4. On April 28, 1863, the Aledo *Weekly Record* published a letter from Ira E. Harsh of the 16th Illinois Infantry to John Miles, a Knox County farmer. One paragraph of the nearly two-column-long letter mentioned "considerable dissatisfaction" in the 102d with Colonel Smith's drunkenness. This brief remark touched off a miniwar in the pages of the *Record*.

About three weeks later there appeared a letter from "An Officer of the 102d Ill. Vol." It denied the charges of drunkenness and indicated that no dissatisfaction existed in the regiment. It went on to say that if the letter had appeared in a Knox County paper (where Smith was known), no refutation would be necessary. The writer hinted that Miles's motive for having the letter published was related to the fact that his two sons had recently been discharged from the 102d under less than honorable circumstances.

In a brief note published just four days later, the editor announced that he had received a letter from Smith saying the paper had "done him great injustice" in publishing Harsh's letter. Smith requested that the paper make inquiries regarding his alleged drunkenness. This was done, according to the editor, with the result that he could find no one whose testimony would establish the colonel as a "temperance man." Most, he said, verified the charges.

On June 6 Miles answered the allegations of the anonymous officer, which had appeared in the paper several weeks earlier, by denying that he had anything to do with publication of the Harsh letter. He took the opportunity, however, to charge that Smith had acted treacherously in securing his election as colonel when McMurtry resigned. He further charged that Smith was drunk when he disciplined ten men early in 1863 for killing a hog that had wandered into camp. Miles went on to claim that Smith promoted his favorites, and that he had broken some of his officers in order to create vacancies for his pets. He said that Smith was "loathed" in Knox County and had been asked not to address the Soldiers' Aid Society of Galesburg earlier in the year because of his scandalous character.

Finally, early in August, two statements signed by various regimental officers appeared in the *Record*. The first, signed by twenty-three officers and by Sergeant Major Fleharty, denied the charges previously published. They desired to "dissent from the policy of attacking officers in the rear, when they are fully occupied by a common enemy in front." They retained "utmost confidence" in Smith as a commander and respected him as a man. Under him, they continued, the regiment had become a "thoroughly disciplined and well drilled" unit. The second statement was published in three parts and signed by eight officers in all. (Not all of the officers signed each part.) The first part absolved Smith of blame in his discipline of the "hog killers." The signers of the second part denied ever seeing Smith drunk, and the third part reported that the colonel had acted fairly with regard to promotions.

With this the commotion faded away. Smith retained his command and served with distinction, apparently pleasing both his regiment and his superiors. At the war's end, Smith was promoted to the brevet rank of brigadier general of volunteers, to date from March 13, 1865. Aledo *Weekly Record,* April 28, 1863, p. 1; May 19, 1863, p. 2; May 26, 1863, p. 3; June 23, 1863, p. 1; and August 4, 1863, p. 1.

5. The 23d Corps, also known during the Atlanta campaign as the Army of the Ohio, was commanded by Maj. Gen. John M. Schofield.

⌀— No. 51 —⌀

Near Marietta, Georgia,
June 25th, 1864.

Sherman's army is still gradually closing in upon the enemy. There has been some heavy fighting during the last few days, and the skirmishing is incessant. On the 20th inst., the right wing of the army moved forward; again continuing its swing around upon the left wing of the rebel army. In completing this movement on the 23d, Geary's Division of Hooker's corps met with strong opposition, but the result was most disastrous to the rebels.[1] The enemy moved forward in heavy column to drive our forces back before they could strengthen the new position they had taken. Our batteries had just been placed in position so as to sweep an open field through which the enemy advanced. When they came within rifle range, the batteries were opened upon them, and the rebel columns were swept away like chaff before the wind. Our division was on the left of the division engaged. The cannonading was terribly grand. The fight continued for nearly an hour, at the end of which time, the rebels had retired, leaving many of their dead upon the field, which were buried by our men the following day. Our loss was c[o]mparatively light. The rebel loss is variously estimated at from 2000 to 4000, in killed and wounded.[2] It is evident that they did not expect such a warm reception. No body of troops could withstand the withering fire which mowed down their ranks. The rebels were commanded by Gen. Hood[.][3]

Our division was under fire during the day but the loss was light. Below I give the list of casualties that have occurred in our regiment since my last letter was mailed.

We are now only a few hundred yards from the enemy's works. Our generals advance their lines cautiously, securing every desirable position as quickly as possible, without recklessly sacrificing life. The army has strong confidence in its leaders, and all feel assured that we will be ultimately successful.

It is very difficult to obtain reliable news from the corps on our right and left. It seems certain, however, that our extreme left has closed in upon the enemy, until it commands the railroad between Marietta and the river. The rebels still hold Merietta [*sic*] and the Kenesaw mountains.

It would perhaps be more proper to speak of the double headed mound called Kenesaw in the singular number. It is an isolated mound, and is traversed by a deep valley by which distinct peaks are formed. Their summits are said to be fourteen hundred feet above the general level.

It is reported that General Ewell is now in command of the rebel army in front of us.[4]—It is not thought that the change will benefit the cause of the Confederacy. It must still be a prime object with the rebels to devote much of their stratigical [sic] talent to making masterly retreats; and Joe Johnston's ability in that line is unquestioned. If the rebel army continues long in its present position I believe the delay will cause its complete overthrow.

As our movements progress, I will at short intervals, by writing short letters, keep you advised of the part played by our own regiment in the great drama that is being enacted.

The friends at home can rest assured that the boys stand up to the work like men.—Deprived of all the comforts at home; constantly exposed to danger and death, they go forward in the performance of their duty with brave hearts and steady nerves. There is but little sickness in the regiment.

List of Casualties.

Killed,	T. J. Maxey, Co. B,
Wounded,	G. D. Russell, B, slight in foot.
"	Joel Hill, K, slight in shoulder.
"	J. J. Myers, K, severely in foot
"	Eugene Calkins, D, both legs.
"	F. Maul, D, left leg, not dangerous
"	Corp. M. Loomis, I, right breast.

S. F. F.

(Rock Island *Union,* July 6, 1864, p. 3)

1. Brig. Gen. John W. Geary's 2d Division, 20th Corps.

2. Fleharty is off by a day when he discusses the battle of Kolb's Farm. Here, late on the afternoon of June 22, 1864, Hood with eleven thousand men impetuously assaulted fourteen thousand entrenched Federals of Hooker's 20th Corps. The rebel attack was soon abandoned after some fifteen hundred casualties were sustained. Historian Albert Castel concludes that the Confederate attack at Kolb's Farm was "more a one-sided slaughter" than a battle. Castel, *Decision in the West,* 291–99; and Scaife, *The Campaign for Atlanta,* 65–67.

3. Lt. Gen. John B. Hood (1831–79) had originally commanded a brigade and a division in the Army of Northern Virginia, where he and his men had earned reputations as hard fighters. Badly wounded at Gettysburg, he recovered sufficiently to accompany Longstreet to

Chickamauga, where he lost his right leg. He commanded a corps in the Atlanta campaign until July 17, 1864, when he succeeded General Johnston as commander of the Army of Tennessee. See Boatner, *Civil War Dictionary*, 407. The most recent biography of Hood is Richard M. McMurry's *John Bell Hood and the War for Southern Independence* (Lexington, Ky., 1982).

4. Lt. Gen. Richard S. Ewell (1817–72) was graduated from the U.S. Military Academy in 1840, in the same class as Sherman and George H. Thomas. He commanded a brigade at First Bull Run and a division under Stonewall Jackson in the Shenandoah Valley. During the campaign of Second Bull Run, Ewell lost a leg in the action at Groveton. He returned to duty in May 1863 as commander of the 2d Corps, Army of Northern Virginia, in place of the slain Jackson. His performance at Gettysburg was less than satisfactory. It is known that Ewell desired to be appointed to command the corps of Lt. Gen. Leonidas Polk (who had been killed resisting Sherman's advance on Atlanta), under his good friend Johnston, but that post was given to Maj. Gen. A. P. Stewart. This perhaps accounts for the rumor Fleharty had heard. See Boatner, *Civil War Dictionary*, 269; and Percy Gatling Hamlin, *"Old Bald Head" (General R. S. Ewell): The Portrait of a Soldier* (Strasburg, Va., 1940), 184.

☙ No. 52 ❧

Near Marietta, Ga.,
June 30, 1864.

It is possible that at this moment you may be wondering what we are doing away down in Georgia, and without professing to be able to inform you fully, I may be able to convey an idea of our situation. So far as I can learn the lines have been changed but little since I last wrote. The enemy still hold Kenesaw mountain, and the two armies confront each other in many places not more than two hundred yards apart. Substantial breastworks have been erected by both parties, and it is difficult for either to gain any advantage by making assaults. The 4th and 14th corps attempted on the 27th inst., to carry the rebel line of works in front of them, but were repulsed with heavy loss. Our corps occupied a position on the right of them, and from a high hill upon which our regiment was stationed we obtained a partial view of the battle. The view would have been perfect but for the dense timber, in which the infantry fought. Our artillery was in an open field on the crest of a hill.—The guns kept up a constant roll of thunder and the musketry sounded not unlike the crashing roar of a hurricane. From our batteries the white smoke would leap—sometime from each gun in succession, and then again from all together—and the bursting shells would leave other white puffs of smoke, suspended as it were for a time, over the rebel line. And the rebel guns were not idle. Volumes of smoke rising from the woods indicated where their batteries were stationed. Occasionally one of their balls made the dust fly on the hill in the vicinity of our batteries, and their shells burst along the crest of the hill. Far beyond the scene of action the rebel guns on Kenesaw Mountain were throwing shot and shell into the lines of our army. At times, above the dense clouds of smoke that had rolled away from the rebel guns on the mountains, shells that had been thrown from some distant point along our line were seen to burst. It was an inspiring spectacle; a magnificent battle scene, without a realization of all the attending horrors. Alas! amid the din of that crashing storm of human strife many true hearts ceased to beat forever.[1]

The battle ended before noon. In the evening we learned that our men had been compelled to fall back to the line from which they had advanced—leaving their dead and wounded upon the field. The dead were afterwards buried under a flag of truce.

In regard to our loss we have only the information that it was *heavy*.[2] The rebel loss could not have equalled ours, as they fought behind good breastworks. The 27th Illinois planted their colors on the rebel works, but being unsupported were compelled to fall back.

The 27th lost one of its best and bravest men—one whom I have ever esteemed as a true friend—private Jonathan Vanmetre, of Berlin, Mercer county.[3] I am informed that he was last seen near the rebel line, standing by the side of a tree, wounded in the head—how badly, none can tell. It is hardly possible that he may be yet alive—in the hands of the enemy. He had been through the principal battles of the war in the West, and had previously escaped unscathed.

The repulse which the 4th and 14th corps met, on this occasion, cannot materially effect our future operations.

Our pickets frequently converse with the rebels. Last evening a member of our regiment endeavored to exchange papers with them. They were willing and anxious to do so, but said they had received no mail for a number of days and had no papers. They thought we had in some way interfered with their communications.

"Whe[n] is Grant going into Richmond," asked one of the rebs.

"He proposes to go into Richmond on the 4th of July," said one of our men in reply, and the rebel evidently recollecting Grant's penchant for celebrating the 4th by such triumphant processions, was silent.[4]

At times the style of conversation is less courteous, and each party black-guard each other with the most choice billingsgate.

Our position has been so close to the rebel line that through one or two openings in the woods, the enemies [*sic*] sharpshooters could readily perceive a man whenever his head was above the breastworks. The rebels fire very low—frequently striking the top log of the works. We were yesterday evening releaved [*sic*] from this advanced position, after having occupied it three days and three nights.

Some of our men narrowly escaped being hit by the rebel balls,—one had his hip slightly cut by a bullet that grazed the breastworks. Another, John Lippencott, of Co. C, was seated upon the ground a short distance in the rear of the breastworks, and was about to sip a cup of coffee, when a ball barked his arm and upset his coffee. Men were wounded a half mile in the rear of us by wandering shot.[5]

We are, at times, amused by the music of these stray balls. One comes along with a *"mew"* like the cry of a kitten, and the boys declare that the reb's [*sic*] are "firing kittens again." Then another comes with a howl as if seeking its Yankee victim. And we have listened to others that would have the wail of winter wind. All these sounds are more musical than the "zip" of the well aimed bullet.

By the way, I must relate an incident that illustrates the effect that the music of musket and cannon balls sometimes has upon the newly initiated soldier. It is said to have occurred at Resacea [*sic*]. In the midst of a charge upon a rebel battery, one of General Hooker's new recruits was observed far in the rear of his regiment, lying behind a tree that effectually secured him from rebel bullets.—he was repremanded [*sic*] by an officer and ordered forward, but protested in this manner: "I do not want to charge upon those guns; I will get shot. If General Hooker wants more cannon let him say so and I will *'throw in and help buy them for him!'*"

The weather is quite warm—yea—most decidedly hot. As regards prospective movements I know nothing.

There is but one casuality [*sic*] to report, in our regiment, since my last letter was written:—Joseph Calhoun, of Co. G., shot through the leg, below the knee. It is a flesh wound and although painful is not at all dangerous.— Joseph is a mere boy, and is a general favorite in the regiment. The wound was inflicted by a stray ball.[6]

Comparatively few of the men are sick.—Exposures and privations which they would once have thought it impossible to endure, are submitted to without a murmur now.

S. F. F.

P. S.—The rebels made a determined attack upon the 4th and 14th corps, last night, and were repulsed with heavy loss.[7]

Last evening a rebel Colonel deserted to our lines. He made the remarkable statement that "there will not be another shot fired by the Rebel army after the 3rd day of July." The reader can interpret the remark as he pleases. I give the statement as it was actually made.

S. F. F.

(Rock Island *Union,* July 20, 1864, p. 1)

1. From June 10 to July 2, 1864, the armies of Sherman and Johnston faced each other along the line of Kennesaw Mountain. The two forces were all but idle, engaging each other in a number of probing actions: Pine Mountain, June 14; Gilgal Church, June 15–17; Golgotha, June 16; Pine Knob, June 19; and Kolb's Farm, June 22. Finally Sherman, frustrated by the stalemate, chose to discontinue his heretofore-successful flanking strategy and ordered a general assault on Johnston's center for June 27 at 9:00 A.M. The attack, known as the battle of Kennesaw Mountain, failed to penetrate the Confederate lines. The day, however, was not a total loss. A late-afternoon dispatch from General Schofield informed Sherman that Cox's division had driven off the rebel cavalry and was in position to turn the enemy's left flank. Castel, *Decision in the West,* 317–18; Miles, *Fields of Glory,* 119; Boatner, *Civil War Dictionary,* 452–53; Scaife, *The Campaign for Atlanta,* 67–71; Sherman, 2: 61–62.

2. Federal losses on June 27 were about 3,000. Exact Confederate casualties are unknown, with estimates ranging from 600 to about 1,000. Castel, *Decision in the West,* 319–20; Miles, *Fields of Glory,* 111; Sherman, *Memoirs,* 2: 61; Boatner, *Civil War Dictionary,* 453.

3. Jonathan Vanmeter had originally enlisted in the 27th Illinois on August 20, 1861, and reenlisted as a veteran on January 1, 1864. Unfortunately, Fleharty's fears proved accurate. Vanmeter was indeed killed in the assault on Kennesaw Mountain on June 27.

4. Grant, of course, did not take Richmond by July 4. On that date his army was bogged down in a siege at Petersburg. That city did not fall until April 2, 1865, and Richmond surrendered the next day.

5. Cpl. John Lippincott was a farmer from Waugh's Grove, Mercer County. See "Descriptive List of Co. C," Record Group 301, Illinois State Archives.

6. Pvt. Joseph O. Calhoun of Keithsburg, Mercer County.

7. Throughout the night of June 29 both sides kept up a brisk fight, in some places separated by a distance of only thirty yards. See Castel, *Decision in the West,* 324–30.

CHAPTER 11

"We Deem the Campaign at an End"

ᕀ— No. 53 —ᕀ

Near Vinings Station, Ga.,
July 8, 1864.

From a tree-top I have seen the spires and domes of the city of Atlanta. Yankee eyes have been fixed upon the coveted prize, and will not be averted until the city is within our grasp. The view of Atlanta is obtained from a high ridge on the north side of the Chattahoochie [*sic*] river. We are encamped along the crest of the ridge which is two and a half miles from the river. Atlanta is nine miles distant.

We have advanced eight or ten miles since I last wrote. The rebels evacuated their strong position at Kenesaw Mountain on the night of July 2d—leaving Marietta in our hands, after a slight show of resistance by their rear guard.

The retreat of the rebel army was doubtless designed to counteract a movement of Sherman's army to the right. It was believed that Sherman proposed to have two or more corps operate against Atlanta, beyond the river, while the main army would keep Johnston occupied on this side. It appears that a want of supplies occasioned some delay in the movement, and Johnston by some means divining the intentions of our commander concluded to retire to a new position in front of Atlanta. His main army is beyond the river. Hardee's corps is between us and the river, strongly entrenched and fortified.[1]

At the time the rebels evacuated their position in front of Marietta the 14th corps was prosecuting a work that would probably have resulted in the capture of the line of works in its front. After the repulse of this corps in the assault of the 27th ult., it threw up breastworks not more than forty yards distant from the rebel line of works. The scheme was to undermine their works and blow them up. The work was progressing finely, and if the rebels had remained a short time longer they would have listened to a little subterranean thunder that would have astonished them, if nothing more.[2]

We followed the enemy early in the morning after they left. Our regiment was in the advance on the road that led to Marietta. We came up with the rear guard of rebel cavalry near that place. Our skirmishers opened a brisk fire. The rebels slowly retired firing irregularly. The regiment, in line of battle across the road, advanced in supporting distance of the skirmishers. It was a lively scene. The skirmishers advanced cautiously but steadily, securing advantageous positions and plying their Spencers whenever an enemy was visible. There were stately residences at the roadside with neatly ornamented grounds, enclosed by picket fences. In advancing it became necessary to pass through these enclosures and it was astonishing to see the boards fly as the boys crashed through the fences.

The rebels had a stronger force in our front. Three times they formed in line of battle to resist our skirmishers, but they were met by such a well directed fire that they were each time thrown into confusion. After the third attempt they retired beyond Marietta.

Capt. D. W. Sedwick, of Co. E, had command of our skirmish line. The Captain, who is one of the coolest and bravest men in the Army of the Cumberland, managed the affair with admirable skill. One of his men had the skin peeled from his cheek very slightly by a passing bullet; with this exception not a man was hurt on our side. The rebels did not fare so well, as a number were seen to fall.[3]

During the advance that morning about two thousand prisoners were captured, and deserters came in by scores. They all reported that others would come in if they had a good opportunity. One of them I observed had the letter "D" printed on his left cheek with India ink. He said it was placed there because he "ran away from them once before."[4]

"If they get you again they will letter you on the other cheek," suggested some one.

"Yes, but they must catch me first," replied the freed rebel, with a triumphant look.

It is estimated that no less than two thousand deserters came into our lines that morning, and still they come. Only last night three came in under such peculiar circumstances that I will tell the story in detail.

One of our men—Beecher Straw, of Co. B—an intelligent, talkative and venturesome Yankee, opened communication with a reb while on picket duty yesterday, and offered to exchange papers.[5] The rebel agreed to exchange, but after a time announced that he could not obtain a paper.

"Then meet me half way and I will give you one," said Beecher.

"Agreed," said the other.

The pickets on both sides were ordered to refrain from firing. The Yankee and the reb met, and shook hands, when something like the following colloquy occurred:

Yankee.—How are you "Johnny."

Rebel.—How are you Jimmy,—and, by the way why do you call us "Johnnies."

Yankee.—Because you live on Johnny cakes.

Rebel.—Well, for a nick-name we must call you "Jimmies." When are you going into Atlanta?

Yankee.—When will you cross the river?

(At this a squad of rebels a short distance from them, laughed heartily, and declared it was a genuine Yankee reply.)

Rebel.—Who commands your corps now?

Yankee.—Joe Hooker.

Rebel.—I thought Joe Hooker was dead.—We have been informed, officially, three or four times, that he had been killed or wounded. I believe the old fellow will live forever.

Yankee.—I think he will live to see the Rebelion [sic] put down. By the way, are you not sick of the war?

Rebel.—Yes. So much so that there are thirteen of us here now who intend to go over to your lines, the first opportunity we have.

Yankee.—Come over here to night then.—We will not fire upon you.

Rebel.—All right. We will come.

After a few more remarks the conversation ended. The parties shaking hands as they separated.

Beecher informs me that the rebel Lieut. in command of their pickets, ordered his men back to their lines two or three times before they separated. The rebel picket was a Tennessean. He stated that the Lieut. was an "Eastern fellow," and it would not do to let him know that they thought of deserting.

During the interview, hundreds of rebels came out of their breastworks to witness the scene. Our men, also, appeared in plain view. Both sides observed the informal armistice, and when the parties retired, the spectators on both sides quietly disappeared.

Now for the result. Our men were relieved from picket duty ere night, but the pickets who relieved them were told to keep a sharp look out for the expected deserters, and were cautioned to refrain from firing upon them.

A short time after dark we heard rapid firing a short distance to the left of the position that had been occupied by the pickets from our regiment, and this morning we were informed that the squad of rebels attempted to [c]ome in there. That their own men discovered their movement and fired a volley at them, whereupon, our pickets supposing they were about to be attacked, opened a rapid fire.—Nevertheless, three of the thirteen escaped to our lines. The fate of the others is not known, though it may be readily divined.

The flanks of the Federal army now rest on the Chattahoochee river,—forming a crescent, between the horns of which, Hardee holds a strong position, covering the Railroad bridge and the main road to Atlanta.—We will probably remain in our present position two or three days, after which time the rebel army will be compelled to fight or get up and travel again.

S. F. F.

(Rock Island *Union,* July 20, 1864, p. 3)

1. On the night of July 1, Sherman moved McPherson's Army of the Tennessee from the left to the right of his line, and commenced yet another of his envelopments of Johnston's position. The next day Johnston withdrew to Smyrna and then to the line of the Chattahoochee River. Lt. Gen. William J. Hardee (1815–73) commanded one of Johnston's corps. Boatner, *Civil War Dictionary,* 453.

2. Unable to carry the Rebel line by assault on June 27, the remnants of Daniel McCook's brigade (3d Brigade, 3d Division, 14th Corps) began a tunnel with the intent of blowing up the Confederate strong point. Castel, *Decision in the West,* 324.

3. Capt. Dan W. Sedwick was from Suez Township, Mercer County. Others also noted Sedwick's valor. One soldier wrote that the Captain was "one of the coolest and firmest men on top of ground." Aledo *Weekly Record,* August 10, 1864, p. 1.

4. Although military courts were empowered to deal harshly with deserters by imposing sentences of death or lengthy prison terms, they often acted far more leniently. Frequently, as in the case cited by Fleharty, the guilty party was branded with a hot iron or marked with indelible ink, usually on the hip, the hand, or the cheek. See Bell Irvin Wiley, *The Life of Johnny Reb: The Common Soldier of the Confederacy* (Baton Rouge, 1978), 225–29.

5. Pvt. Lyman B. Straw of Henderson, Knox County, was killed twelve days later (July 20) at Peachtree Creek.

No. 54

Peach Tree Creek, near Atlanta, Ga.,
July 21st, 1864.

Yesterday the rebels made a desparate [*sic*] attempt to break through and crush the center of Sherman's army. The blow fell upon Hooker's corps and one division of the 4th corps.[1] General Hooker had been ordered to take up a position south of Peach Tree Creek, filling a gap between the 4th and 14th corps. The 1st division had been ordered to form on the left of the 14th corps; the 2d division on the left of the 1st; and the 3d on the left of the 2d.[2]

The movement to assume these positions commenced early in the morning, but had not been completed when the rebels advanced.—Our division had formed in line of battle at the foot of a range of hills on the south side of Peach Tree Creek. Geary's division was on our right, but some of the regiments in his command were closed en mass [*sic*]; and the 1st division was yet in the rear of the 2d.—About four o'clock p. m. the rebels were observed rapidly advancing through the open fields south of the creek. Our line was immediately ordered to move forward to the crest of the hill in front of us, and the opposing forces instantly became engaged.

The 102d occupied an advantageous position on the extreme right of the division, our line resting upon a knoll which commanded a hill in an open field down the slope of which the enemy were moving in heavy masses upon the left of our brigade, and upon the center of our division. A clump of wood obscured them from our view, in the immediate front of the regiment.

Without faltering or wavering, the enemy moved down the slope of the hill on the left. Sheets of fire blaze along the line of musket in their front; their advance actually pierces the center of the division, and the body of greys, moving forward with apparent irresistable [*sic*] momentum, is intermingled with the line of blue. All this time they received a withering fire from their immediate front, and are subjected to a terrible fire from the regiments. comprising the right of our brigade. A perpetual sheet of flame bursts from the line of Spencer rifles, in the hands of our boys, and the terrific fire of their guns enfilade their lines as they advance.[3] On the right of our regiment, a battery sweeps the hillside with shot and shell, and yet, in the face of this storm of death, for a time they press on. The rebel flag waves defiantly in their front line, and is carried right up to the line where waves the stars and stripes.

A hand to hand contest ensues at that point. Amid fire, and smoke and dust, the combatants continue the terrific struggle. For a time there appears to be some confusion in our line, at one point towards the left of the division. But the faltering are checked, and the long line of blue, stands immovable and unconquerable. At last the enemy waver; numbers drop to the rear; others quickly follow, and finally the entire body, in utter rout and confusion is rolled back by our advaceing [sic] lines; and then from our men, a shout goes up, and rises high above the r[o]ar of battle; the wild, thrilling, prolonged shout of victory!

During all this time the most of us were utterly ignorant of the state of affairs, on our immediate right. Geary's division was unable to form in line of battle, before the enemy were upon them, and was pressed back in some confusion. The rebels followed up their advantage with the utmost impetuosity, and their columns swaged [sic] around on our right until they had nearly reached the rear of our regiment. At this critical moment, the 1st division was ordered into position, on the right of the 2nd. The men of this division, moved gallantly forward and drove the enemy before them. Geary then succeeded in restoring order among his troops, and they moved forward again. The enemy could not withstand the onset, and retired in confusion. At the critical moment previous to the advance of the 1st. division, when a portion of the line on our right was giving way, an Aid [sic] came riding breathlessly up to Capt. Wilson, who commanded our regiment, and told him that if he did not retire, his regiment would be captured in less than five minutes. Capt. Wilson, "didn't see it."[4] There was a battery on his immediate right, that had been served with unexampled bravery and skill. He determined to stand by it to the last. And he did. The tide turned; the rebel hordes, were rolled back, and we had the satisfaction of knowing that at the perilous moment when the day seemed nearly lost on our right, and when there was signs [sic] of confusion on the left of our own division, the 1st. brigade never wavered, and the 102nd, gave back not an inch.

With the repulse of the enemy the main struggle ended; although an irregular fight was kept up until dark.

Owing to the nature of the ground in front of our regiment, the rebels could not advance successfully against us, and we were not subjected to as heavy a fire, as the regiments on our right and left. The position enabled us to give them a terrible cross-fire. We were however in an extremely critical situation. If the enemy had broken through on our left, and the tide of battle had pressed Geary's division a little farther back upon the right, we would have been isolated and surrounded.

The 3d. division had no support. Each brigade held one regiment in reserve. And this weak line, fighting in an open field, was all that could impede the advance of the enemy to the Chattahoockee [*sic*] river. If they had succeeded in carrying their point, our Grand army would have been cut in twain, and the result must have been terribly disastrous; as it was, they met with a most disastrous defeat. The open fields in front of our division were everywhere strewn thickly with their dead, and many of their wounded fell into our hands.

The loss of Hooker's Corps in killed[,] wounded and missing was 1500 men. Of this number, our division lost 528. Our brigade lost 170 in killed and wounded. The division captured seven stands of colors; of these our brigade captured three.

The entire rebel loss, is estimated at 6000, and this is considered a moderate estimate.

Honorable Mention.

I must not close this account without paying a tribute to our brigade commander Col. Harrison. The Colonel is a nephew of "Old Tippecanoe" and seems to possess all of his natural spirit. Encouraging his men and enspiring [*sic*] them with his own ardor, he moved from point to point along his lines, utterly reckless of flying bullets.[5]

Until recently, Col. Harrison has had command of the 70th Indiana regt., in our brigade. When Gen. Butterfield relinquished the command of the 3d division our brigade commander, Gen. Ward, was appointed to fill his place, and Col. Harrison was ordered to assume command of the brigade.[6]

Of our Regimental Officers, I can say this; every one done his duty. To particularize, would be unjust. Col. Mannon though unwell was on the ground, encouraging his men. The immediate command, devolved upon Capt. Wm. A. Wilson of Co. K., who was ably assisted by Capt. D. W. Sedwick of Co. E.

List of Casualties in the 102d.

Killed—Segt. Hermon C. Shinn, Co H., private Lyman B. Straw, Co. B.,

Wounded.—Co. C., corpl. J. H. Lippencott, right shoulder, slight; private David Fitzemaier, slightly in foot.

Co. K., R. A. Kiddoo, leg broken. D. W. McKee slightly in left arm.

Co. G., 1st Sergt. J. C. Reynolds, severely in arm, Sergt. J. C. McWard, severely in left side.

Co. B., Sergt. Alonzo Beswick, slightly in leg, David R. Boyd, finger shot off, Manuel Trout, severely in head.

Respectfully,

S. F. F.

(Rock Island *Union*, August 3, 1864, p. 3)

1. This was actually Brig. Gen. John Newton's division of the 4th Corps.

2. The cautious and defensive strategy of Johnston had worn thin with Jefferson Davis, and on July 17 the Confederate president replaced him as commander of the Army of Tennessee. The new commander, John Bell Hood, was a combative man whose natural impulse was to attack. As Sherman maneuvered to cut the railroads supplying Atlanta, Hood saw a chance to hit Thomas's Army of the Cumberland while it crossed Peachtree Creek. The attack was scheduled for 1 P.M. on July 20 but did not materialize until three hours later. By this time Thomas had the 4th, 14th, and 20th Corps across the creek and assuming defensive positions when the assault began. Hood's attack was driven back with heavy losses.

At Peachtree Creek the 1st Division of the 20th Corps was commanded by Brig. Gen. Alpheus S. Williams, the 2d Division by Brig. Gen. John W. Geary, and the 3d Division by Brig. Gen. William T. Ward. Harrison's brigade held the extreme right of the corps' front with the 102d on the right of the brigade line. See Catton, *This Hallowed Ground*, 420–22; McPherson, *Battle Cry of Freedom*, 754; Kelly, *Kennesaw Mountain*, 46–47; Scaife, *The Campaign for Atlanta*, 88–89; *OR*, Vol. XXXVIII, Pt. 2, p. 356.

3. With no enemy in their front, the 102d changed position and opened an enfilading fire on the advancing rebel column, "pouring volley after volley in quick succession, such as the Spencer rifle alone can give." Sgt. Thomas Simpson of Company E recorded in his diary the scene that afternoon: "The Johnnies did not appear to be in force on our immediate front. If they was we failed to see them, but we saw them on our left as thick as ducks in a mill pond. And we pumped a crossfire into them from our Spencers that made the poor Devils think it was raining lead." The regiment's losses in this engagement were two killed and nine wounded. One regimental historian estimated that the 102d expended five thousand rounds of Spencer ammunition alone at Peachtree Creek. See *History of Mercer County*, 410; Thomas Simpson Diary, July 20, 1864, MS in possession of Melvin Simpson, Alexis, Ill.

4. Capt. William A. Wilson of Company K, a thirty-three-year-old Mercer County farmer, led the regiment that day because Lieutenant Colonel Mannon was ill. In his report of the day's action, Col. Benjamin Harrison wrote that "Captain Wilson . . . though unused to regimental command, managed the regiment with marked skill, and deserves special mention." As Fleharty noted, the commendation resulted partly from Wilson's ignoring a staff officer's order to have the 102d retire to another position. About the incident, Harrison wrote: "The captain very cooly replied [to the officer] that his regiment had been placed there by me and should stay there until I ordered it away." After the Atlanta campaign, Wilson resigned his commission and returned to his farm. *History of Mercer County*, 94–95, 409; *OR*, Vol. XXXVIII, Pt. 2, pp. 346–47.

5. Col. Benjamin Harrison was the grandson, not the nephew, of President William Henry Harrison. He would serve as president of the United States from 1889 to 1893. One soldier, in writing of Harrison's action at Peachtree Creek, proclaimed, "Col. Harrison deserves a star in place of an eagle on his shoulder. He deserves it. So says the 1st Brigade." The soldier added that it was Harrison's decision to have the brigade occupy a piece of high ground that stopped the rebel attack. The high command agreed. While riding the 20th Corps line the next day, General Hooker came upon Harrison and, shaking his hand, exclaimed, "Harrison, by God, I'll make you a Brigadier for this fight." See Harry J. Sievers, *Benjamin Harrison: Hoosier Warrior, 1833–1865* (Chicago, 1952), 178–85, 259–62; Miles, *Fields of Glory,* 137; Aledo *Weekly Record,* August 10, 1864, p. 1.

6. Maj. Gen. Daniel Butterfield (1831–1901), who is rightly or wrongly credited as the composer of "Taps," had been a brigade commander in the Army of the Potomac on the Peninsula, at Second Bull Run, and at Antietam. He then briefly commanded a division before being given the 5th Corps, which he led at Fredericksburg. During the Chancellorsville and Gettysburg campaigns he was chief of staff of the Army of the Potomac. When Hooker came west in 1863, Butterfield accompanied him and served as his chief of staff during the Chattanooga campaign and in the early stages of Sherman's operations against Johnston. In April 1864 he was given command of the 3d Division, 20th Corps. Boatner, *Civil War Dictionary,* 110.

Fleharty was very unhappy with General Ward's advancement, considering him "utterly unfit for the place he holds." Earlier in the year he had noted in a letter home that "I have yet to see the man in the 102d that likes Gen. Ward." Ward and Colonel Smith had not been on good terms, and consequently Fleharty concluded that the General "will be slow to show us any favors." Fleharty to Stephen W. Fleharty, July 14, 1864; and Fleharty to his parents, February 3, 1864; both in possession of Mrs. Sarah E. Glass.

◦— No. 55 —◦

North Bank of the Chattahoochie River,
September 4, 1864.

The "objective point" of our long campaign has at length been reached. The stripes and stars wave over Atlanta. Yet it does not appear that the campaign is ended. One of our men remarked when he heard of Sherman making his onward movement, that "he is a glorious General but don't know when to close his campaign."

So far as this regiment is concerned, however, we deem the campaign at an end. When the last movement to the right commenced, the 2d corps[1] was marched back to the river and placed in position on the south side to guard the railroad bridge, the pontoon bridges, and the wagon train, commissary stores, etc., north of the river. In the disposition of our troops our brigade was finally ordered to take up a position north of the river about one mile from the railroad bridge, to guard against a cavalry dash from that direction. It will be perceived, therefore, that we did not participate in the final contest for the possession of Atlanta. It was not a little mortifying to be debarred the privilege of marching into the city after the four months' campaign which placed it at our mercy.[2]

The city was occupied by our troops on the morning of the 2d inst—at which time part of our corps, including one brigade of our division, took possession, and unfurled the old flag where the emblem of treason had so long defiantly waved.[3]

The long interval that has passed since I last wrote has not been prolific of exciting events in the history of our regiment. It is true that from the 22d of July to the 25th of August we were almost all the time in the front line of works; were frequently shelled, and much of the time were exposed to flying bullets, yet we had very few casualties. We will not soon forget the grand artillery duels that took place around Atlanta. During the first days of the siege (if such it could be called) the rebel guns were constantly busy, but when the Union guns had been placed in position along the line, the rebels were subjected to a galling fire, which made them glad to purchase comparative quiet by preserving a respectful silence.

Over one month we remained almost inactive before Atlanta. Our lines were occasionally advanced a few rods, but the general progress seemed slow, indeed. At length the question began to be mooted around "What will be done next?" "Is Sherman at last brought to a dead lock?—is our army paralyzed [sic]?"—and some even predicted that nothing would be done until the new levies could be placed in the field. And one might have supposed that Gen. Sherman himself felt thus, to have seen him, as I observed him a day or two previous to the movement, riding leisurely along, attended by a single officer, and appearing as unconcerned as if no such grand movement was on foot. It may be, however, that at that moment he was revolving in his mind the details of the brilliant strategic move, which has thus far resulted so gloriously. All honor to our noble General! He has *wrested* Atlanta from the hands of the enemy, notwithstanding their most determined efforts to hold the place.

It is said that the rebels were sadly non-plussed when they found the Yankee army had vacated the line of works north and north-east of the city. At first they supposed we would make a sudden dash at some other point to force an entrance into the city, but finally they decided that our army was about to retreat, and a large lot of commissary stores was brought into the city by railroad to supply Hood's pursuing forces! We are informed that 5,000 bags of meal and a "ware-house full" of hard bread were captured by our troops, and that from these stores the suffering citizens are regularly supplied with rations.[4]

As I have received no authentic details in regard to the capture of munitions of war, or of prisoners, in the battles which resulted in in [sic] the fall of Atlanta, I will make no effort to give such statistics. We are assured, however, that our captures have everywhere been important.[5]

The 102d is having a much-needed relaxation from the privations of active campaign. When the regiment left Waughatchie [sic], May 2d, it reported 450 enlisted men for duty.—When we left the front line, August 25th, there were reported for duty but 280 enlisted men. Disease and rebel bullets have thinned our ranks.

Those who have participated in this ever-memorable campaign, will find a sad pleasure in permitting the mind to wander back to the varied scenes of the eventful months that have passed—passed forever, thank God,—with their visions of blood and their burden of sighs and groans. Are there others in the near future as dark and bloody? Heaven forbid!

We will often think of the weary night marches—of the marches by day, when the burning sun and the suffocating dust reduced us to the last degree of wretchedness. And we will think of the bivouac by the roadside, where we lay perhaps with a stone for a pillow, while drenched by a pelting rain. And our minds will wander to the battle-fields, where brave comrades fell—and dropping a tear to their memory, we will recall our thoughts to the duties of to-day, and to the living brave,—to those true friends who have been tried as by fire, and whom we have learned to love as brothers—bound more closely together in a common cause by the memory of perils and privations shared together, and we will thank Heaven that with our poor lives theirs have been spared.

With the apparent close of the campaign, I conclude my series of letters to the UNION. If any of your readers are inquisitive and wish to know why I discontinue the correspondence, I will tell them that my reasons are weighty and most decidedly confidential. I may assure them that I remain on the best of terms with the UNION, and I trust also, that I have the good will of those who have read my rambling productions.

Respectfully,

S. F. F.

(Rock Island *Union*, September 21, 1864, p. 2)

1. The 102d was actually part of the 20th Corps. Since it is unlikely that Sergeant Fleharty did not know to which corps his regiment belonged, this mistake is probably the result of a misreading of the original letter.

2. On August 27 Colonel Harrison was ordered by Maj. Gen. Henry W. Slocum (1827–94), commanding the 20th Corps, to move the 1st Brigade to the north side of the Chattahoochee River and occupy the Confederate works there, to protect the supply trains and the commissary and ordnance depots. The brigade remained in this position until after the surrender of Atlanta. See Harrison's report in *OR*, Vol. XXXVIII, Pt. 1, pp. 348–50.

3. The city of Atlanta was surrendered the morning of September 2 to elements of the 2d and 3d brigades of Ward's Division under the command of Col. John Coburn. See the report of Capt. Henry M. Scott (acting assistant inspector general on Ward's staff), who accompanied Coburn, in *OR*, Vol. XXXVIII, Pt. 2, pp. 332–34.

4. Union hospitality to Atlanta's citizens was short lived. On the same day Fleharty wrote this letter, Sherman telegraphed General Halleck in Washington and laid out his plan to evacuate all of Atlanta's civilian population and make the city a military installation. By September 21, more than sixteen hundred civilians had been shipped south. Castel, *Decision in the West*, 548–49.

5. In his memoirs, Sherman reports the aggregate loss to the Confederate army through the entire campaign as 34,979, including 12,983 prisoners. Sherman, *Memoirs*, II, 132.

Epilogue

The two men who made possible Fleharty's contribution to the history of the 102d Illinois and the war continued to lead productive lives after the conflict came to an end. J. B. Danforth's opposition to the Lincoln administration never subsided. But as the war's final outcome became evident, his editorials lost both their appeal and significance. With Lincoln's assassination his bitterness disappeared altogether.

In 1869 Danforth sold the *Argus* for a second time and reentered the business world. He moved to New York and engaged in a manufacturing venture with his brother. The move proved to be a financial disaster, and he returned to Rock Island in May 1872 to purchase a minority interest in the *Argus.* Unable to control the political policy of the paper, he left it again for the final time.[1]

In December 1877, with the backing of the local labor movement, Danforth started the *Rock Islander* as an "advocate of the interest of the working men." About the fledgling paper he wrote the following:

> It will be a working-men's paper, a greenback paper, a silver paper, a grange paper, a business newspaper, a good family paper, a paper through which the men and women who work in factories, shops, mills, or for railroads or other corporations, and in which laborers and farmers and business men can all find a friend.[2]

---

1. *Portrait and Biographical Album of Rock Island County, Illinois,* 638, 714; *The Biographical Encyclopedia of Illinois of the Nineteenth Century,* 248.

2. *Portrait and Biographical Album of Rock Island County,* 638–39; Newton Bateman and Paul Selby, eds., *Historical Encyclopedia of Illinois and History of Rock Island County,* 738.

In 1892, at the age of seventy-two, Danforth sold the *Rock Islander* and moved to San Jose, California, where he died on January 11, 1896.[3]

In April 1864, Congressman Isaac N. Arnold's efforts to expunge Colonel Myron S. Barnes's court-martial conviction (see Introduction, note 26) finally succeeded when the War Department informed Governor Yates that Barnes could be recommissioned. On May 6 Barnes was notified by the adjutant general's office that he was "authorized and requested" to recruit a hundred-day regiment. Barnes helped organize the 140th Illinois Infantry, but he did not enter the field.[4]

In August 1864 Barnes sold the *Union,* but the new owner was unable to pay for it, and the paper reverted to Barnes in November. Resuming control, he kept on for another two years, finally selling out in December 1866. Barnes either owned or edited three different papers in the next six years. From Rock Island he went to Dubuque, Iowa, where he published the *Daily Times.* For a short while he operated the Aurora (Illinois) *Daily Herald,* and in the fall of 1871 he helped organize the *Daily News* in Chicago, which existed solely to support Horace Greeley's run for the presidency in 1872. After Greeley's "disastrous campaign" and loss to the incumbent Grant, Barnes left Chicago to purchase the *Free Press* in Galesburg, Illinois. In poor health, he finally retired from the newspaper business in February 1883. He died in Galesburg on November 3, 1889.[5]

3. Bateman and Selby, eds., *Historical Encyclopedia of Illinois,* 738; [Rock Island] *Argus,* January 13, 1896, p. 5.

4. Michael A. Mullins, *The Fremont Rifles: A History of the 37th Illinois Veteran Volunteer Infantry* (Wilmington, N.C., 1990), 125; Allen C. Fuller to Barnes, May 6, 1864. National Archives, Records of the Adjutant General's Office, RG 94, Rolls, Returns, and Other Records of the Regular and Volunteer Armies, 1789–1912; *History of Knox County,* 650.

5. *Portrait and Biographical Album of Knox County,* 783; *History of Knox County,* 650; *Portrait and Biographical Album of Rock Island County,* 717; *The Past and Present of Rock Island County,* 162; Bateman and Selby, eds., *Historical Encyclopedia of Illinois,* 738.

BIBLIOGRAPHY

BOOKS AND ARTICLES

Anderson, Nancy, and Dwight Anderson. *The Generals: Ulysses S. Grant and Robert E. Lee.* New York: Alfred A. Knopf, 1988.

Ash, Stephen V. "Tennessee." In *Encyclopedia of the Confederacy,* edited by Richard N. Current, IV, 1574–80. New York: Simon and Schuster, 1993.

Baird, Lewis C. *Baird's History of Clark County, Indiana.* Indianapolis: B. F. Bowen, 1909.

Barnett, James. "Willich's Thirty-Second Indiana Volunteers." *Cincinnati Historical Society Bulletin* XXXVII (1979), 48–70.

Basler, Roy P., ed. *The Collected Works of Abraham Lincoln.* 9 vols. New Brunswick, N.J.: Rutgers University Press, 1953.

Bassett, Isaac Newton. *Past and Present of Mercer County, Illinois.* 2 vols. Chicago: S. J. Clarke, 1914.

Bateman, Newton, and Paul Selby, eds. *Historical Encyclopedia of Illinois and History of Rock Island County.* 2 vols. Chicago: Munsell, 1914.

Baumann, Ken. *Arming the Suckers: A Compilation of Illinois Civil War Weapons.* Dayton, Ohio: Morningside House, 1989.

The Biographical Encyclopedia of Illinois of the Nineteenth Century. Philadelphia: Galaxy, 1878.

Black, Robert C. III. *The Railroads of the Confederacy.* Chapel Hill: University of North Carolina Press, 1952.

Blanchard, Ira. *I Marched with Sherman: Civil War Memoirs of the 20th Illinois Volunteer Infantry.* San Francisco: J. D. Huff, 1992.

Boatner, Mark M. III. *The Civil War Dictionary.* New York: David McKay, 1959.

Bruce, Robert V. *Lincoln and the Tools of War.* Indianapolis: Bobbs-Merrill, 1956.

Byers, S. H. M. *Iowa in War Times.* Des Moines: W. D. Condit, 1888.

Byrne, Frank L. "Prisoners of War." In *Encyclopedia of the Confederacy*, edited by Richard N. Current, III, 1256–64. New York: Simon and Schuster, 1993.

———. "Prisons." In *Encyclopedia of the Confederacy*, edited by Richard N. Current, III, 1265–68. New York: Simon and Schuster, 1993.

Castel, Albert. *Decision in the West: The Atlanta Campaign of 1864.* Lawrence, Kans.: University Press of Kansas, 1992.

Catton, Bruce. *Terrible Swift Sword.* Garden City, N.Y.: Doubleday, 1963.

———. *This Hallowed Ground: The Story of the Union Side of the Civil War.* Garden City, N.Y.: Doubleday, 1956.

Cole, Arthur C. *The Era of the Civil War, 1848–1870.* Centennial History of Illinois, Vol. III. Springfield: Illinois Centennial Commission, 1919.

Curti, Merle E. "Young America." *American Historical Review* 32 (October 1926): 34–55.

Dictionary of American Biography. 20 vols. New York: Charles Scribner's Sons, 1928–36.

Dorris, Mary C., comp. *The Hermitage: Home of General Andrew Jackson, Seventh President of the United States.* Rev. ed. Hermitage, Tenn.: The Ladies Hermitage Association, 1957.

Dyer, Frederick H. *A Compendium of the War of the Rebellion.* Des Moines: Dyer, 1908.

England, Otis Bryan. *A Short History of the Rock Island Prison Barracks.* Rev. ed. Rock Island, Ill.: Historical Office, U.S. Army Armament, Munitions, and Chemical Command, 1985.

Fitch, John. *Annals of the Army of the Cumberland.* Philadelphia: J. B. Lippincott, 1863.

Fleharty, George. *The Illustrated Life of the Flehartys.* Pleasonton, Nebr.: n.p., 1920.

Fleharty, Stephen F. *Our Regiment: A History of the 102d Illinois Infantry Volunteers, with Sketches of the Atlanta Campaign, the Georgia Raid, and the Campaign of the Carolinas.* Chicago: Brewster and Hanscom, 1865.

Forman, Jacob G. *The Western Sanitary Commission: A Sketch of Its Origin, History, Labors for the Sick and Wounded of the Western Armies, and Aid Given to Freedmen and Union Refugees, with Incidents of Hospital Life.* St. Louis: R. P. Studley, 1864.

Geary, James W. *We Need Men: The Union Draft in the Civil War.* DeKalb, Ill.: Northern Illinois University Press, 1991.

Glatthaar, Joseph T. *The March to the Sea and Beyond: Sherman's Troops in the Savannah and Carolinas Campaigns.* New York: New York University Press, 1985.

Gorn, Elliott J. "Sports Through the Nineteenth Century." In *Encyclopedia of American Social History*, edited by Mary Kupiec Cayton et al. III, 1627–41. New York: Charles Scribner's Sons, 1993.

Hamlin, Percy Gatling. *"Old Bald Head" (General R. S. Ewell): The Portrait of a Soldier.* Strasburg, Va.: Shenandoah, 1940.

Heaps, Willard A., and Porter W. Heaps. *The Singing Sixties: The Spirit of the Civil War Days Drawn from the Music of the Times.* Norman: University of Oklahoma Press, 1960.

Heitman, Francis B. *Historical Register and Dictionary of the United States Army.* 2 vols. Washington, D.C.: Government Printing Office, 1903; rpr. Urbana, Ill.: University of Illinois Press, 1965.

Hicken, Victor. *Illinois in the Civil War.* Urbana, Ill.: University of Illinois Press, 1966.

Hirshson, Stanley P. *The Lion of the Lord: A Biography of Brigham Young.* New York: Alfred A. Knopf, 1969.

History of Knox County, Illinois. Chicago: Charles C. Chapman, 1878.

History of Mercer County, Together with Biographical Matter, Statistics, etc. . . . Containing Also a Short History of Henderson County. Chicago: H. H. Hill, 1882.

House Reports, 39th Cong., 1st Sess., No. 101, p. 259, "Memphis Riots and Massacres."

Hunt, Frazier, and Robert Hunt. *Horses and Heroes: The Story of the Horse in America for 450 Years.* New York: Charles Scribner's Sons, 1949.

Hyman, Harold M. *Era of the Oath: Northern Loyalty Tests During the Civil War and Reconstruction.* Philadelphia: University of Pennsylvania Press, 1954.

Ingersoll, Lurton D. *Iowa and the Rebellion.* Philadelphia: J. B. Lippincott, 1866.

Kautz, August V. *Customs of Service for Non-Commissioned Officers and Soldiers, as Derived from Law and Regulations, and Practiced in the Army of the United States: Being a Handbook for the Rank and File of the Army, Showing What Are the Rights and Duties, How to Obtain the Former and Perform the Latter, and Thereby Enabling Them to Seek Promotion and Distinction in the Service of Their Country.* Philadelphia: J. B. Lippincott, 1864.

Kelly, Dennis. *Kennesaw Mountain and the Atlanta Campaign: A Tour Guide.* Marietta, Ga.: Kennesaw Mountain Historical Association, 1990.

Knox Directory: 1837–1963. Galesburg, Ill.: Knox College, 1963.

Leffel, John C., ed. *History of Posey County, Indiana.* Chicago: Standard, 1913; rpr. Evansville, Ind.: Unigraphic, 1978.

Leverett, Rudy H. "Jones County, Mississippi." In *Encyclopedia of the Confederacy,* edited by Richard N. Current, II, 870. New York: Simon and Schuster, 1993.

Long, E. B. *The Civil War Day by Day: An Almanac, 1861–1865.* Garden City, N.Y.: Doubleday, 1971.

Lord, Francis A. *Civil War Collector's Encyclopedia.* Harrisburg, Pa.: Stackpole, 1965.
———. *Civil War Sutlers and Their Wares.* New York: Thomas Yoseloff, 1969.

Lund, Jennifer. "Conscription." In *Encyclopedia of the Confederacy,* edited by Richard N. Current, I, 396–99. New York: Simon and Schuster, 1993.

Lutz, Jane (Shaull). *A Historical Account of the Trago/Trego Family.* Grand Rapids, Mich: n.p., 1983.

McCune, Calmar. "Early Days in Polk County." In *Collection of Nebraska Pioneer Reminiscences,* 248–51. N.p.: Nebraska Society of the D.A.R., 1916.

McPherson, James. *Battle Cry of Freedom: The Civil War Era.* New York: Oxford University Press, 1988.

Maxwell, William Quentin. *Lincoln's Fifth Wheel: The Political History of the United States Sanitary Commission.* New York: Longmans, Green, 1956.

Merrill, James. "Cairo, Illinois: Strategic Civil War River Port." *Journal of the Illinois State Historical Society* LXXVI (1983), 242–56.

Mickey, David H. *Of Sunflowers, Coyotes, and Plainsmen.* Lincoln, Nebr.: Augstums Printing, 1992.

Miles, Jim. *Fields of Glory: A History and Tour Guide of the Atlanta Campaign.* Nashville: Rutledge Hill Press, 1995.

Muelder, Hermann R. *A Hero Home from the War: Among the Black Citizens of Gales-burg, Illinois, 1860–1880.* Galesburg: Knox College Library, 1987.

Mullins, Michael A. *The Fremont Rifles: A History of the 37th Illinois Veteran Volunteer Infantry.* Wilmington, N.C.: Broadfoot, 1990.

Paludan, Phillip Shaw. *The Presidency of Abraham Lincoln.* Lawrence, Kans.: University Press of Kansas, 1994.

The Past and Present of Rock Island County, Illinois. Chicago: L. H. F. Kett, 1877.

Peterson, Harold L., ed. *Encyclopedia of Firearms.* New York: E. P. Dutton, 1964.

Portrait and Biographical Album of Knox County, Illinois. Chicago: Biographical, 1886.

Portrait and Biographical Album of Rock Island County, Illinois. Chicago: Biographical, 1885.

Ramage, James A. *Rebel Raider: The Life of General John Hunt Morgan.* Lexington, Ky.: University Press of Kentucky, 1986.

Remini, Robert V. *Andrew Jackson and the Course of American Democracy, 1833–1845.* New York: Harper and Row, 1984.

———. *Andrew Jackson and the Course of American Empire, 1767–1821.* New York: Harper and Row, 1977.

———. *Andrew Jackson and the Course of American Freedom, 1822–1832.* New York: Harper and Row, 1981.

Report of the Adjutant General of the State of Illinois. 8 vols. Springfield: Phillips Bros., 1901.

Scaife, William R. *The Campaign for Atlanta.* Saline, Mich.: McNaughton and Gunn, 1993.

Scott, H. L. *Military Dictionary: Comprising Technical Definitions; Information on Rai-sing and Keeping Troops; Actual Service, Including Makeshifts and Improved Materiel;*

and Law, Government, Regulation, and Administration Relating to Land Forces. New York: D. Van Nostrand, 1864.

Sears, Stephen W. *George B. McClellan: The Young Napoleon.* New York: Ticknor and Fields, 1988.

Sheppley, Helen Edith. "Camp Butler in the Civil War Days." *Journal of the Illinois State Historical Society* XXV (January 1933), 285–317.

Sherman, William T. *Memoirs of Gen. W. T. Sherman.* 4th ed., rev., cor. and complete. 2 vols. in 1. New York: C. L. Webster, 1891.

Sievers, Harry J. *Benjamin Harrison: Hoosier Warrior, 1833–1865.* Chicago: Henry Regnery, 1952.

Silber, Irwin. *Songs of the Civil War.* New York: Columbia University Press, 1960.

Slocum, Henry W. "Sherman's March from Savannah to Bentonville." In *Battles and Leaders of the Civil War,* edited by Robert U. Johnson et al. IV, 681–95. New York: Century, 1888.

Terrell, W. H. H. *Indiana in the War of the Rebellion.* Indianapolis: Douglass and Conner, 1869.

Van Horne, Thomas B. *History of the Army of the Cumberland, Its Organization, Campaigns, and Battles.* 3 vols. Cincinnati: Robert Clarke, 1875.

The War of the Rebellion: A Compilation of the Official Records of the Union and Confederate Armies. 130 vols. Washington, D.C.: Government Printing Office, 1880–1901.

Warner, Ezra J. *Generals in Blue: Lives of the Union Commanders.* Baton Rouge: Louisiana State University Press, 1964.

Welcher, Frank J. *The Union Army, 1861–1865: Organization and Operations.* 2 vols. Bloomington: Indiana University Press, 1989–93.

White, Robert H. "Tennessee's Four Capitals." In *Tennessee Old and New, Sesquicentennial Edition, 1796–1946.* 2 vols. Kingsport, Tenn.: Kingsport Press, 1946.

Wiley, Bell Irvin. *The Life of Billy Yank: The Common Soldier of the Union.* Garden City, N.Y.: Doubleday, 1971.

————. *The Life of Johnny Reb: The Common Soldier of the Confederacy.* Baton Rouge: Louisiana State University Press, 1978.

Wilson, James Grant. *Biographical Sketches of Illinois Officers Engaged in the War Against the Rebellion of 1861.* Chicago: J. Barnet, 1862.

NEWSPAPERS

(All papers published in Illinois unless noted)
Aledo *Democrat,* 1901
Aledo *Weekly Record,* 1862–64, 1870, 1872

Chicago *Tribune,* 1865, 1872

Galesburg *Republican-Register,* 1873–75, 1891

Keithsburg *Observer,* 1864–65

Monmouth *Atlas,* 1863

Osceola [Nebr.] *Home News,* 1880

Osceola [Nebr.] *Homesteader,* 1876

Rock Island *Argus* [variously *Weekly Argus, Daily Argus,* and *Evening Argus* at different times], 1861–63, 1896

Rock Island *Union,* 1863–64

Rock Island *Weekly Union,* 1863

Manuscript Sources

Cochran, William F. Papers. Illinois State Historical Library, Springfield.

Fleharty, Stephen F. Papers. Henry M. Seymour Library, Knox College, Galesburg, Illinois.

Fleharty, Stephen F. Papers in possession of Sarah E. Glass, Warren County, Illinois.

Illinois State Archives. Adjutant General (Military and Naval Department). RG 301. Administrative Files on Civil War Companies and Regiments. 301.18.

National Archives. Records of the Adjutant General's Office. RG 94. Records of the Record and Pension Office of the War Department. 94.12.

Ricker, Eli S. Papers. Nebraska State Historical Society, Lincoln.

Simpson, Thomas. Diary in possession of Melvin Simpson, Alexis, Illinois.

U.S. Census MSS, Mercer County, Illinois, 1860. Microfilm.

Index